The Soccer Games and Drills Compendium

FABIAN SEEGER

THE SOCCER GAMES AND DRILLS COMPENDIUM

350 SMART AND PRACTICAL GAMES TO FORM
INTELLIGENT PLAYERS – FOR ALL LEVELS

Meyer & Meyer Sports

Original title: *Spielnahes Fußballtraining*, Meyer & Meyer Aachen, 2015
Translated by: AAA Translation, St. Louis, Missouri
British Library Cataloguing in Publication Data
A catalogue record for this book is available from the British Library

The Soccer Games and Drills Compendium
Maidenhead: Meyer & Meyer Sport (UK) Ltd., 2016
ISBN 978-1-78255-104-1

© 2016 by Meyer & Meyer Sport, Aachen, Germany
Auckland, Beirut, Dubai, Hägendorf, Hong Kong, Indianapolis, Cairo, Cape Town,
Manila, Maidenhead, New Delhi, Singapore, Sydney, Teheran, Vienna
Member of the World Sports Publishers' Association (WSPA)
www.w-s-p-a.org
Printed by: Print Consult GmbH, Munich
ISBN 978-1-78255-104-1
Email: info@m-m-sports.com
www.m-m-sports.com

TABLE OF CONTENTS

Preface 16

1   Games 18

  1.1   Passing 18

    1.1.1   5-on-3 (on mini goals) 20

    1.1.2   4-on-4 plus 4 (on mini goals) 21

    1.1.3   4-on-4 (on passing goals) 22

    1.1.4   4-on-4 plus 4 (playing deep) 23

    1.1.5   4-on-4 (playing deep with changing direction) 24

    1.1.6   4-on-4 plus 2 (play through the wing player) 25

    1.1.7   4-on-4 plus 2 (passing squares) 26

    1.1.8   4-on-4 plus 4 (for possession) 27

    1.1.9   4-on-4 plus 2 (switching play) 28

    1.1.10   4-on-4 (superior number in possession) 29

    1.1.11   4-on-4 (offense vs. defense) 30

    1.1.12   3-on-3 plus 3 (seams) 31

    1.1.13   3-on-3 plus 3 (for possession) 32

    1.1.14   3-on-3 plus 4 (narrow for possession) 33

    1.1.15   3-on-3 (against 3-on-2) 34

    1.1.16   6-on-6 plus 6 (for possession) 35

  1.2   Dribbling 36

    1.2.1   4-on-4 (dribbling and first touch) 36

    1.2.2   4-on-4 (on dribble goals, outside) 37

    1.2.3   4-on-4 (on dribble goals, center) 38

    1.2.4   4-on-4 (on dribble goals with finish) 39

    1.2.5   4-on-4 (on dribble lines with finish) 40

    1.2.6   4-on-4 (on dribble lines with follow-up action) 41

    1.2.7   4-on-4 (through dribble fields) 42

    1.2.8   4-on-4 (on central dribble field) 43

    1.2.9   4-on-4 (on dribble goals with subsequent pass) 44

    1.2.10   4-on-4 plus 2 (with outside players) 45

    1.2.11   4-on-4 plus 2 (with dribbling players) 46

    1.2.12   4-on-4 (touch competition) 47

1.3   Transitioning and reacting 48

   1.3.1   3-on-3 plus 4 (on mini goals) 48

   1.3.2   4-on-4 (on mini goals with transition after finish) 49

   1.3.3   4-on-4 plus 1 (with changing objectives) 50

   1.3.4   4-on-4 plus 2 (on alternating mini goals) 51

   1.3.5   4-on-4 plus 2 (with transition toward the goal) 52

   1.3.6   4-on-4 (with changing game objectives) 53

   1.3.7   4-on-4 (on alternating goals) 54

   1.3.8   8-on-8 (with 3 balls) 55

   1.3.9   4-on-4 (with change of direction) 56

   1.3.10 4 plus 1 against 4 plus 1 (with changing objectives) 57

   1.3.11 2-on-2 (with transition to 3-on-2 and change of direction) 58

   1.3.12 4-on-8 (on 4 mini goals with transition to offense) 59

1.4   Small games 60

   1.4.1   Catch (duel) 60

   1.4.2   Catch (team competition) 61

   1.4.3   Catch (1-on-1) 62

   1.4.4   Handball header (open passing game) 63

   1.4.5   Handball header (on goals) 64

   1.4.6   Handball (shot on goal) 65

   1.4.7   Numbers soccer (1) 66

   1.4.8   Numbers soccer (2) 67

   1.4.9   The Great White 68

   1.4.10 Moveable goals 69

   1.4.11 Calling names 70

   1.4.12 Memory® 71

1.5   Tactics 72

   1.5.1   Defensive tactics (defend with a high line) 72

   1.5.2   Defensive tactics (block passing lanes) 73

   1.5.3   Defensive tactics—pressing (1) 74

   1.5.4   Defensive tactics—pressing (2) 75

   1.5.5   Defensive tactics—pressing (3) 76

   1.5.6   Offensive tactics (transition to offense 4-on-4 plus 4) 77

1.5.7   Offensive tactics (transition to offense 8-on-5 plus 3) 78

1.5.8   Offensive tactics (diagonal passes) 79

1.5.9   Offensive tactics (playing with a wing player) 80

1.5.10   Offensive tactics—opening the game (1) 81

1.5.11   Offensive tactics—opening the game (2) 82

1.5.12   Offensive tactics—opening the game (3) 83

1.6   Kick-off variations 84

1.6.1   Kick-off (tennis ball) 84

1.6.2   Kick-off (open passing game) 85

1.6.3   Kick-off (roll the ball) 86

1.6.4   Kick-off (wing player) 87

1.6.5   Kick-off (passing sequence) 88

1.6.6   Kick-off (dribbling competition) 89

1.6.7   Kick-off (positional technique) 90

1.6.8   Kick-off (reacting) 91

1.6.9   Staggered 3-on-3 (finish) 92

1.6.10   Staggered 3-on-3 (transitioning) 93

1.6.11   Staggered 3-on-3 (passing sequence and finish) 94

1.6.12   Staggered 4-on-4—passing sequence (1) 95

1.6.13   Staggered 4-on-4—passing sequence (2) 96

1.6.14   Staggered 5-on-5 (passing sequence and finish) 97

1.7   Chaos and action 98

1.7.1   From 1-on-1 to 2-on-2 98

1.7.2   From 1-on-1 to 3-on-2 99

1.7.3   From 2-on-1 to 3-on-2 100

1.7.4   From 1-on-1 to 4-on-3 101

1.7.5   Chaos 1-on-1 102

1.7.6   Chaos 3-on-3 (on 6 goals) 103

1.7.7   Chaos 3-on-3 (on 3 goals) 104

1.7.8   Fast 2-on-2 105

1.7.9   4-on-4 (ball in hand) 106

1.7.10   Integrated playing fields 107

1.8   Tournaments, playing fields, and rule variations 108

    1.8.1   Tournament (Champions League) 108

    1.8.2   Tournament (4-on-4) 109

    1.8.3   Tournament (4-on-4)—explanations 110

    1.8.4   Tournament (touches) 112

    1.8.5   Tournament (goal hunt) 113

    1.8.6   Tournament (winner plays) 114

    1.8.7   Playing field (vertical field in the center) 115

    1.8.8   Playing field (vertical field to the goal) 116

    1.8.9   Playing field (switching play) 117

    1.8.10   Playing field (play through the center) 118

    1.8.11   Playing field (breadth and depth) 119

    1.8.12   Playing field (target zones) 120

    1.8.13   Creative rule variations 121

2   Drills 124

  2.1   Passing (loops) 126

    2.1.1   Triangle passing (simple passing) 126

    2.1.2   Triangle passing (ball control and first touch) 127

    2.1.3   Triangle passing (first-touch control and tempo dribbling) 128

    2.1.4   Triangle passing (double-double pass) 129

    2.1.5   Triangle passing (dropping off) 130

    2.1.6   Passing square (Ping-Pong straight) 131

    2.1.7   Passing square (Ping-Pong diagonal) 132

    2.1.8   Passing square (Ping-Pong alternate) 133

    2.1.9   Passing square (double pass) 134

    2.1.10   Passing square (third man running) 135

    2.1.11   Passing square (looking for position) 136

    2.1.12   Passing square (play through the center) 137

    2.1.13   Diamond passing (double pass) 138

    2.1.14   Diamond passing (double pass and pursuit) 139

    2.1.15   Diamond passing (overlapping) 140

    2.1.16   Diamond passing (overlap and third man running) 141

    2.1.17   Passing rectangle—overlap and play deep (1) 142

    2.1.18   Passing rectangle—overlap and play deep (2) 143

    2.1.19   Passing hexagon (double pass and third man running) 144

    2.1.20   Passing hexagon (looking for position) 145

2.1.21 Passing star (competition) 146

2.1.22 Double passing square 147

2.1.23 Double passing loop 148

2.1.24 Passing loops (organized as a competition) 149

2.2 Passing Game (passing circles) 150

2.2.1 Passing circle (basic passing game) 150

2.2.2 Passing circle (double pass) 151

2.2.3 Passing circle (double-double pass) 152

2.2.4 Passing circle (overlapping) 153

2.2.5 Passing circle (instep shot and header) 154

2.2.6 Passing circle (third man running) 155

2.2.7 Expanded passing circle (overlap and third man running) 156

2.2.8 Combination passing circle and open passing game (interfering player) 157

2.2.9 Passing circle (passing and looking for position) 158

2.2.10 Passing circle (6er behavior) 159

2.3 Open passing 160

2.3.1 Open passing (commands) 160

2.3.2 Open passing (groups of three) 161

2.3.3 Open passing (groups of three plus hand ball) 162

2.3.4 Open passing (color game) 163

2.3.5 Open passing—sequence (1) 164

2.3.6 Open passing—sequence (2) 165

2.3.7 Open passing in groups of two—cone goals (1) 166

2.3.8 Open passing in groups of two—cone goals (2) 167

2.3.9 Open passing in groups of three (cone goals) 168

2.3.10 Open passing in groups of three (around triangles) 169

2.3.11 Open passing in groups of four (play on triangles) 170

2.3.12 Open passing (catcher) 171

2.4 Dribbling 172

2.4.1 Individual dribbling 172

2.4.2 Shadow dribbling 173

2.4.3 Linear dribbling 174

2.4.4 Linear dribbling (feints) 175

2.4.5   Individual dribbling (field changes) 176

2.4.6   Individual dribbling (dribble through cone goals) 177

2.4.7   Individual dribbling (dribble figure-8s) 178

2.4.8   Dribbling (competition) 179

2.4.9   Dribbling (fields) 180

2.4.10   Combination individual and linear dribbling 181

2.5   Shot on goal 182

2.5.1   Basic shot on goal 182

2.5.2   Shot on goal (first-touch control) 183

2.5.3   Shot on goal with passing (1) 184

2.5.4   Shot on goal with passing (2) 185

2.5.5   Shot on goal with passing (3) 186

2.5.6   Shot on goal with passing (4) 187

2.5.7   Shot on goal with passing (5) 188

2.5.8   Shot on goal with passing (6) 189

2.5.9   Shot on goal with passing (7) 190

2.5.10   Shooting competition (dribbling) 191

2.5.11   Shooting competition (squaring) 192

2.5.12   Shooting competition—passing (1) 193

2.5.13   Shooting competition—passing (2) 194

2.5.14   Shooting sequence with two finishes 195

2.5.15   Shooting sequence with two finishes (plus 2-on-2 and 3-on-3) 196

2.5.16   Shooting sequence with three finishes (1) 197

2.5.17   Shooting sequence with three finishes (2) 198

2.5.18   Shooting sequence with three finishes (3) 199

2.5.19   Shooting sequence with five finishes 200

2.5.20   Shot on goal (duels) 201

2.6   Feints and juggling 202

2.6.1   Basic feints (1) 202

2.6.2   Basic feints (2) 203

2.6.3   Basic feints (3) 204

2.6.4   Feint competition (team) 205

2.6.5   Feint competition (individual) 206

2.6.6   Feints (1-on-1) 207

2.6.7   Feints (shot on goal) 208

2.6.8   Juggling (1) 209

2.6.9   Juggling (2) 210

2.6.10 Juggling (3) 211

2.7   1-on-1 212

2.7.1   Basic 1-on-1 212

2.7.2   1-on-1 (transition) 213

2.7.3   1-on-1 (decision) 214

2.7.4   1-on-1—reaction (1) 215

2.7.5   1-on-1—reaction (2) 216

2.7.6   1-on-1—reaction (3) 217

2.7.7   1-on-1—reaction (4) 218

2.7.8   1-on-1—reaction (5) 219

2.7.9   1-on-1—reaction (6) 220

2.7.10 1-on-1—reaction (7) 221

2.7.11 Frontal 1-on-1 222

2.7.12 Diagonal 1-on-1 (1) 223

2.7.13 Diagonal 1-on-1 (2) 224

2.7.14 Diagonal 1-on-1 (3) 225

2.7.15 1-on-1 (wing) 226

2.7.16 1-on-1—two goals (1) 227

2.7.17 1-on-1—two goals (2) 228

2.7.18 1-on-1—arena (1) 229

2.7.19 1-on-1—arena (2) 230

2.7.20 1-on-1—arena (3) 231

2.7.21 1-on-1—arena (4) 232

2.7.22 1-on-1—arena (5) 233

2.8   Active defense 234

2.8.1   Chase and capture (1) 234

2.8.2   Chase and capture (2) 235

2.8.3   Chase and capture (team of two) 236

2.8.4   Chase and capture (finish) 237

2.8.5   Chase and capture (plus 1-on-1) 238

2.8.6   Chase and capture (team of three) 239

3   Fitness training 240

   3.1   Soccer-specific speed training 242

       3.1.1   Speed (repetition method) 242

       3.1.2   Speed (shuttle race) 243

       3.1.3   Speed (reaction and change of direction) 244

       3.1.4   Fast 1-on-1—follow-up action (1) 245

       3.1.5   Fast 1-on-1—follow-up action (2) 246

       3.1.6   Fast 1-on-1 (dribbling with follow-up action) 247

       3.1.7   Fast 1-on-1—shot on goal (1) 248

       3.1.8   Fast 1-on-1—shot on goal (2) 249

       3.1.9   Fast 1-on-1 (circuits) 250

       3.1.10   Fast 1-on-1 (shot on goal and catch) 251

       3.1.11   Fast 1-on-1—duel and shot on goal (1) 252

       3.1.12   Fast 1-on-1—duel and shot on goal (2) 253

       3.1.13   Speed (catching game) 254

       3.1.14   Speed—sprinting game (1) 255

       3.1.15   Speed—sprinting game (2) 256

       3.1.16   Quick reaction and orienting 257

       3.1.17   Fast 3-on-7 258

   3.2   Soccer-specific athletic training (strength, stretching, stabilization and coordination) 259

       3.2.1   Stretching (Balance Pad®) 259

       3.2.2   Strength training (Balance Pad®) 261

       3.2.3   Strength training—posture (1) 264

       3.2.4   Strength training—posture (2) 266

       3.2.5   Strength training—posture (3) 268

       3.2.6   Strength training—posture (4) 269

       3.2.7   Strength training—posture (5) 270

       3.2.8   Strength training—posture (6) 272

       3.2.9   Strength training—posture (7) 274

       3.2.10   Strength training—posture (8) 276

       3.2.11   Strength training—Thera-Band® (1) 278

       3.2.12   Strength training—Thera-Band® (2) 279

       3.2.13   Strength training—Pezzi exercise ball (1) 280

       3.2.14   Strength training—Pezzi exercise ball (2) 282

       3.2.15   Strength training—Pezzi exercise ball (3) 283

       3.2.16   Regeneration and massage—Blackroll® (1) 284

       3.2.17   Regeneration and massage—Blackroll® (2) 285

3.3   Soccer-specific endurance training 286

    3.3.1   Endurance course (continuous method) 286

    3.3.2   Endurance course (passing) 287

    3.3.3   Endurance course—shot on goal (1) 288

    3.3.4   Endurance course—shot on goal (2) 289

    3.3.5   4-on-2 (interval runs) 290

    3.3.6   Endurance game (3-on-2 plus 1) 291

    3.3.7   Endurance game (4-on-4) 292

    3.3.8   Endurance game (4-on-4 plus 4-on-2) 292

4   Indoor training **294**

4.1   Indoor training 296

    4.1.1   Line drills 296

    4.1.2   Movement tasks (hoops) 297

    4.1.3   Movement tasks (benches) 298

    4.1.4   Movement tasks (jump ropes) 299

    4.1.5   Chain tag 300

    4.1.6   Bridge tag 301

    4.1.7   Twin soccer 302

    4.1.8   Soccer baseball 303

    4.1.9   Shot on goal game (wall target) 304

    4.1.10   Shot on goal game (cone target) 305

    4.1.11   Shot on goal game (clean half) 306

    4.1.12   Shot on goal game (3 plus 3 vs. 3 plus 3) 307

    4.1.13   Team dodgeball 308

    4.1.14   Individual dribbling 309

    4.1.15   Dribbling (movement competition) 310

    4.1.16   Dribbling (coordination competition) 311

    4.1.17   Group passing game 312

    4.1.18   Passing loop (benches) 313

    4.1.19   Passing (benches) 314

    4.1.20   Shot on goal (1) 315

    4.1.21   Shot on goal (2) 316

    4.1.22   Shot on goal (3) 317

    4.1.23   Shot on goal (4) 318

    4.1.24   Shot on goal (roundabout) 319

    4.1.25   Variable 1-on-1 320

4.1.26   Diagonal 1-on-1 or 3-on-2 321

4.1.27   2-on-2 plus 4-on-4 322

4.1.28   From 1-on-0 to 4-on-3 323

4.1.29   4-on-3 plus 2 324

4.1.30   Double 3-on-3 325

4.1.31   Game—against the boards (1) 326

4.1.32   Game—against the boards (2) 327

4.1.33   Game (diamond) 328

4.1.34   Game (deep neutral players) 329

5   Goalkeeper training 330

5.1   Goalkeeper training 332

5.1.1   Warm-up (1) 332

5.1.2   Warm-up (2) 333

5.1.3   Warm-up (3) 334

5.1.4   Legwork (follow-up action) 335

5.1.5   Legwork—low balls (1) 336

5.1.6   Legwork—low balls (2) 337

5.1.7   Legwork—low balls (3) 338

5.1.8   Reacting (1) 339

5.1.9   Reacting (2) 340

5.1.10   Catching high balls (1) 341

5.1.11   Catching high balls (2) 342

5.1.12   Throw-out and punt 343

6   Team building 344

6.1   Teamwork 345

Chain competition – ball transport – group run – one-leg hop 345

Throwing and catching 1 – throwing and catching 2 – sorting – jumping rope 346

Jumping rope – flying – field running – supporting legs 347

Dribbling chain – 2-on-2 challenge – trust fall – 1-on-1 equilibrium 348

Rock–paper–scissors – caterpillar – flying carpet – mass revolt 349

5-on-1 with task – 1-on-1 with task – figures 350

7   Background knowledge 352

7.1   Soccer-specific training principles 353

7.2   Soccer-specific training management 354

7.3   Coaching for training and game management 354

    7.3.1   Defensive coaching with individual tactics 355

    7.3.2   Offensive coaching with individual tactics 356

    7.3.3   Defensive coaching with group tactics 357

    7.3.4   Offensive coaching with group tactics 357

8   Appendix 358

8.1   Legend 358

8.2   Definitions and reading support 360

8.3   References 361

8.4   Photo credits 362

PREFACE

Stephan Kerber

In my capacity as DFB (German Football Association) basecamp coordinator for the Hamburg Soccer Association (HFV), it has been my job since 2002 to expose the regional talent to cutting-edge training content.

360 basecamps are located all over Germany. Around 40 to 50 kids from age 11 to 15 are trained by over 1,200 DFB coaches and are coached with no additional costs for the talents. 29 basecamp managers coordinate the efforts nationwide. In Hamburg 300 young players are coached by 20 DFB-coaches. This system is unique—worldwide! The DFB invests huge sums in the upbringing of talents to ensure Germany's top position in soccer. By now representatives of many European soccer associations visit our training basecamps to learn about our training system.

As successful as German youth soccer has been in recent years, thanks to the increasingly better-functioning support structure, it is still important to analyze which training system will ensure success in years to come. Which new elements will be needed to be competitive in top soccer? This compilation of attractive training exercises offers versatile content that makes it possible to specifically emphasize technical or tactical goals.

The goal was to create age-appropriate effective training units for the hard-working, hard-running, and technically accomplished team player. This was done primarily in close communication with the DFB basecamp trainers and the Hamburg Soccer Association's select team coaches, whose good ideas had to be developed further and put into a form that readers could comprehend.

This book contains many variations that did not just go straight from the desk into the book, but nearly all of the drills were tested, modified, and refined with the help of the DFB talent development program's different age groups in Hamburg and within the HFV's select soccer program, chiefly the age groups 1998, 1999, 2000, 2001, 2002, and 2003 (U19 to U12—a broad bandwidth).

Fabian Seeger started the process on October 1, 2009, as DFB basecamp coach at the DFB basecamp Sachsenweg in Hamburg. Working with the different age groups and constantly trying out his ideas and tips from other sources resulted in a broad spectrum that allowed for the content of this book to develop into this user-friendly version. Since then, there has been an awesome exchange, and I congratulate him on his diligence in creating something new from what he saw and for adding a new spin and realistic stimuli to standard drills. I still, today, feel greatly motivated by our joint efforts to devise complex exercises for top talent that create meaningful learning processes with a variety of guidelines. Counteracting monotony while creating experience-oriented, fun training units for long-term fun and learning success.

I hope this book will be widely read and the training exercises well used.

Enjoy!

Stephan Kerber

1 GAMES

A significant and universal goal of training is the best possible preparation for a competition. Ideally, it is particularly those movement patterns and behaviors required and practiced in a competition that are practiced during training. During a competition, a player is confronted with different situations and various decision-making options. What matters in the end is which problem-solving approach he chooses to purposefully reach the situation-specific result.

And yet successfully solving a game situation does not always consist of scoring a goal or winning the ball. In fact, there are many sub-goals that, in the end, result in successfully scoring goals and preventing goals. For the purpose of realistic training, chapter 1, Games, focuses on the development of certain drills that reproduce the complexity of 11-on-11 play on a smaller scale. The many challenges of different competitive situations can be combined as areas of focus in training to allow the conception of different drills with different objectives. In the process, individual training parameters, such as field size, team size, or number of goals, can be purposefully used to work on the current training topic. In doing so, the listed training parameters are in no way intended as mandatory factors, but rather should always be adapted to the team's respective performance and skill level as well as age group by the implementing coach.

Competitive soccer consists of widely different situations in which the players must largely act together. During training, the complexity of 11-on-11 is decreased, and segments of the game are separated. Looking at specific game situations and scaled-down game sequences generates drills that, next to fitness-related and technical requirements, focus primarily on individual and group tactics.

Depictions and descriptions of the individual drills generally leave out field measurements. Determining the field size, passing distances, or the distance between players and goals is considered part of a coach's toolbox. The coach determines measurements based on the specific training emphasis and, along with the topic's focus, is guided by variables such as age and capability of players, number of training participants, or the desired training intensity.

Playing ability
Pressure from the opponent
Action speed
Creativity
Decision-making
Time pressure   Cognition
Orientation skills
Transition skills

1.1   PASSING

1.1.1   5-on-3 (on mini goals)

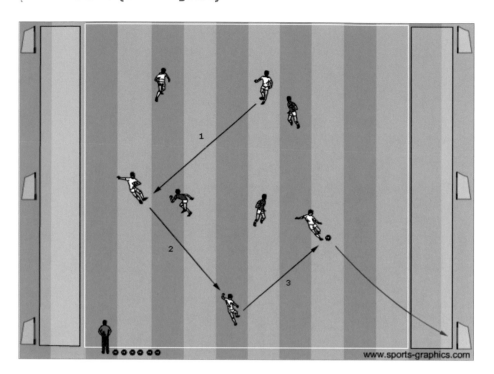

Execution

The WHITE team plays the outnumbered RED team. After the finish the coach brings each new ball into the game to the WHITE team. Players are not allowed to step on the edge areas marked in YELLOW. The WHITE team must have played at least three passes within their own ranks before they can finish. The RED team can play freely and, after winning the ball, is allowed to immediately take shots on the goals with unlimited touches.

Concept

The superior number simplifies and prompts the desired passing game. Playing on mini goals also facilitates precise passing during the finish. The YELLOW areas (passing zone) induce and prompt forceful passes and finishes across the field.

Variations

* Limit the number of touches for the superior number team.
* Direct play with every other pass from the superior number team.
* Prerequisite for a shot on goal: 4 or 5 passes within the ranks of the superior number team.
* Specify the technique for the shot on goal: inside foot/laces kick/direct finish.

1.1.2   4-on-4 plus 4 (on mini goals)

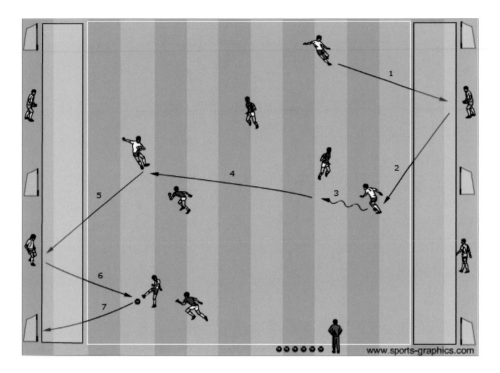

Execution

Two teams of four players each play in the center of the field. Four additional players are positioned in the outside zones. The team in possession is allowed to involve all four players. No players are allowed to enter the YELLOW zones. Shots on goal must be direct (see 7) and after first involving an outside player (double pass or third man running). If a direct finish is not possible after the pass from outside (see 3), the team remains in possession. After a finish, the coach brings a new ball into the game.

Concept

Involving the outside players forces double passes, third man running, and deep forward passes. The YELLOW passing zone prompts forceful passes. Since only direct finishes are possible, precision is required during the finish. In addition, the finishing situation must be well prepared using reliable combination play.

Variations

* ★ Limited touches for the team in possession.
* ★ Limited touches for outside players.
* ★ Double score for finishes with the weak leg.

1.1.3   4-on-4 (on passing goals)

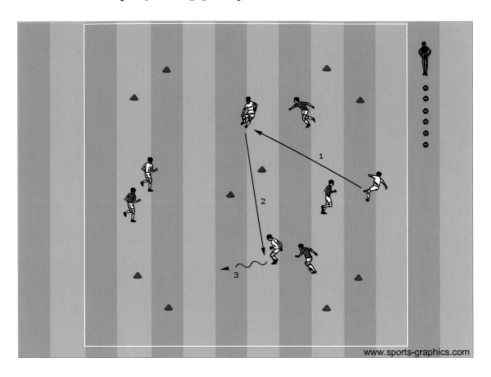

Execution

The RED team plays 4-on-4 (see 1) against the WHITE team. The team in possession tries to play a pass to a teammate through one of the passing goals (see 2). After a successful pass through a passing goal (see 2), the team stays in possession and continues the game without interruption (see 3). If a ball goes off the field, the coach brings a new ball into the game.

Concept

Playing a pass through one of the passing goals requires primarily well-timed and practical offers to help get open.

Variations

* Simplify or expand to 4-on-4 (plus two neutral players in possession).
* Specify the passing technique for playing through cone goals: direct passing.
* Vary or modify the array of passing goals.
* Limit touches for the team in possession.

1.1.4   4-on-4 plus 4 (playing deep)

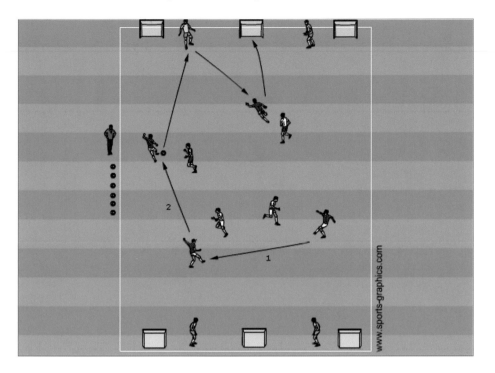

Execution

The teams play 4-on-4 on the field. After two passes in the own ranks, the team in possession is allowed to involve the outside players. A shot on the mini goals is only possible if a pass from outside is turned into a direct shot. If a pass from outside is not turned into a direct shot but is handled and kept in the game, another outside player can be involved in an attempt to score through him as the game continues. After the finish, the coach brings a new ball into the game.

Concept

After playing 4-on-4 in a tight space, the game is opened up to the outside after two forward passes. After a pass to an outside player, immediate reaction and pursuit, or rather getting open, is required to bring on the finish. The direct finish in the form of a pass on a mini goal requires major concentration and precision.

Variations

* Vary or modify the array of passing goals (e.g., diagonally staggered).
* Specify the direction of play (e.g., RED team can only finish on the three upper goals).
* Prerequisite for a shot on goal: 3 (or 4) passes in the ranks of the team in possession.
* Outside players are not allowed to play direct return passes to the passing player.

1.1.5   4-on-4 (playing deep with changing direction)

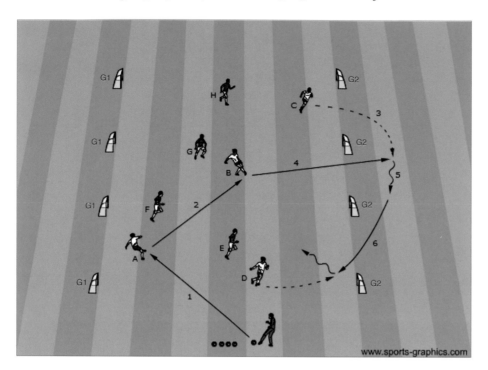

www.sports-graphics.com

Execution

The RED team plays 4-on-4 against the BLUE team. Initially, players cannot play on the mini goals. After the coach's opening ball (see 1), the players pass each other the ball within the own ranks (see 2). Initially, the objective is to play a deep pass to a teammate through two mini goals (see 4). The player who gets open behind the mini goals (see 3) controls the ball (see 5) and dribbles back onto the field or plays a direct pass to a teammate on the field (passing game; see 6). Playing on the mini goals becomes possible after the successful deep pass. The direction of play depends on the deep pass. If the deep pass is played between the G2 goals, the team in possession attacks the goals on the opposite side (see figure). The defending team (here the RED team) attacks the G2 goals and can immediately start pressing. After a team finishes, the coach brings a new ball into the game.

Variations

- Simplify or expand to 4-on-4 (plus two neutral players in possession).
- Prerequisite for the deep pass: 3 (or 4) passes in the own ranks.
- Limit the number of passes prior to deep pass (e.g., no more than five).
- Limit touches for the teammate receiving the deep pass.

1.1.6   4-on-4 plus 2 (play through the wing player)

www.sports-graphics.com

Execution

4-on-4-play in the center. Shots on the mini goals can only be taken after first passing to an outside player (see 1 and 2). Players cannot enter the outside zones where the outside players are positioned. The same applies to the passing zones in front of the mini goals. After the finish, the coach brings a new ball into the game.

Concept

Play through the outside player must be initiated prior to the finish. Passing zones in front of the mini goals prompt forceful shots on goal. The possession team's superior number makes play through the outside player easier.

Variations

*   Specify the shooting technique (see 3): inside foot/instep/direct shot.
*   Prerequisite for a shot on goal: Involve both outside players (switching play).
*   Prerequisite for a shot on goal: Additional pass after a pass from an outside player.
*   Prerequisite for a pass to the outside player: 3 (or 4) passes within the own ranks.

1.1.7   4-on-4 plus 2 (passing squares)

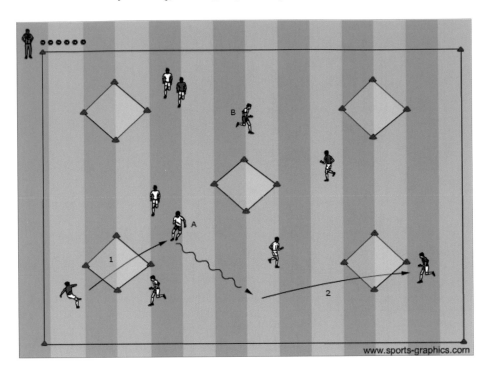

www.sports-graphics.com

Execution

The RED team plays 4-on-4 against the WHITE team on the field. The team in possession can also pass to the neutral players (see players A and B). Players cannot enter the cone squares (passing squares). The game's objective is to pass the ball to a teammate through the passing square. After scoring, or rather successfully passing the ball, the game continues without interruption. The successful team remains in possession and can score additional points.

Concept

Having to play through the passing squares prompts forceful and sometimes longer passes. The array of the passing squares also facilitates demand for diagonal passes. Receiving the ball through one of the passing squares requires purposefully getting open and signaling availability.

Variations

 ★ Specify the passing technique for playing through passing squares: direct passing.
 ★ Scoring: short pass (one point; see 2) and long pass (two points; see 1).
 ★ Even numbers play without neutral players (e.g., 4-on-4).

1.1.8   4-on-4 plus 4 (for possession)

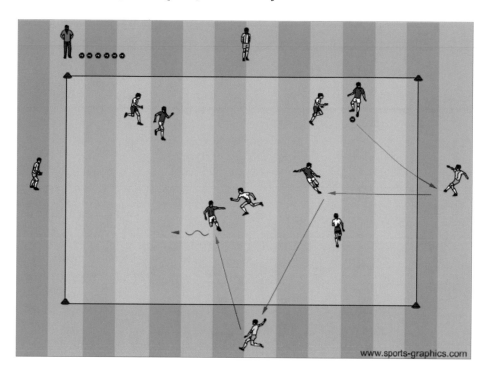

Execution

The RED team and the BLUE team play 4-on-4 on the marked field. The team in possession is allowed to involve the outside players. The game's objective is to play as many passes as possible in the own ranks. One player from each team counts the passes out loud.

Concept

The large superior number makes passing or keeping the ball in the own ranks relatively easy. This drill facilitates lots of back-to-back passes in the own ranks and practicing passing techniques without too much pressure from the opponents.

Variations

* Limited touches for outside players.
* Limited touches for field players.
* No passes allowed between two outside players.
* Points scored after every 10 passes in a row.

1.1.9   4-on-4 plus 2 (switching play)

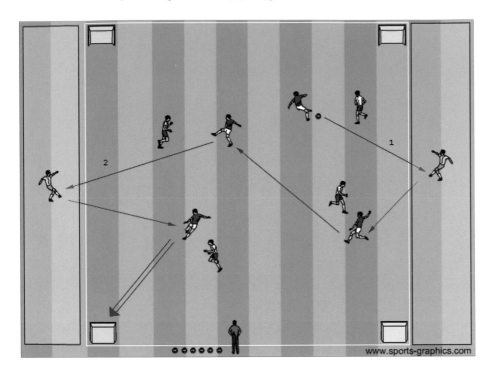

Execution

The RED team and the BLUE team play 4-on-4 on the field. The team in possession is allowed to pass to the two permanent outside players. Once the possession team has involved both players (see 1 and 2), they are allowed to shoot on the mini goals. After the finish, the coach brings a new ball into the game.

Concept

The possession team's superior number situation makes passing easier. The specified prerequisites for the finish force switching play. In terms of training emphasis, the required behavior for finishing on the mini goals prompts forceful passes instead of shots on goal.

Variations

* Specify the technique for shots on goal: inside foot/instep/direct finish.
* Limited touches for outside players.
* Limited touches for field players.

1.1.10   4-on-4 (superior number in possession)

Execution

The RED team and the BLUE team play 4-on-4 on the field, whereby possession creates a constant majority–minority relationship. Each team has a position between its own mini goals (see A and B) where there is always a player from the defending team who does not participate in the game (here from team A). As soon as a team has possession, that player is once again allowed to complete his team. When the opponent has possession, one player must always withdraw and fall back to that position.

Concept

The superior number during possession makes passing play easier.

Variations

* Option for the team in possession: Involve the waiting opponent.
* Active players are not allowed to run into zones #A and #B.
* Shots on goal from zones #A and #B are not allowed.
* Game is continued with a ball from the coach.
* Game is continued with a ball placed in a corner.

1.1.11   4-on-4 (offense vs. defense)

www.sports-graphics.com

Execution

A centerline divides the playing field into two halves. The two teams play 4-on-4 on the two large goals (see team A/a and team B/b). In doing so, two players from each team position in their own half and two in the opposing half. Players are not allowed to leave their zones.

Concept

Two players from each team are defenders and open the game in possession (see players A and b). The two remaining players are attackers and continue the plays (see players a and B). This arrangement allows the players to practice their position-specific tasks and content, such as game build-up and joint defense (see players A and b) as well as pressing and creating goal-scoring chances (see players a and B).

Variations

★ Third offensive player possibly moves up for 3-on-2.

★ Limit no more than one additional pass between the two offensive players.

★ Use time limit for shot on goal after the pass into the offensive zone (e.g., 6 seconds).

1.1.12   3-on-3 plus 3 (seams)

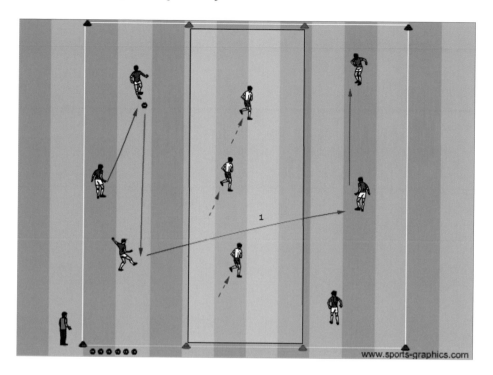

www.sports-graphics.com

Execution

The three players in each of the outside zones can circulate the ball within their own groups of three and have the goal of passing the ball through the center zone to the zone on the opposite side (see 1). In doing so they can insert the ball between the two players in the center or play past the three players on the outside. The players in the center zone shift and try to stop the balls. When a ball is intercepted, the coach brings a new ball into the game.

Concept

The passing game is generally easier without pressure from the opponents in the outside zones, allowing for time to prepare the pass to the other side. Pushing the ball through players prompts diagonal passes, and passing play from outside becomes easier if a quick switch in play precedes it.

Variations

* Limit touches in outside zones.
* Specify the passing technique for play through the center zone: direct passing.
* Organize as a competition: Switch tasks after three turnovers.
* Scoring: outside pass (one point); pass through the center (two points).

1.1.13   3-on-3 plus 3 (for possession)

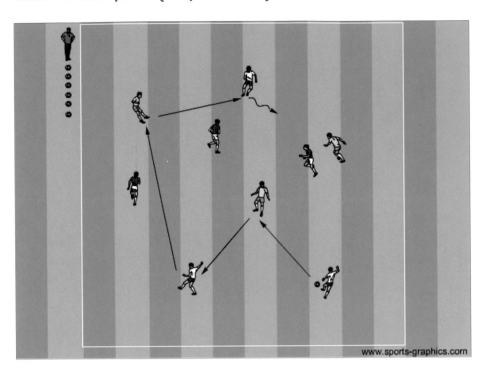

Execution

Three teams of three players each play for possession on the field and try to play as many passes in a row as possible. As the figure shows, the BLUE team and the GRAY team play together against the RED team. When the RED team wins the ball, it keeps possession and plays together with the team that did not lose the ball. The team with the player who lost possession becomes the outnumbered team.

Concept

The superior number makes passing play easier. Still, the player in possession is under pressure because if he makes a mistake, he and his team become the minority without the ball.

Variations

★   Limit touches for the team in possession.

★   Direct play with every second or third pass from the team in possession.

1.1.14   3-on-3 plus 4 (narrow for possession)

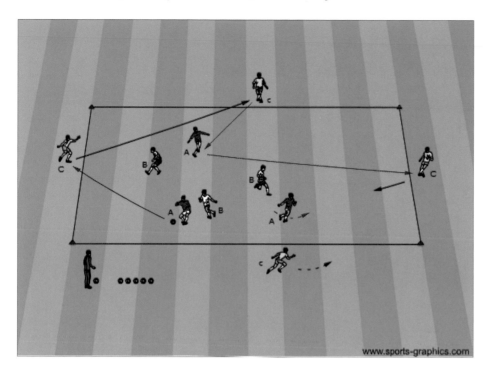

www.sports-graphics.com

Execution

The RED team (see player A) and the BLUE team (see player B) each have three players on the field. Four players are positioned off the field and can only be passed to by the team currently in possession. The team in possession (see player A) attempts to keep the ball within the own ranks with the help of the outside players and, in doing so, tries to switch play to the short sides of the field through player C. The outside players can signal their availability to receive a pass along the entire length of their side (see player c). As soon as the ball goes out of bounds, the coach brings a new ball into the game.

Variations

* Limit touches for outside players.
* Limit touches for field players.
* Specify 2 or 3 mandatory touches for the player in possession.
* Specify the free leg (left/right) for outside players.
* Organize as a competition: Which team switches play most often?

1.1.15   3-on-3 (against 3-on-2)

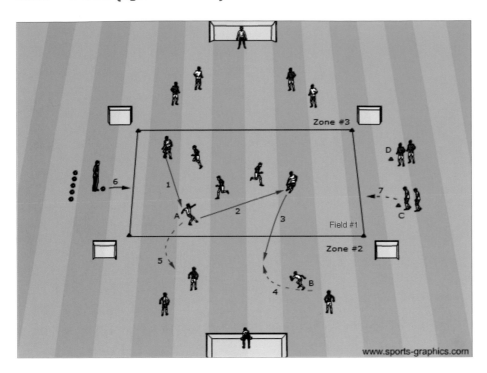

Execution

All players are assigned to a RED or a BLUE team. Three players from each team are positioned in the center of the field (see field #1). In addition, two players from each team are positioned in the zones in front of the goals (see zones #2 and #3). Waiting players are in positions C and D. The game always starts with 3-on-3 in the center (see field #1). The team in possession tries to play two consecutive passes (see 1 and 2) and then has the option of passing to a teammate in zone #2 or #3. Here the pass to player B in zone #2 is successfully completed (see 3). After a successful pass into an offensive zone, a player from the center can move up for 3-on-2 (here player A; see 5). The three attackers try to get a shot on the big goal. After winning the ball, the two defenders can counter on the two mini goals. As soon as a pass from the center has been successfully played into one of the two offensive zones, the coach brings a new ball into the game (see 6), and one player (here player C) completes the 3-on-3 of the waiting position in the center (see 7).

Concept

A fast passing game and, after two successful passes, a switch in play or vertical deep play is needed in the center. Each team's two players in the offensive zones must be ready for defense or offense.

1.1.16   6-on-6 plus 6 (for possession)

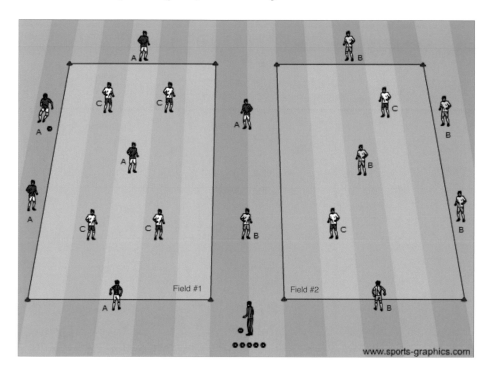

www.sports-graphics.com

Execution

Three teams of six players each (see teams A, B, and C) spread out on a playing field that consists of two outside fields (see fields #1 and #2) and a center zone. Two teams always play together in possession (here teams A and B) against one team (here team C), which must split up between the two fields (see team C). Team A has possession and plays two-touch combinations. To switch the ball to the second field, the ball must always be passed to the players in the center zone. Only these players can pass the ball to the other field. The defending team (here team C) is always arranged in a 4:2 ratio. In doing so, four players are always on the same field as the team in possession. When there is a field switch, two players also move to the other field.

Guidelines

It is considered an error if the defending team touches the ball, a bad pass is played, the ball is passed into touch, or one player has more than two touches. After each error, the coach plays a new ball into the game, and each ball from the coach prompts a switch of play. The defending team must provoke three errors, or rather, win the ball. After winning the ball three times, the team switches positions with the team that caused the third error. The two players in the center have a special function. They decide whether the own team keeps possession or there will be a switch of play.

1.2 DRIBBLING

1.2.1 4-on-4 (dribbling and first touch)

Execution

The RED team plays 4-on-4 against the BLUE team. The players pass each other the ball by hand (see 1). At first, both goalkeepers can participate, making it initially 4-on-4 plus 2. The goal is to do a brief dribble by hand. The player in possession must bounce the ball 3 times in a row (see 2). Possession changes immediately if the ball first touches the floor or the player only bounces it once or twice. If a player is able to bounce the ball 3 times, he must then play at least one pass to a teammate (see 3). A shot on both goals using a volley or a dropkick from the hand (see 4) can follow immediately after.

Concept

One objective can be to get a player open so he has space to bounce or dribble the ball. The players should courageously use available spaces to bounce or dribble the ball. Precise and sensible first touches (if applicable with change of direction) are promising.

Variations

* Prerequisites for a shot on goal: 2 or 3 additional passes after bouncing or dribbling.
* Specify the shooting technique: dropkick/header/inside foot/instep.
* Specify the shooting technique: direct shot out of the air without first catching the ball.
* Playing with the foot: dribbling with at least four touches.

1.2.2   4-on-4 (on dribble goals, outside)

Execution

The RED team plays 4-on-4 against the BLUE team. Players are allowed to approach the dribble lines after completing three passes within the own team. The game's objective is to dribble across one of the RED dribble lines (see 1). Most important here is the ball control after crossing the line.

Concept

The players are asked to demonstrate target-oriented, dynamic dribbling. This requires recognizing gaps and courageously approaching them in a 1-on-1. A minimum number of touches (see variations) prompts more dribbling and also more 1-on-1 dribbling situations due to easier access for the opponents.

Variations

* Specify 2 or 3 mandatory touches for players in possession.
* Make target lines smaller: Play on the BLUE dribble lines.
* Specify the direction of play: RED team on line #A/BLUE team on line #B.
* Play on the opposite side after scoring and transitioning.

1.2.3   4-on-4 (on dribble goals, center)

Execution

The RED team plays 4-on-4 against the BLUE team. On the field, cone goals are set up in no particular order. The goal is to dribble through one of these cone goals with the ball at the foot (see 1).

Concept

Force courageous starts with the ball into appropriate spaces or gaps, depending to the configuration of the cone goals. Dribbling should be properly prepared with passing combinations so a dribble through the goal can be completed without a 1-on-1-situation and a follow-up action (pass to the partner) is possible.

Variation

* Specify 2 or 3 mandatory touches for the player in possession.
* Simplify or expand to 4-on-4 (plus two neutral players in possession).
* Use precision dribbling through the cone gate with the first touch.
* Follow-up action: shot on mini goals after successful dribble.

1.2.4   4-on-4 (on dribble goals with finish)

Execution

The RED team plays 4-on-4 against the BLUE team. A goalkeeper is positioned in a marked-off diamond in the center of the field. No field player is allowed to enter the diamond. The game's objective is to dribble through one of the cone goals from the outside (one point) and, if possible, finish with a shot into the diamond afterward (two points). After the finish, the coach brings a new ball into the game.

Concept

Courageous dribble into the center is rewarded with a possible shot on goal.

Variations

* Option for the team in possession: Involve the goalkeeper in a 4-on-4 plus 1.
* Simplify or expand to 4-on-4 (plus three neutral players in possession).

1.2.5   4-on-4 (on dribble lines with finish)

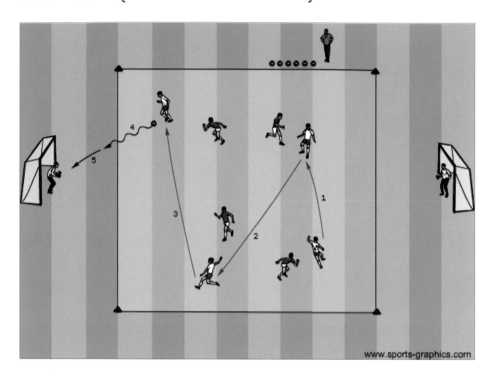

Execution

The RED team plays 4-on-4 against the BLUE team inside the area of the field marked in YELLOW. After three consecutive passes (see 1, 2, and 3) within the own team, players are allowed to leave the field on both sides by dribbling toward the goal (see 4). Next, the player with the ball can take a shot on the goal (see 5).

Concept

After a preparatory passing relay, players should leave the field with a fast target-oriented dribble toward the goal. The dribble should be followed by a fluid follow-up action as the finish.

Variations

* Specify the shooting technique after dribbling across the line (see 5): direct finish.
* Simplify or expand to 4-on-4 (plus two neutral players in possession).
* Specify 2 or 3 mandatory touches for the player in possession.
* Specify play against the goalkeeper: Dribble past the goalie.
* Option of moving one defensive player up for 1-on-1.

1.2.6   4-on-4 (on dribble lines with follow-up action)

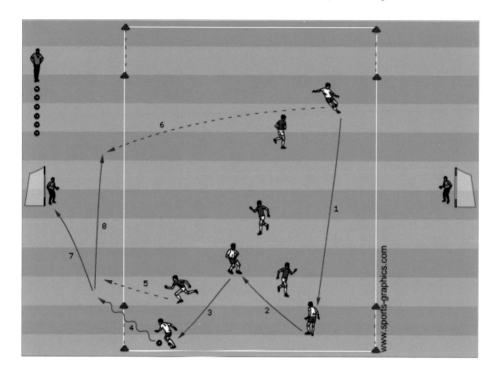

Execution

The RED team plays 4-on-4 against the BLUE team. After three passes within the team in possession (see 1, 2, and 3), the objective is to dribble through one of the small dribble goals toward the large goal (see 4). One opponent (see 5) and one player of the own team (see 6) are allowed to follow the player in possession. The player in possession can take a shot on goal (see 7) or pass to his teammate (see 8). After the finish, the coach brings a new ball into the game, and the players who were previously active off the field now immediately return to the field for 4-on-4.

Concept

The preparatory passing game should be followed by a target-oriented dribble. The pursuing players will generate pressure, so additional opportunities for action open up.

Variations

* Specify 2 or 3 mandatory touches for the player in possession.
* Simplify or expand to 4-on-4 (plus two neutral players in possession).
* Specify the shooting technique (see 7 and 8): inside foot/instep/direct finish.

1.2.7   4-on-4 (through dribble fields)

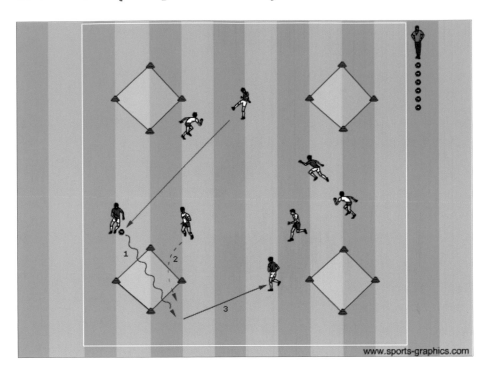

Execution

The RED team plays 4-on-4 against the BLUE team. Players are not allowed to enter the small square fields. The game's objective is to dribble across one of the fields marked in YELLOW (see 1 with the ball at the foot). As soon as a player decides to dribble across a field, a defender is allowed to follow him onto that field and interfere (see 2). Another goal is a subsequent pass to the teammate immediately after the field has been crossed (see 3).

Concept

The dribble action must be well prepared so the player in possession has space and is able to cover a long distance (with the ball at his foot)—ideally without a lot of pressure from the opponent. This requires confident dribbling preferably followed by an additional action.

Variations

* Vary or modify the way the fields are arranged (e.g., another field in the center).
* Specify how to exit the field: on the side/through the opposite side.
* Precision dribble with the first touch onto the field.

1.2.8   4-on-4 (on central dribble field)

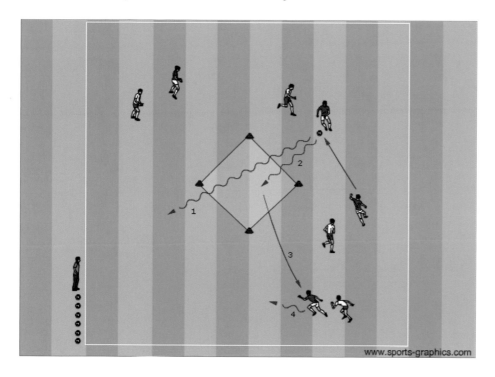

Execution

The RED team plays 4-on-4 against the BLUE team. Players are not allowed to enter the YELLOW dribbling field. The game's objective is that one player from the team in possession can penetrate the opposing lines with a dribble and enter the center field. In doing so, he has the option of leaving the field using a dribble (see 1) or passing the ball from the field to a teammate (see 2 and 3). After the successful pass or dribble, the game continues without interruption (see 4).

Concept

A preparatory passing game is used to prepare a suitable dribbling situation, which the player in possession must recognize and utilize. The game's objective is to exploit gaps in the defense with a dribble.

Variations

* Organize as a competition with a points system:

    One point: dribbling across two of the field's lines (see 1).

    Two points: dribbling with subsequent pass (see 2 and 3).

    Three points: receiving player dribbles (three touches) without losing the ball (see 4).

1.2.9   4-on-4 (on dribble goals with subsequent pass)

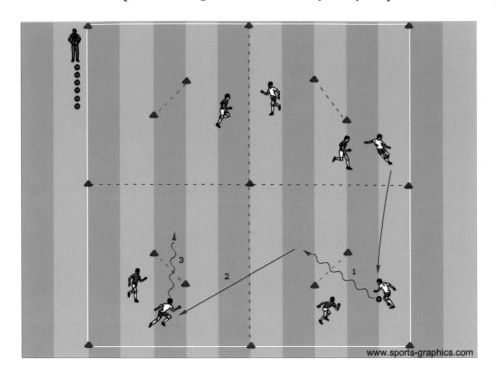

www.sports-graphics.com

Execution

The RED team plays 4-on-4 against the BLUE team. All players can move about freely and are not bound to the marked quarters. The game's objective is to dribble through one of the four dribble goals after receiving a pass (see 1). After dribbling through the goal, the player must play a pass to a teammate (see 2). The pass must be long and deep and, therefore, must be played into one of the adjacent fields.

Concept

A target-oriented passing game and successful dribbling must be followed by a follow-up action in the form of a pass to the teammate who is getting open. Group tactical behavior is required for the preparatory and follow-up phases.

Variations

*   Organize as a competition with a points system:

    One point: dribbling through the cone goal (see 1).

    Two points: dribbling through the cone goal with the first touch.

    Three points: pass into a different quarter of the field after a successful dribble (see 2).

    Four points: dribble through a second cone goal as a follow-up action.

1.2.10   4-on-4 plus 2 (with outside players)

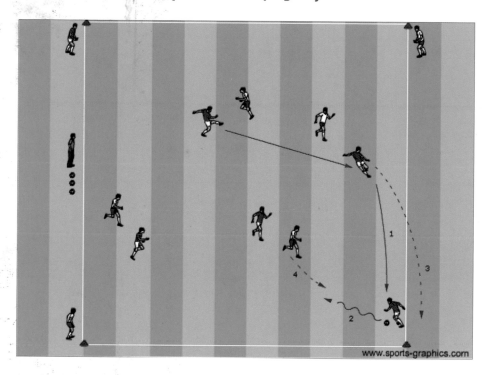

www.sports-graphics.com

Execution

The RED team plays 4-on-4 against the BLUE team. Each team has two outside players who are positioned diagonally opposite each other at the markings. The game's objective is to play lots of passes to the outside players (see 1). As soon as an outside player has received a pass, he dribbles onto the field and has to complete three mandatory touches (see 2) before he is able to pass the ball. The passing player on the field switches to the position opening up outside (see 3). The opposing team tries to put pressure on the dribbling player (see 4).

Concept

Because of the three mandatory touches, dribbling onto the field from outside is often done with opponent pressure from the front and side. Even before the first touch, the outside player anticipating the pass should have a problem-solving approach in place and should, for instance, employ running and body feints before handling the ball.

Variations

* Specify 2 or 3 mandatory touches for the player in possession.
* Increase number of mandatory touches for outside players (see 2).
* Specify receiving leg (left/right) for outside players (see 2).

1.2.11   4-on-4 plus 2 (with dribbling players)

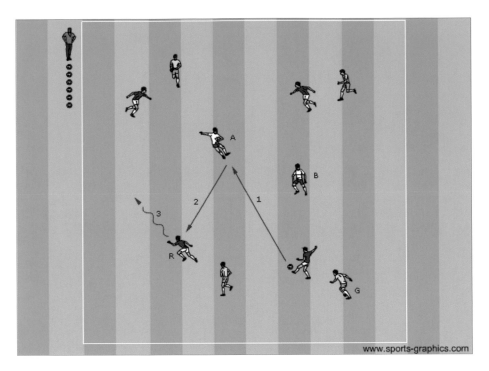

www.sports-graphics.com

Execution

The RED team plays 4-on-4 against the GRAY team. The team in possession (here GRAY) is allowed to pass to the two neutral players A and B (see 1). Each team designates a dribbling player (see R and G). The dribbling players are obligated to always use at least three touches (see 3). Dribbling players change regularly.

Concept

Passes to the dribbling players must be target oriented and well prepared. Furthermore, the team's positional play must open up space for the potential dribbling player to dribble.

Variations

* Specify 2 or 3 mandatory touches for neutral players.
* Increase the number of mandatory touches for the dribbling player.
* Designate two dribbling players.

1.2.12   4-on-4 (touch competition)

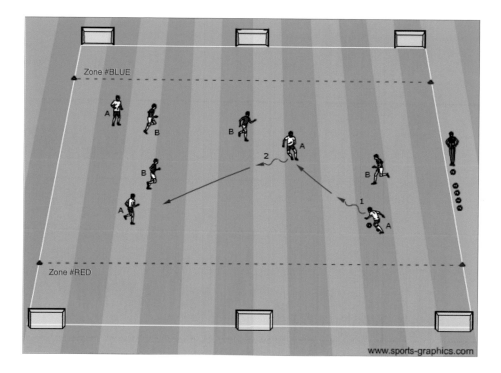

Execution

The BLUE team (see A) plays 4-on-4 against the RED team (see B). Both teams are not allowed to play direct passes, which means every ball received must be handled (see 1 and 2). The teams try to score on three mini goals. Shots on mini goals can only be taken from the outer zones (for the BLUE team, see zone #BLUE; for the RED team, see zone #RED). The zones can only be dribbled in. After a successful shot, the opponent's minimum number of touches goes up. If the BLUE team scores first, each player on the RED team has to use at least three touches. If the BLUE team scores a second time, every player on the RED team has to use at least four touches, and so on. The first team to score three times wins.

Concept

Since only dribbling is permitted in the zones, it forces a dribble before every finish. Even in the 4-on-4-drill, the rising number of touches requires constant dribbling. Important factors are precise ball control and passing that facilitates carrying the ball into open spaces.

1.3   TRANSITIONING AND REACTING

1.3.1   3-on-3 plus 4 (on mini goals)

www.sports-graphics.com

Execution

The RED team plays 3-on-3 against the BLUE team. The team in possession can also pass to the outside players who can only return it as a direct pass. A finish on the mini goal is possible after a successful pass to an outside player. But players can only play on two mini goals. The passing leg with which the outside player returns the ball is critical here. If the outside player passes with the right leg (see 3), the top and bottom goals must be played on (see 2). If the outside player passes with the left leg, the goals on the left and right (see 1) must be played on. As soon as another outside player receives a pass, the goals to be played on change based on which passing leg is used.

Concept

Here emphasis is placed on training cognition (here with respect to the passing leg). Immediate reaction, or rather quick transition, based on the passing leg and the resulting mini goals to be played on as well as orientation in space are also important.

Variation

*   Specify the mini goals to be played on by a command from the outside player.

1.3.2   4-on-4 (on mini goals with transition after finish)

Execution

The RED team plays 4-on-4 against the BLUE team. After three consecutive passes in the own ranks, the team in possession (see RED team) can finish on one of the four mini goals (see 1). After the finish, the coach immediately brings a second ball into the game (see 3). All players must quickly transition and react to the new ball (see 2). Unlike the direction of the finish (here left), the direction of play during the second ball is now specified so that the RED team attacks on the opposite side (here right), and the BLUE team defends the right side.

Concept

Alertness must be maintained after the finish. It is about quick transitions with a change in the direction of play. Important here is alternating between tactics for attacking or defending all four goals, or switching to the specified direction of play with the second ball.

Variations

* Continue play: ball from the coach for the RED team after a successful finish by the RED team.
* Continue play: ball from the coach for the BLUE team after an unsuccessful finish by the RED team.

1.3.3   4-on-4 plus 1 (with changing objectives)

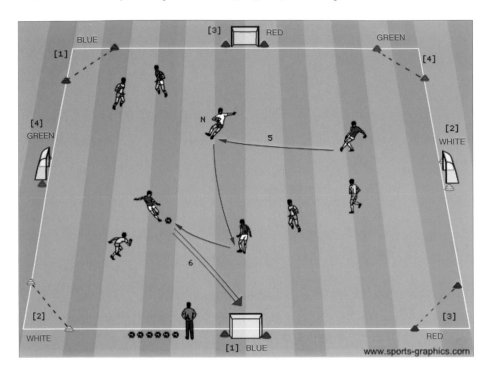

Execution

Four mini goals and four dribble lines are set up around the playing field. On the field, the RED team plays 4-on-4 against the GRAY team. The team in possession (see 5) can also pass to a neutral player (see N). The initial objective is to keep the ball in the own ranks. During the course of the game, the coach designates a color (here BLUE) and opens up a mini goal and a dribble line. Now both teams can attack the BLUE mini goal (see 6) or dribble on the BLUE dribble line (see [1]) and score a point until the next signal from the coach.

Concept

After the signal from the coach, a quick transition from possession to a target-oriented finish is critical and is needed as quickly as possible. The coach determines the amount of time between two signals and the frequency of transitions, changing the game situation.

Variations

* Vary or modify coach's signal (e.g., designate numbers).
* Vary or modify coach's signal (e.g., alternately designate color and number).

1.3.4   4-on-4 plus 2 (on alternating mini goals)

Execution

The RED team plays 4-on-4 against the BLUE team. The team in possession can involve the two neutral players. The neutral players are marked A and B. The game's objective is to involve the two neutral players in the game one after the other (see 1, 2, and 3). After that, a shot on goal is an option. Two goals open up, depending on which of the two neutral players played the second pass (see A).

Concept

Alertness and cognition are trained here. After playing with the neutral players, the other players ideally position themselves so the game can continue with a follow-up action.

Variations

* Specify the mini goals to be played on by assigning colors to the neutral players.
* Specify the mini goals to be played on using a command from one of the neutral players.

1.3.5   4-on-4 plus 2 (with transition toward the goal)

Execution

The RED team plays 4-on-4 against the BLUE team. The two large goals are manned by goalkeepers and marked with WHITE or BLACK cones. The initial objective is to keep the ball in the own ranks. Both goalkeepers can be involved (see G). As soon as the coach designates one of the goals by calling out its color (here BLACK), the direction of play has been specified until there is a finish. The team in possession attacks the designated goal (see 1). The team without the ball defends that goal and attacks the opposite goal.

Concept

Quick transitions from possession without a target to a specific direction is required. Important for the defense is defensive transitioning and, specifically, compressing in the center.

Variations (goalkeeping techniques)

* The goalkeeper has the option of picking up and rolling the ball during the possession phase.
* Specify 2 or 3 times of mandatory contact with the ball for goalkeepers during possession.

1.3.6   4-on-4 (with changing game objectives)

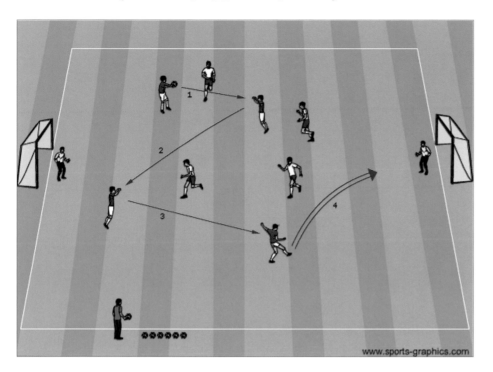

Execution

The RED team plays 4-on-4 against the BLUE team on the field. The ball is passed by hand. Possession changes if the ball touches the ground. After a team has played three passes (see 1, 2, and 3), they can finish on one of the goals (see 4). The finish can be in the form of a volley or a dropkick from the hand of the kicker.

Concept

Reaction or transition from possession to target-oriented goal-scoring takes place with the third pass.

Variations

- ☀ Option for the team in possession: Involve the goalkeepers while holding on to the ball.
- ☀ Specify the direction of play after the ball-holding phase (see 4).
- ☀ Specify the shooting technique: header/volley/dropkick (see 4).

1.3.7   4-on-4 (on alternating goals)

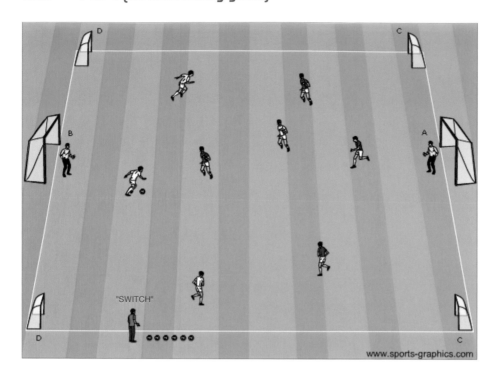

Execution

The WHITE team with goalkeeper B plays against the RED team with goalkeeper A. Initially, players only play on the large goals. After the coach signals by calling "switch," players can only play on the mini goals. Next, the WHITE team plays on goals C, and the RED team attacks goals D.

Concept

The basic idea is the quick transition from playing through the center to playing on the wing. Using the signals allows the coach to decide in which situations players should demonstrate a quick transition.

Variations

* Specify the shooting technique on the mini goals: direct finish.
* Option for the team in possession: Pass to the goalkeeper during play on the mini goals.

1.3.8   8-on-8 (with 3 balls)

Execution

The WHITE team plays for possession against the RED team. There are always three balls in play (see 1, 2, and 3). If a ball goes off the field, the coach brings a new ball into the game. The game's objective is to keep all three balls in the own ranks for five seconds (one point).

Concept

The players must recognize where on the field the own team is in a minority situation and fill in. Furthermore, coaching each other with clear commands is necessary to even out the minority situations and break up unnecessary majority situations.

Variations

- Adjust the player–ball ratio relative to the performance level.
- Specify 2 or 3 mandatory touches for players in possession.
- Simplify or expand by adding neutral players.

1.3.9   4-on-4 (with change of direction)

Execution

The WHITE team plays against the RED team. The WHITE team initially attacks the three dribble goals (see A, B, and C). The WHITE team's objective is to get through one of the goals to the dribble field D. The RED team tries to prevent this and while in possession attacks the large goal (see E). After the WHITE team successfully dribbles through (see 1), the objectives change so that the WHITE team must now play on the large goal and the RED team on the dribble goals.

Concept

Quick transitions are also required after a dribble goal has been reached so there is always a follow-up action. The transition is in the change in direction and alternating between playing through the center and on the wing.

Variations

* Automatic change in direction of play after 10 passes in the own ranks.
* Organize as a competition with a points system:

    One point: Dribble through a cone goal into zone #D (see 1).

    Two points: Successful shot on goal #E.

    Three points: Combination of dribble (see 1) and a goal without opposing possession.

    Four points: Combination of dribble and goal by the same player.

1.3.10   4 plus 1 against 4 plus 1 (with changing objectives)

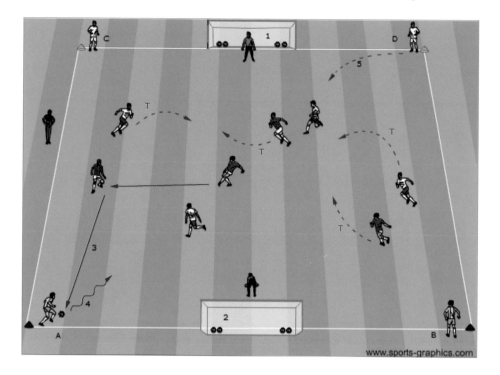

Execution

The RED team plays 4-on-4 against the WHITE team. After three passes in the own ranks, the team in possession can pass to an outside player (see 3). With the outside pass, the outside player (see A) dribbles onto the field (see 4) and becomes a part of the RED team, and the player positioned opposite him (see D) joins the WHITE team. The transition (see T) and the play on the two large goals (see 1 and 2) begin with the outside pass (see 3), and then the RED team attacks goal 1 and the WHITE team goal 2, depending which outside player the team in possession passed to.

Concept

Generally, transitions are prompted by the search for position from playing for possession to target-oriented play on the large goals. Determining which large goal must be defended or played on depends on situation— which outside player is passed to.

Variations

* Continue play as 4-on-4 plus 1 by activating the outside player who received the pass.
* Continue play as 6-on-6 by activating all outside players.

1.3.11   2-on-2 (with transition to 3-on-2 and change of direction)

www.sports-graphics.com

Execution

Play starts on the field as 2-on-2 on both large goals. As soon as a team finishes, shot on goal or past the goal, the direction of play changes, and one outside player of the team that finished dribbles a new ball onto the field for 3-on-2. In doing so, the outside players coordinate who will start and alternate the follow-up actions. The teams of two in the center switch play and play on or defend the other goal. The outside player, who dribbles onto the field for the 3-on-2, has to play at least one pass. The players in the center regularly switch with the outside players. Two goals per round count as a point scored. Compete to see which team is the first to score 10 goals.

Concept

The finish on a goal is rewarded with a second ball. Deep tempo runs are promising after the double transition (second ball and change in direction of play).

Variations

* Option of a shot on goal without an additional pass for the receiving outside player.
* Designate the outside player using two field players (e.g., call the name).
* Continue play as 3-on-3: additional activation of a defending outside player.

1.3.12 4-on-8 (on 4 mini goals with transition to offense)

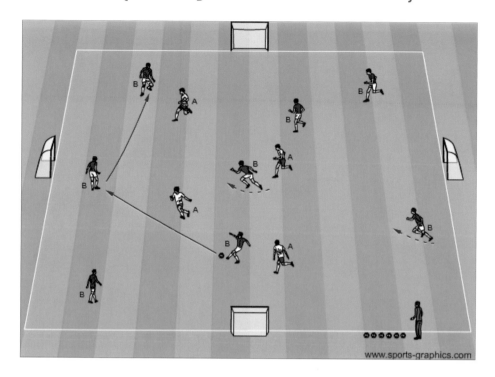

Execution

Team B in possession consists of eight players and plays for possession on a marked field. When team B loses the ball, it must immediately switch to counterpressing. Team A consists of four players and plays in minority to quickly win the ball. After successfully winning the ball, team A can finish on the four mini goals. After a finish or if the ball goes into touch, the coach immediately brings a new ball into the game. The minority team has 90 seconds to win as many balls and score as many goals as possible. After 90 seconds, four new players switch to the minority situation.

Concept

The minority team (here team A) plays against the clock and is encouraged by motivated coaching to hunt for and quickly win the ball. In addition, fast and target-oriented transitions should be forced.

Variations

* Specify 2 or 3 mandatory touches for the majority team.
* Prerequisites for a shot on goal by the minority team: dribble across an outside line.

1.4   SMALL GAMES

1.4.1   Catch (duel)

Execution

A discretionary number of players (here 8) are on a marked field. The players do not need to wear identifying bibs. Some players are in possession (see A), whereas others don't have a ball (see B). Player A tries to remain in possession and defend his ball (see 1). Player B tries to steal the ball from a player in possession with a tackle (see 2). If this is successful and player A loses his ball, he immediately tries to regain possession with his next action.

Learning goals

* Dribbling with lots of feints and keeping the ball close.
* Body feints and changing direction with the ball.
* Shielding the ball from the opponent.
* Keeping an eye on multiple potential attackers.

Variation

* Organize as a competition: The players without a ball pass a stolen ball out of bounds. At the same time, player A, who lost the ball, is eliminated from the game. Have players see long it takes the B players to eliminate all of the balls, or rather players, from the game.

1.4.2   Catch (team competition)

Execution

A group of catchers is positioned at an outside cone (see RED team). On the field is an opposing group in which every player has a ball (see 1 and BLUE team). After a starting signal, a player from the RED team starts onto the field (see 2) and tries to tag one of the players with his hand. If he succeeds, he quickly returns to the group and exchanges high-fives with the next player on his team. Now that player starts onto the field to tag another player.

Learning goals

* Dribbling with lots of feints and keeping the ball close.
* Body feints and changing direction with the ball.

Variations

* Increase active players on the RED team: Starting signal applies to two catchers.
* Organize as a competition: How long will it take the RED team to tag 10 players?
* Organize as a competition: How many players can the RED team tag in two minutes?

1.4.3   Catch (1-on-1)

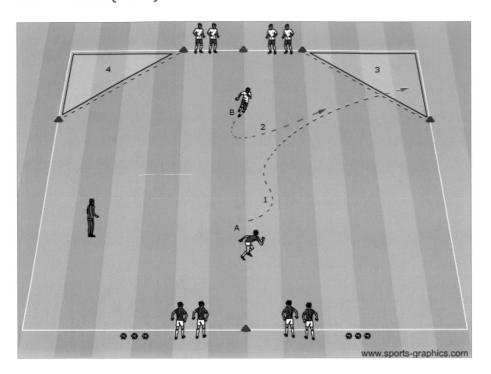

Execution

The players on the RED team (see A) are positioned at the RED cone and act as attackers. The players on the BLUE team (see B) are positioned at the opposing BLUE cone and are the defenders. After a signal from the coach, one player from each group starts onto the field. The player from the RED team (see A) must try to reach one of the end zones (see 3 and 4) and ideally chooses a running path with lots of feints and changes in direction. The B players from the BLUE team try to tag him by hand (see 2) before he reaches one of the two end zones or target lines. With the next signal from the coach, two new players start. Tasks change after each round.

Learning goals

* Running paths with lots of changes in direction and body feints.
* Smart changes to running speed (i.e., highest speed after change in direction).

Variations

* Execute with ball: Reach the end zone by dribbling with the ball at the foot.

1.4.4   Handball header (open passing game)

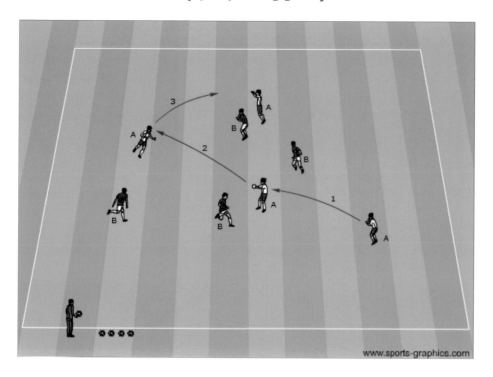

www.sports-graphics.com

Execution

Players are divided into two teams. The ball is passed by hand. The goal is to remain in possession (see 1 and 2) without the ball touching the ground (turnover) or an opposing player intercepting the ball. A team is awarded one point if it is able to play a header pass (see 3). In doing so, the ball can be headed back to the player who played the pass (one point) or to another teammate as third man running (two points).

Concept

Quick passing play is supposed to create a header opportunity and should be prepared accordingly. Ideally, the players should recognize when to play a header without opposing pressure and with a high probability of success and when it makes more sense to simply catch and pass the ball.

Variations

* Organize as a competition with a points system:

   One point: header to a teammate (see 3).

   Two points: direct volley pass by foot to the partner (see 3).

   Three points: two successive headers (see 2 and 3).

1.4.5   Handball header (on goals)

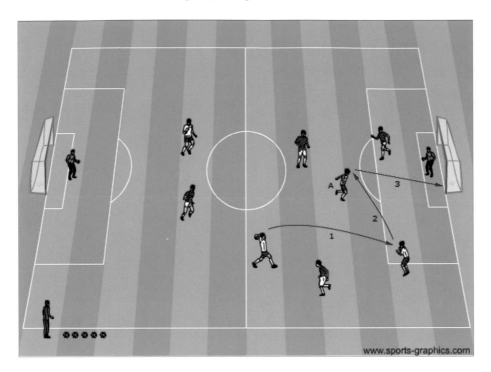

www.sports-graphics.com

Execution

The RED team plays 4-on-4 against the BLUE team on the two large goals, each manned with a goalkeeper. The ball is passed by hand (see 1 and 2) and cannot touch the ground. Goals can only be scored using a header (see A and 3). When a goal is scored or a ball goes out of bounds, the coach immediately brings a new ball into the game.

Learning goals

* Fast passing game to create space for the player heading the ball.
* Practicing getting open using simplified passing by hand.

Variations

* Eliminate direction of play: opportunity to play on both goals.
* Simplify or expand to 4-on-4 (plus two neutral players in possession).
* Prohibit play by hand for defenders when a cross is played into the box (header defense).

1.4.6   Handball (shot on goal)

Execution

Players are divided into two teams. The team in possession passes the ball by hand. If the ball touches the ground, possession changes immediately. Players can take no more than three steps while holding the ball. The team in possession (see A and a) tries to create a gap in the opponent's chain (see B) using a quick passing game and appropriate getting-open tactics (see 1 and 2). The shot on goal can be taken as a volley by hand or a dropkick (see 3). After the finish, the coach immediately brings a new ball into the game. If a goal is scored, the successful offense remains in possession. If no goal is scored, the coach plays the next ball to the defense, which then switches to offense.

Concept

Offense focuses on playing wide and courageously exploiting gaps. Defense practices shifting as a unit.

Variations

* Simplify or expand to 4-on-4 (plus two neutral players in possession).
* Specify constant alternating between ground passes and direct passes.
* Add a counterattack opportunity for the defense: dribble lines/mini goals.

1.4.7   Numbers soccer (1)

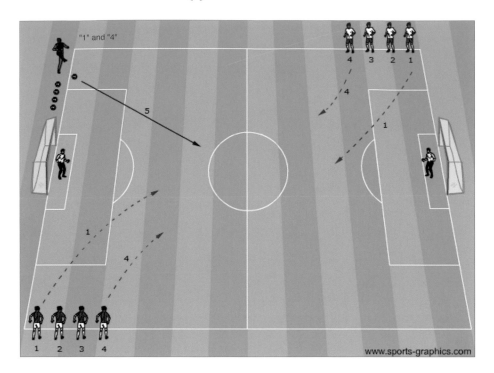

Execution

Two teams are positioned in two corners of the field. Each of the BLUE and RED players is assigned a number. The coach brings a ball into the game and at the same time calls one or more numbers (here 1 and 4). The respective players start onto the field against the large goals (here 2-on-2). The game ends when a goal is scored. As the game progresses, the coach can also call additional numbers, allowing those players to come into the game. If a number is called twice, the respective players have to exit the field during the game.

Learning goals

* Quick reaction to the coach's signal.
* Quick orientation in space and coordinated manning of positions.

Variations

* Call up players using an arithmetic problem (e.g., 8 - 4 and 10 - 9 = players 4 and 1).
* Call up different players (e.g., BLUE 3 and 4 against RED 1 and 2).

1.4.8 Numbers soccer (2)

Execution

Only two of the players on the RED team are active (see A). Two other players each sit out one round (see B). For each round, a varying number of players from the BLUE team are allowed to intervene in the game. The players on the BLUE team are numbered (here 1 to 4). The coach brings a ball into the game (see 5) and calls out one or more numbers. The players he calls (here players 2, 3, and 4) start into the game and on the large goals. The players on the RED team start with the coach's touch on the ball.

Learning goals

* Quick reaction to the coach's signal.
* Quick orientation in space and coordinated manning of positions.
* Offensive and defensive orientation of the BLUE team depending on actual numbers ratio.

Variations

* Call up players using an arithmetic problem (e.g., 8 - 4 and 10 - 9 = players 4 and 1).
* Vary the coach's ball: Alternate passes to the BLUE and the RED team.

1.4.9   The Great White

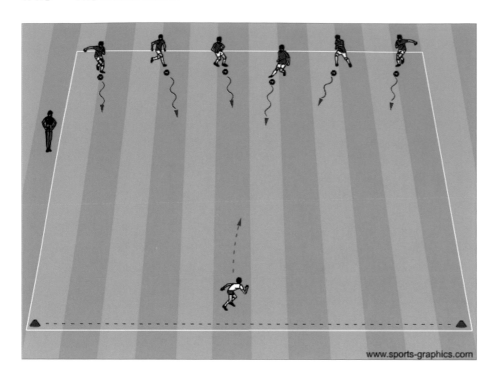

www.sports-graphics.com

Execution

Multiple players are positioned along one edge of a playing field (here the RED team). On the other side of the field is a single player without a ball—the Great White. At a signal from the coach, the RED players approach with a dribble and try to reach the end zone on the other side of the field (see RED dribble lines) without getting tagged by the catcher, the Great White. When a player is tagged, he also becomes a catcher when the coach gives his next signal.

Learning goals

⋆   Courageous dribble when a gap opens.

⋆   Situation-specific tempo dribble with changes in direction.

Variations

⋆   Execute without ball: reach the end zone without a ball at the foot.

⋆   Execute with ball: reach the end zone with a ball at the foot.

⋆   Specify the free leg (left/right) for outside players.

⋆   Prohibit running paths in reverse direction.

1.4.10   Moveable goals

www.sports-graphics.com

Execution

On the field are several players with multiple balls (see RED team). The number of players on the RED team is not important. The number of balls is geared toward the number of players from the RED team (here six players and three balls). In addition, players pair up, holding an agility bar between them (see a and b), and run around the field as moveable goals. By dribbling, the players on the RED team try to get into position (see 1) to play a pass through the moving goal to a teammate who doesn't have a ball (see 2).

Learning goal

★   Determine pairs within the RED team (one ball per pair of players).

Variations

★   Designate pairs within the RED team (one ball per pair of players).

★   Organize as a competition: How many passes will be played during a certain period of time?

★   Organize as a competition: Which pair allows more goals through their moving goal?

★   Organize as a competition: Which pair allows fewer goals through their moving goal?

1.4.11   Calling names

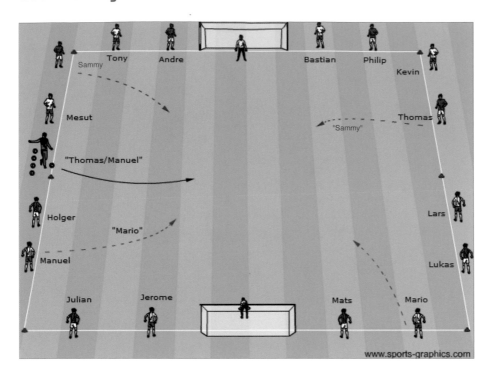

Execution

Players from the RED team and the BLUE team are positioned equal distance all along the edge of the field, alternating teams. The coach specifies the ratio of RED to BLUE players for the game (here 2-on-2). The players from the BLUE team always attack the upper goal, and the players from the RED team always attack the lower goal. The coach plays the ball into the center and designates two players, one player from the BLUE team and one player from the RED team. The designated players (here Thomas and Manuel) run onto the field to the ball, and each calls one teammate to join them on the field. The called-up player (here Mario for the BLUE team and Sammy for the RED team) also start onto the field and participate in the 2-on-2 on the two large goals.

Concept

Depending on the position of the ball, the players called up by the coach try to designate one or more players who can start from tactically advantageous positions in a given situation. Here the players can be asked to designate primarily offensive or defensive positions or players.

Variations

* Vary the player ratio (3-on-3/4-on-4).
* Vary the coach's ball (e.g., center/wing/near the goal).

1.4.12   Memory®

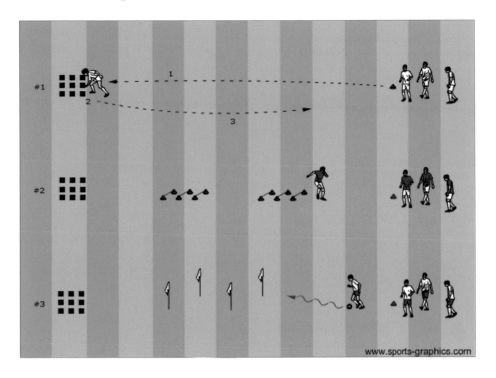

Execution

Players are divided into several groups and compete against each other. Each group plays on a target field with memory cards placed on it. The first player from each team runs from the start cone toward the memory cards (see 1). He is allowed to uncover two cards per lap (see 2) and then return to his group (see 3) to send the next team member into the race with a high-five. If he uncovers a matching pair of memory cards, he can take them back to the group. The goal is to bring the entire set of memory cards back to the group. Players are allowed to communicate with each other to share already known positions of images.

Variations

#1: Complete running paths in versatile running ABCs.

#2: Complete running paths with coordination tasks.

#3: Complete running paths as an obstacle dribble.

* Prohibit communication and exchanging of information.
* Use a card game: Uncover all hearts.
* Vary games (e.g., dice, Jenga, stack the cups, solve arithmetic problems).

1.5   TACTICS

1.5.1   Defensive tactics (defend with a high line)

Execution

The RED team (defense) plays against the BLUE team (offense). The BLUE team has one less player than the RED team. Depending on the performance level, player C can be added for 6-on-6. The RED team's goalkeeper (see GK1) opens each new action with a goal kick or throw-out (see 1) to one of the opposing players, A or B (here player A). Prior to every action, the players of the RED team position flat side by side and are allowed to start on the field only after the goalkeeper's goal kick (see 2). The attacker receiving the pass (here player A) controls the ball after the pass (see 3), and the BLUE team attacks. The RED team defends and, after winning the ball, is also allowed to attack one of the large goals.

Tactical learning goals

* Come out and decrease distance to opponent (see 2).
* Build up staggered depth and safeguard each other.
* Two levels (form back four and 6er).
* High defense and no passive waiting.
* Active defense (objective: win the ball and counter).

1.5.2   Defensive tactics (block passing lanes)

Execution

The RED team (defense) plays against the BLUE team (offense). The BLUE team has one less player than the red team. Depending on the performance level, player C can be added to the 6-on-6. The RED team's goalkeeper (see GK1) opens each new action with a goal kick or throw (see 1) to one of the opposing players, A or B (here player B). Prior to every action, the players of the RED team position flat side by side and are allowed to start on the field only after the goalkeeper's goal kick (see 3 and 4). The attacker receiving the pass (here player B) controls the ball after the pass (see 2), and the BLUE team attacks. The RED team defends and, after winning the ball, is also allowed to attack one of the large goals. The BLUE team can score additional points by either dribbling across the dribble line in the center (see L) and the game continues or finish in one of the two mini goals (see G).

Tactical learning goals

* Block passing lanes between central defender and wingback (see G and 4).
* Block passing and dribble lanes between central defenders, or rather, 6ers (see L and 3).
* Come out and decrease distance (see 3 and 4)/staggered depth/safeguard.
* Form two levels (back four and 6er)/high defense/no passive waiting.
* Create a majority in the center (see 3 and 4).

1.5.3   Defensive tactics—pressing (1)

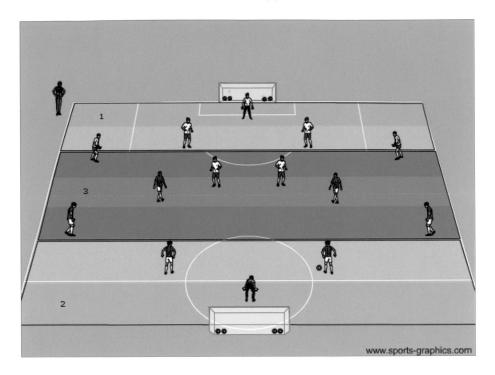

Execution

The tactical goals in passing (active defense with the objective of winning the ball) apply to the RED as well as the BLUE team. Both teams have six players, and each form a back four with two 6ers (i.e., a back four with two forwards). The field is divided into three pressing zones. The following point system applies to force-pressing during this drill and rewards successful counterpressing (see 1 and 2) or midfield-pressing (see 3):

Two points: RED team wins the ball in zone 3 and scores a subsequent goal.

Three points: RED team wins the ball in zone 1 and scores a subsequent goal.

Two points: BLUE team wins the ball in zone 3 and scores a subsequent goal.

Three points: BLUE team wins the ball in zone 2 and scores a subsequent goal.

One point: All unlisted successful goals (e.g., after goalkeeper's opening).

Tactical learning goals

* Acting as a unit, pressuring the opponent, approaching, hunting, and situational double-teaming.
* Winning the ball with transition to offense.

1.5.4   Defensive tactics—pressing (2)

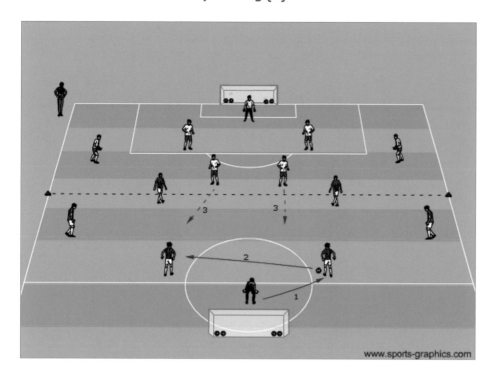

Execution

The tactical goals in passing (active defense with the objective of winning the ball) apply to the RED as well as the BLUE team. Both teams have six players and each form a back four with two 6ers (i.e., a back four with two forwards). A centerline is marked with two cones. The game is always opened with a throw-out by one of the two goalkeepers to one of the central defenders (see 1). At the time of the throw-out, all players from both teams are in their own half. Play opens with the central defender's first touch, and the centerline can be crossed (see 3). The team in possession (here the RED team) must initially play at least five passes in their own half (see 1 and 2) before the centerline can be crossed. The mandatory minimum touches in the own half make pressing as well as access (i.e., tackling) easier.

Tactical learning goals

* Quick forward movement into the opposing half.
* Early interference with the opponent's game start.
* Act as a unit, pressuring the opponent, approaching, hunting, and situational double-teaming.
* Winning the ball with transition to offense.

1.5.5   Defensive tactics—pressing (3)

Execution

The tactical goals in passing (active defense with the objective of winning the ball) apply only to the RED team. If necessary, tasks can be switched after a period of time. The RED team has six players (back four and two forwards), and the BLUE team has five players (back four and one 6er). A sixth player from the BLUE team (see A) serves as the neutral player. The BLUE team's goalkeeper always opens the game with a throw-out to one of the two central defenders (see 1). During every throw-out, the players from the RED team stand at their position-specific marking cones and can only leave that position with the goalkeeper's throw-out to start pressing (see 2). The BLUE team's objective is to cross one of the two dribble lines (see 3 and 4) or to play a pass to neutral player A in the central passing field (see 5). The RED team tries to prevent this or to immediately build pressure when the goalkeeper throws out to win the ball and transition to offense (see 2). The start of pressing is variable and adaptable: pass to a wingback, pass from central defender to central defender, pass to a certain "pressing victim," or poor ball control by an opposing player.

Tactical learning goals

*   Coordinated start pressing (here the goalkeeper's throw-out).
*   Mutual language/communication/code word for the start of pressing.

1.5.6   Offensive tactics (transition to offense 4-on-4 plus 4)

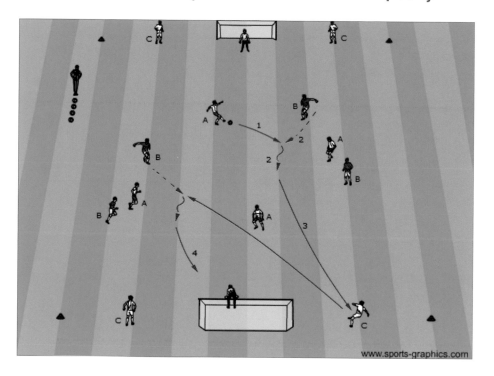

Execution

Teams A and B play 4-on-4 with the objective of holding up the ball (see 1). The team without the ball tries to win the ball. When a team (here team B) manages to intercept a pass or win the ball (see 2), they can play on the large goals and should immediately transition to offense. After winning the ball, they can pass to the deep wing players (see C and 3). Wing players can only play direct passes.

Concept

Focus on actively winning the ball through joint pressing. Use a quick transition to offense with the first forward glance right after winning the ball (see 3), and as many players as possible move up toward the deep pass (see 4).

Variations

* Prerequisite for a shot on goal: pass/involve wing players (see 3).
* Prerequisite for a shot on goal: direct finish (see 4).

1.5.7   Offensive tactics (transition to offense 8-on-5 plus 3)

Execution

Players on field #1 play an 8-on-5 game. The team with the majority (here the RED team) plays for possession (see 1). Here the rule is "1 to 2." Direct passes are always an option. When a player uses two touches (see 2), the next player must play a direct pass and can only use one touch (see 3). The outnumbered team (here WHITE) tries to win the ball and pass it to one of the players waiting on field #2. If the switch in play is successful, all of the players on the WHITE team and five of the players from the RED team switch to field # 2.

Concept

Immediately after winning the ball, the outnumbered team must quickly switch to offense and perform a switch of play. In the case of a turnover, the majority team has the opportunity to counterpress.

Variation

★   Provoke a transition with a ball from the coach (here with a pass to field #2).

1.5.8   Offensive tactics (diagonal passes)

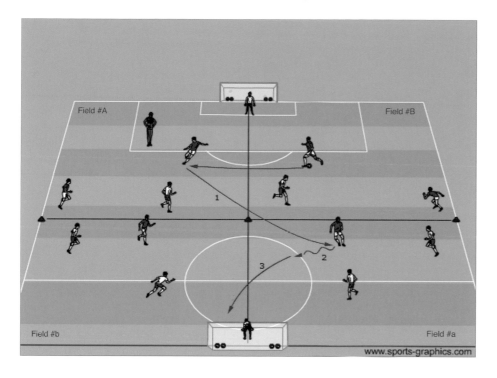

Execution

Both teams have six players (back four and two forwards). There are no guidelines; play is open with the objective of successfully scoring on the opposing goal. To force offensive diagonal passes, the field is divided into four zones. The following rules apply:

Two points: RED team scores on field a after a pass from field #A or on field #b after a pass from field #B.
Two points: BLUE team scores on field A after a pass from field #a or on field #B after a pass from field #b.
Three points: A goal scored with no more than two touches after a diagonal pass (see 2 and 3).

Tactical learning goals

* Offensive passing game in the form of diagonal passes (see 1).
* Purposeful play toward the goal after receiving a pass (see 2 and 3).

1.5.9   Offensive tactics (playing with a wing player)

Execution

Form two teams of four players each. Players position on two levels as offensive midfielders and forwards in the center field. One neutral player positions as an outside midfielder or wing player in each of the two outside zones. The wing players are always a part of the team in possession and can be involved in the game through an outside pass. The game's objective is to play diagonal passes to the outside wing players (see 2) and to score a goal using a cross from the wing (see 4). To make it easier, the wing player (here player A) cannot be interfered with while he controls the ball and plays the cross (see 3 and zone R). Thus, no field players are allowed to enter the outside zones marked in YELLOW. The RED team can send the wing players to zones R (see 2); the BLUE team can attack in zones B (see 1). Three successful passes played in 4-on-4 (see 1) can serve as a prerequisite for a pass to the wing. Moreover, allowing goals to be scored from 4-on-4 without involving a wing player can also be an option.

Tactical learning goals

* Offensive passing using the wing player in the form of diagonal passes (see 2).
* Occupying the striker position after the pass to the wing (see running lane 4).

1.5.10   Offensive tactics—opening the game (1)

Execution

The tactical goals for opening the game (quick, reliable, target-oriented, combination play) apply to both teams. For this reason, the goalkeepers alternate bringing one ball into the game. The goalkeepers start each new action with a throw-out to one of the two central defenders (see 1). The first six passes are specified (see 1 to 7) and must be completed prior to playing on the large goals. The 6-on-6 on the two large goals only starts after the sixth pass has been received (see 7). During the first six passes, the defenders act as passive opponents and do not attempt to win the ball by tackling, but rather semi-actively. The formations, the specified order of passes, and the timing of active intervention by the defense can be changed.

Tactical learning goals

* Reliable and automated passing play by the back four in coordination with the 6ers.
* Working out goals for opening the game (switching play or pass to a 6er).
* Creative problem solving after specified game opening (see from 7).

1.5.11   Offensive tactics—opening the game (2)

www.sports-graphics.com

Execution

The tactical goals for opening the game (quick, reliable, target-oriented combination play) apply to both teams. For this reason, the goalkeepers alternate bringing one ball into the game. The goalkeepers start each new action with a throw-out to one of the two central defenders (see 1). During the throw-out by one of the goalkeepers, all the players from both teams position themselves in their own half. The game's objective is to score a goal in 6-on-6 play. After the goalkeeper opens the game (see 1), the team in possession must first play five passes in their own half before the centerline can be crossed. At the same time as the goalkeeper throws out the ball, the opponents (see 1) are allowed to run across the centerline and interfere with the game build-up. Depending on the performance level, the timing of interference by the defending team (here RED) can be adjusted as follows:

* Defense is allowed to cross the centerline after the third pass.
* Defense can cross the centerline during the throw-out to the central defender.
* Limit the number of players allowed to cross the centerline (e.g., two players).

Tactical learning goal

* Controlled game opening under opponent pressure.

1.5.12   Offensive tactics—opening the game (3)

Execution

The tactical goals for opening the game (quick, reliable, target-oriented combination play) apply to both teams. For this reason, the goalkeepers alternate bringing one ball into the game. The goalkeepers start each new action with a throw-out to one of the two central defenders. To meet the game's objective and score on the opponent's goal, players must dribble through one of the three dribble goals (see 1 and 2). Depending on the performance level, the following rules can be added:

★ Only wing players (see B) are allowed to dribble through the outer goals (see 1).

★ Only 6ers are allowed to dribble through the inner goal (see 2).

★ Players must always cross the line of the cone goal with the first touch.

★ Only two opposing defenders (see C) are allowed to interfere when the goalkeeper throws out the ball.

★ All opposing defenders (here the BLUE team) are allowed to interfere when the goalkeeper throws out the ball.

Tactical learning goals

★ Game opens into a specific space (see 1 and 2).

★ Game opens to specific players (see A and B).

1.6   KICK-OFF VARIATIONS

1.6.1   Kick-off (tennis ball)

www.sports-graphics.com

Execution

Eight players throw four tennis balls back and forth on a playing field. The number of tennis balls varies based on the size of the group. The tennis balls are constantly swapped, passed, and caught. The game begins after a signal from the coach. The coach brings a ball to one of the eight players in the game. Team affiliation is based on possession of the tennis balls. All players holding tennis balls play together against the players without tennis balls (see A and B). The team with tennis balls always plays on the goal of GK1.

Concept

All players must position themselves in line with the coach's signal and the focus of the respective game. Shifting the focus from tennis balls (catching) to soccer balls (passing) is required.

Variations

* Vary the number of tennis balls to create majorities or minorities.
* Vary the equipment (e.g., bibs, cones, soccer balls, or Frisbees).

1.6.2   Kick-off (open passing game)

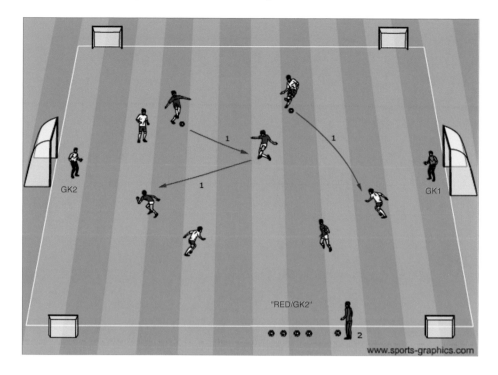

Execution

The RED team and the BLUE team each circulate one ball within their own ranks (see 1) in open passing play. The coach calls one team and one goalkeeper as the start of a subsequent game. The team that is called plays together with the goalkeeper who was called and their own ball on the goal of the goalkeeper who was not called (here the RED team with GK2 in possession against the BLUE team with GK1). The team that was not called passes the own ball to the coach. After the first game ball exits the game from, for instance, a scored goal, the coach brings a second ball (see 2) into the game.

Concept

After open positioning during passing play, the players now must quickly orientate themselves for the subsequent game and position based on the new direction of play. The player in possession must quickly pass the ball used in passing play to the coach or toward the mini goals so he is then able to quickly participate in the 4-on-4.

Variations

* Specify for the team not called: Try to score on the four mini goals with the own ball.
* Option for the team in possession: Involve the goalkeeper in play on the mini goals.

1.6.3   Kick-off (roll the ball)

Execution

The BLUE team plays 4-on-4 against the RED team. Initially, the ball is only passed by hand. The objective is to play three consecutive passes within the own team (see 1, 2, and 3). After three passes by hand, the ball can be rolled to one of the goalkeepers (see 4). After the ball was successfully rolled, 4-on-4 play on the two large goals ensues. The successful team together with the goalkeeper who received the pass play on the opposite goal (here the BLUE team with GK1 on the goal of GK2). The opposing team automatically plays defense.

Concept

After the ball is successfully rolled, the transition from hand to foot must be made. At the same time, the direction of play changes to the two large goals. The players must get in the appropriate positions (see 5) according to the new direction of play and, as a team, focus on defense or offense.

Variations

* Simplify or expand to 4-on-4 (plus two neutral players in possession).
* Expand the game's preliminary objective: prerequisite of 4 or 5 passes by hand.
* Option for the team in possession: involve the goalkeeper.

1.6.4   Kick-off (wing player)

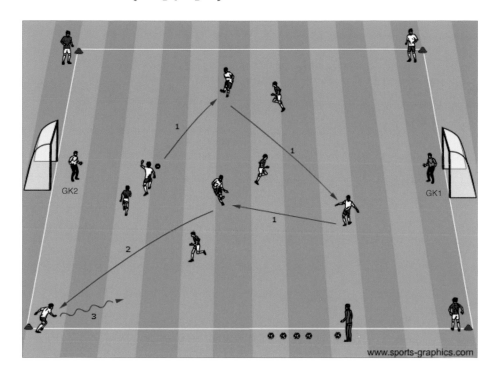

Execution

The RED team plays 4-on-4 against the BLUE team. The players initially let the ball circulate for possession within their own ranks and without a specific direction of play (see 1). The objective is to pass to one of the own wing players (see 2). The wing player receiving the pass dribbles onto the field for a 4-on-5. Depending on which wing player is involved, play is directed on the large goals (here the BLUE team plays on the goal of GK1).

Concept

After the pass to the wing player, both the direction of play and the position-specific orientation of the own team toward the large goals change. All players must quickly orientate themselves and get in position as a team.

Variations

* Prerequisite for a pass to the wing player: 3 or 4 passes in the own ranks (see 1).
* Option for the team in possession during preliminary play: Involve the goalkeeper.
* Prerequisite for a pass to the wing player: direct pass (see 2).
* Continue play as 5-on-5: additional activation of a defending wing player.

1.6.5   Kick-off (passing sequence)

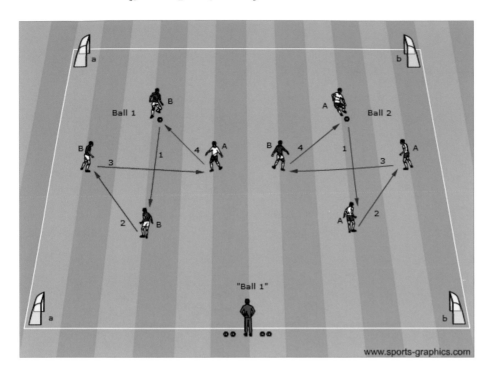

Execution

Players position in two groups of four as shown in the figure. Each group initially executes a specified passing sequence (see 1, 2, 3, and 4) for a certain period of time. The game balls have been numbered beforehand as "Ball 1" and "Ball 2." The coach gives a signal and calls up a ball (here "Ball 1"). The called ball is now the game ball and will be used in the subsequent 4-on-4 on mini goals. The ball that wasn't called must be put in the back of one of the mini goals by the player who was in possession at the time the starting signal was given. That takes the ball out of the game.

Concept

The switch from passing sequence to game requires a transition. Each team starts in diamond formation in a predetermined direction of play (and with players arranged as shown in the figure) with one player in an offensive position.

Variations

   ★   Specify the direction of play (e.g., team A attacks mini goals a).

   ★   Eliminate the direction of play: option of play on all mini goals.

   ★   Prerequisite for playing on goals: 3 or 4 passes in the own ranks.

   ★   Continue play with a ball from the coach (here with "Ball 2").

1.6.6   Kick-off (dribbling competition)

Execution

Two players from the BLUE and RED teams position on the field. With a signal from the coach, a dribbling competition starts on the wings. This dribbling competition determines which players will start in 3-on-2 on the field and how the players must position and align on the field. The two A players start the dribbling competition (see 1) and try to dribble as quickly as possible through the mini goal from outside (see 2). Only the quicker player keeps dribbling onto the field (here the RED team player; see 3) and plays 3-on-2 on the opposing goal with his team (here the RED team on the goal with GK2). The defeated dribbling player lines up again for the dribbling competition without a playing action. In a close dribbling race, the coach determines the faster dribbler.

Concept

The players in the center must react according to the situation and, depending on their position, get ready for defensive or offensive action.

Variations

* Vary or modify the dribbling route.
* Dribble with the weak leg.

1.6.7   Kick-off (positional technique)

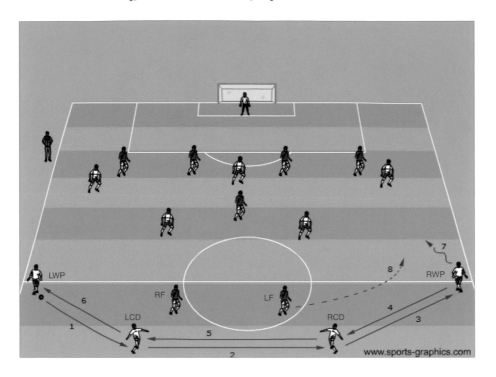

Execution

All players position according to their playing position, as shown in the figure. After a passing sequence, 6-on-6 play ensues in the upper half of the field. The four players from the BLUE team (see LWP, LCD, RCD, and RWP) pass each other the ball as specified (see 1 to 6). All of the uninvolved players shift with the position of the ball. After receiving the ball, the wing players (LWP and RWP) can start a 6-on-6 any time by dribbling into the upper half (here RWP; see 7). One forward (see LF and 8) can also intervene in the game and put direct pressure on the player in possession.

Concept

The specified passing sequence shows the passing technique required in the game. The passive shifting by all players prior to the start of the game guarantees a very realistic opening to the game. The defense must align itself left or right according to an attack. The participating forward must support his team defensively so the defense isn't outnumbered.

Variations

*   Vary the passing sequence (e.g., by involving one or both 6ers).
*   Option of central defenders starting the game (see CD).

1.6.8   Kick-off (reacting)

Execution

A central corridor separates two playing fields with one large and two mini goals in each section. After a signal from the coach (here "START"), the A and B players dribble toward each other (see 1). Player A makes a decision and dribbles either onto the left or the right field (here left; see 2). Player B reacts and dribbles onto the opposite field (here right; see 3). 3-on-2 play ensues on both fields. The team in possession attacks the large goal; the outnumbered team counters on the mini goals.

Concept

The waiting players on the fields don't know whether they will be offense of defense as a majority or minority during the 3-on-2. The goal is for the players to react as fast as possible, correctly assess the situation, and make sure their alignment within the team is position appropriate.

Variations

- ★ Vary or modify the coach's signal for the start of the game (visual/audible).
- ★ Vary the player ratio (4-on-3/5-on-4).
- ★ Coach picks the player who gets to choose the field while dribbling (see 1).
- ★ After both balls finish, continue play in 2 x 3-on-3 through a subsequent action.

1.6.9   Staggered 3-on-3 (finish)

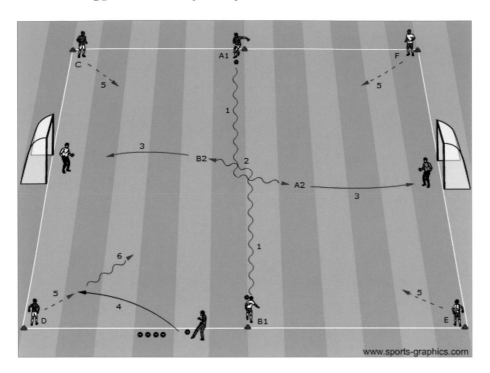

Execution

Players A1 and B1, each with his own ball at his foot, dribble toward each other (see 1), first passing to each other on the right side (see 2) and then turning left and taking a shot on goal (see 3). The two balls that were shot are taken out of the game. At the same time as A1 and B1 take their shots, the coach brings a ball into the game for a 3-on-3 (see 4). The player the coach passes to (here player D) starts toward the pass (see 5) and dribbles onto the field for the 3-on-3 (see 6). All six players participate in the game, whereby the two shooters start from their new positions in the center of the field (see A2 and B2).

Concept

Depending on which wing player received a pass, all players must now transition to their new offensive or defensive positions. With a configuration like the one stated above, the 3-on-3 begins with a staggered arrangement. In doing so the shooters take an offensive position.

Variation

★   Vary the game start with a ball from the coach to one of the two goalkeepers.

1.6.10   Staggered 3-on-3 (transitioning)

Execution

The RED and BLUE teams are arranged in echelons in their starting positions. The RED team plays on the two upper mini goals, and the BLUE team plays on the two lower mini goals. The coach passes the first game ball to one of the two players positioned in the center (see a, b, and 1). 3-on-3-play ensues. As soon as the first game ball has been put in the back of one of the goals or is out of the game, the coach points to one of the four balls positioned off the field. The next 3-on-3 is played with the ball he pointed to. The players from both teams can react to the coach's signal and take possession of the new game ball.

Concept

At the start of the game, both teams are already in a basic staggered formation. Prior to the first ball, the teams do not know whether they will play offense or defense. Quick orientation and swift offensive or defensive alignment are promising. After each finish, players must again transition and react to possession or defensive play.

1.6.11   Staggered 3-on-3 (passing sequence and finish)

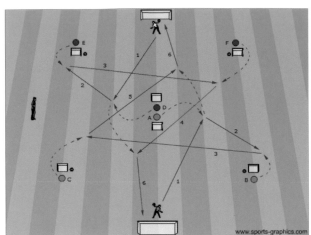 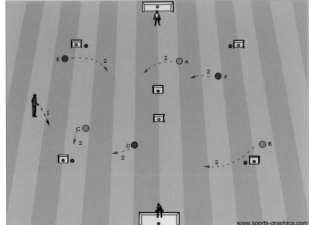

Execution

The RED team and the BLUE team simultaneously begin the described passing sequence with a throw-out by the goalkeepers and subsequent shot on goal (see left figure, 1 to 6). After the shots, the coach points to one of the four balls (see right figure, 1). 3-on-3-play with that ball ensues after a signal from the coach. The players near the ball try to get possession, and all the other players position according to the resultant situation (offense or defense) and the goals to be played on. The BLUE team is allowed to finish on the three mini goals marked BLUE and the large goal marked BLUE. The RED team is allowed to finish on the three mini goals marked RED and the large goal marked RED. Whenever a team is able to play a pass through the two mini goals in the center, that team then has the opportunity to finish on all eight goals. As soon as the first ball is out of the game, the coach points to one of the three remaining game balls. A total of four balls is used one after another during each round.

Points system

One point: Goal scored on a mini goal.

Two points: Goal scored on a large goal.

Three points: Pass through the center mini goals/goal scored on a mini goal.

1.6.12   Staggered 4-on-4—passing sequence (1)

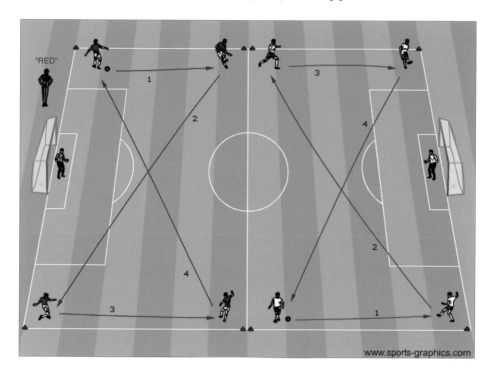

Execution

The RED team and the BLUE team each let a ball circulate in their own ranks in a specified passing order (see 1, 2, 3, and 4). The coach chooses one team (here the RED team). After a signal, the chosen team plays on the opposite goal with the own ball. The team that wasn't chosen plays the used ball to the own goalkeeper. The goalkeeper puts it in the own goal, and the ball is then out of the game.

Concept

All players must transition from a passing sequence to a game and purposefully adapt their positions according to the direction of play. Due to their positioning during the passing sequence, both teams are already in a staggered formation.

Variations

* Vary the passing sequence: direct play/two mandatory touches.
* Continue the game 4-on-4 with a new ball from the coach after a goal is scored.

1.6.13   Staggered 4-on-4—passing sequence (2)

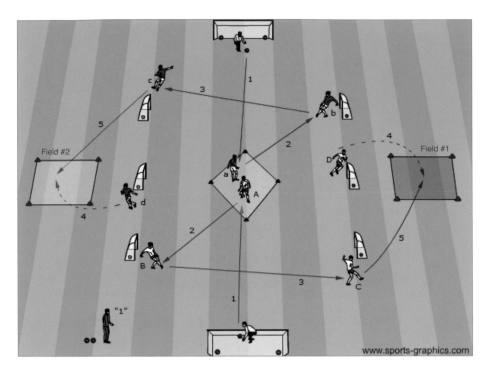

Execution

The BLUE team and the RED team simultaneously start a specified passing sequence and try to finish it as quickly as possible on the target fields #1 and #2. To do so, the goalkeepers simultaneously roll their ball to player A/a (see 1); player A/a plays to player B/b (see 2) who passes the ball to player C/c (see 3). At the same time, player D/d runs onto the target field (see 4) and receives the pass from player C/c (see 5). After the pass onto the playing field, a game ensues in which the RED team plays on the mini goals marked in RED, and the BLUE team plays on the mini goals marked in BLUE. If a player in possession dribbles into the center diamond, the team in possession can also play on the two large goals. The team in possession at the beginning of the game is always the one that finished the passing sequence first and was able to pass the ball onto the target field. To do so, the coach calls the target field (here field #1), which must be passed to first, and thereby determines the team in possession. The opposing team deposits the own game ball on the target field (here player d in field #2). After the first ball exits the game through a finish, the deposited ball is used as the second game ball, and a second playing action takes place. After the successful finish with the first ball, all players are allowed to run for the second ball in field #2 and try to get possession.

1.6.14   Staggered 5-on-5 (passing sequence and finish)

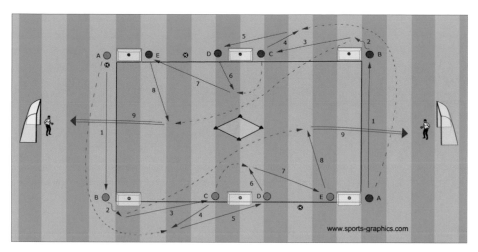

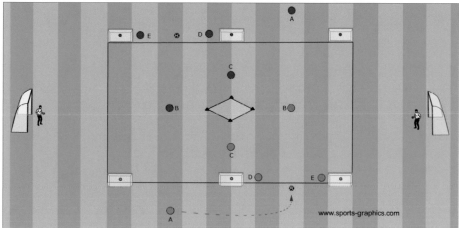

Execution

The RED and BLUE teams simultaneously start the described passing sequence and end with a closing shot on goal by the B players (see top figure). The faster team gets possession for the subsequent drill (announced by the coach). Here the BLUE team finishes first. Only player A (here on the BLUE team) is allowed to bring the ball into the game for the drill. In the now ensuing 5-on-5 drill, the BLUE team defends three mini goals (marked BLUE), and the RED team defends three mini goals (marked RED). Whenever a player dribbles or passes through the center diamond, the two large goals can also be played on. After the finish, the second ball comes into the game. Both teams can run to claim it. If the BLUE team reaches it first and brings it into the game, the mini goals switch (i.e., BLUE attacks the BLUE mini goals).

One point: Goal scored on a mini goal.

Two points: Playing inside the diamond plus a goal scored on a mini goal.

Three points: Playing inside the diamond plus a goal scored on a large goal.

1.7   CHAOS AND ACTION

1.7.1   From 1-on-1 to 2-on-2

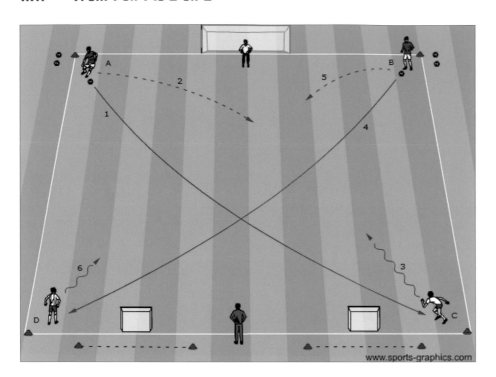

www.sports-graphics.com

Execution

Each round consists of two balls played back to back. Players A and B are the defenders, and players C and D are the attackers. Player A plays the first ball diagonally to player C (see 1) and then moves toward the center of the field (see 2). Player C controls the ball and dribbles toward the large goal for 1-on-1 (see 3). 1-on-1 play ensues between attacker C and defender A. The 1-on-1 ends with a shot on goal or a scored goal by player C or with player A winning (and clearing) the ball. The end of the 1-on-1 is also the starting signal for the subsequent 2-on-2 with the second ball. To this end, B plays a diagonal pass to D (see 4) and moves toward the center of the field (see 5). Attacker D controls the ball and, together with player C, plays against defenders A and B. The two active players in the 1-on-1 (here players A and C) must quickly transition and intervene in the 2-on-2.

Variations

* Counter opportunity on mini goals or dribble line for the defender.
* Specify the passing leg (left/right) for passes 1 and 4.
* Specify the passing technique (e.g., volley) for passes 1 and 4.

1.7.2   From 1-on-1 to 3-on-2

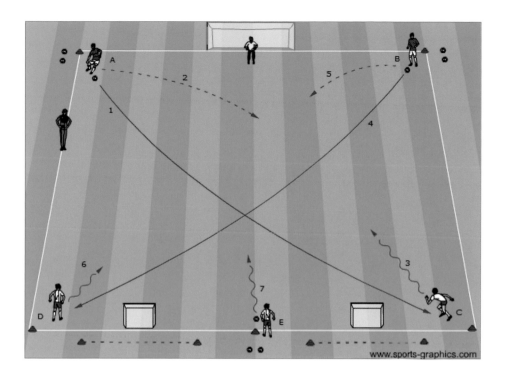

Execution

Each round consists of three balls played back to back. Players A and B are the defenders, and players A and C are the attackers. To start, players A and C play 1 on-1, and the second ball initiates a 2-on-2 between A and B against C and D (see game in 1.7.1). After the 2-on-2, a 3-on-3-situation ensues with the third ball. The 2-on-2 ends with a shot on goal, a goal scored by the offense, or with the defense winning (and clearing) the ball. At the end of the 2-on-2, player F immediately brings the third ball into the game, and the closing 3-on-2-situation begins (see 7).

Variations

* Create a handicap delay for player E: Dribble around the start cone.
* Create a counter opportunity on the mini goals for the defense after winning the ball.
* Specify the passing leg (left/right) for passes 1 and 4.
* Specify the passing technique (e.g., volley) for passes 1 and 4.

1.7.3   From 2-on-1 to 3-on-2

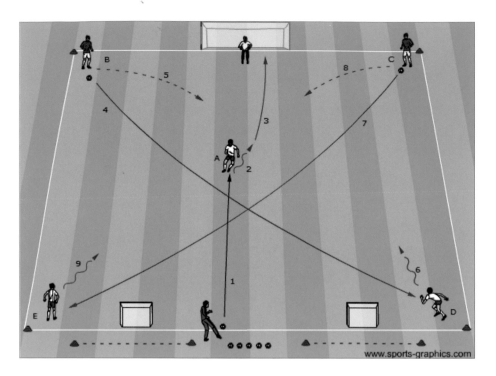

Execution

Each round consists of three balls played back to back. Players B and C are the defenders, and the players A, E, and D are the attackers. To start, player A receives the first ball as a pass from the coach (see 1). Player A controls the ball in the direction of the goal (see 2) and finishes (see 3). As A finishes, defender B passes the second ball to player D (see 4). 2-on-1 play begins between A and D against B. With the conclusion of the 2-on-1, situation C plays the third ball as a pass to player E (see 7), starting the 3-on-2-situation between the attackers A, D, and E and defenders B and C. Compare to the game in 1.7.1 for the sequence starting with pass 4.

Variations

* Specify the shooting leg for player A with a signal from the coach during the pass.
* Specify the first defender with a signal from the coach during the pass.
* Specify the passing technique (e.g., volley) for passes 1, 4, and 7.
* Create a counter opportunity on mini goals for the defense after winning the ball.
* Specify the passing leg (left/right) for passes 4 and 7.
* Perform a feint before passes 4 and 7.
* Resume play in 3-on-2 with a fourth ball from the coach.

1.7.4   From 1-on-1 to 4-on-3

Execution

Player A positions himself centrally in front of the goal as the attacker. Three players stand at each of the cones marked accordingly (see B, C, D, E, F, and G). The coach plays a pass to A (see 1). Player A controls the pass toward the large goal (see 2), finishes on that goal (see 3), immediately transitions, and assumes a defensive position (see 4). The coach calls a player (here player C), determining the next player to dribble his ball onto the field. Player C reacts to the coach's signal and dribbles onto the field as the attacker in a 1-on-1 against player A (see 5). As soon as the coach calls another player, that player also dribbles onto the field. If the coach would subsequently call, for example, "E," a 2-on-1 situation would ensue between E and A against C. This means that an alert and quick transition is required after each action, whereby it is often unclear whether the players are acting defensively or offensively. Players regularly switch positions.

Variations

* Specify the shooting leg for player A with a signal from the coach during the pass.
* Create a counter opportunity on mini goals for the defense after winning the ball.
* Resume play in 4-on-3 with an eighth ball from the coach.

1.7.5   Chaos 1-on-1

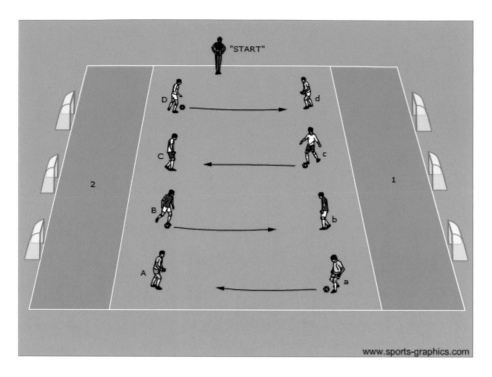

Execution

Multiple 1-on-1 situations take place simultaneously on a field (here four 1-on-1-situations). The field has no boundaries or specific goal. Players are divided into pairs. Each player has a specific opponent. For example, player A plays against player a. The pairs position opposite each other and play direct passes back and forth. As soon as the coach gives a starting signal, each 1-on-1 situation begins. Players A, B, C, and D try to reach end zone 1 and score a goal on one of the three mini goals. Accordingly, a, b, c, and d try to enter end zone 2 and score there. The player in possession during the direct passing sequence at the time of the coach's signal begins the 1-on-1 as the attacker. Each player in possession is able to utilize the entire width of the field and finish on all three mini goals.

Variations

* Specify the passing technique: direct passes/two touches.
* Specify the technique for shot on goal: inside foot/instep/left/right/weak foot.

1.7.6   Chaos 3-on-3 (on 6 goals)

www.sports-graphics.com

Execution

Players are divided into four teams of three players each. Team A plays against team B, and team C plays against team D. If possible, the coach and assistant coach (or a designated player) continue to play new balls into the game if balls have been shot or have left the field. The coach (see left) always plays the ball to team A or B, and the assistant coach always plays the ball to team C and D. A field player must actively call for a new ball. The game's objective is to initially keep the ball in the own ranks in 3-on-3 and play four consecutive passes. If four consecutive passes were played without in between touches by the opponent, the team in possession can finish on one of the six mini goals. Afterward, the coach gives the group a new ball. The players are intentionally not marked with bibs so the players are forced to be more alert.

Variations

* Increase number of teams (e.g., 3 x 3 against 3).
* Simplify or expand by adding neutral players.
* Specify the technique for shot on goal: inside foot/instep/left/right/weak foot.
* Simplify by playing the game by hand.

1.7.7   Chaos 3-on-3 (on 3 goals)

Execution

The playing field is marked with three large goals (each guarded by a goalkeeper) and three cones (each guarded by a neutral player; see G). Players are divided into seven teams of three players each (see team A to team G). Exact team numbers depend on the total number of players. Team A plays against team B; team C plays against team D; and team E plays against team F. Team G initially only serves as neutral players, whereby each player always plays new balls to two opposing teams (see 4 to E/F). The game's objective is to initially keep the ball in the own ranks in 3-on-3 play and to play four consecutive passes. Once four consecutive passes have been played without an in-between touch by the opponent, the team in possession is allowed to finish on one of the large goals. Afterward, that group receives a new ball from a neutral player. If a receiver runs out of balls, the two teams can also ask for balls from the other neutral players. Play continues until none of the neutral players have any balls left outside. The outside players (here G) now come on the field, and the team with the fewest goals scored during that round switch to the cones outside and become neutral players.

Variations

* Adapt the number of teams according to the number of available players:
  18 field players = 2 x 4 against 4 + 2 receivers / 15 field players = 2 x 3 against 3 + 1 + 2 receivers.

1.7.8   Fast 2-on-2

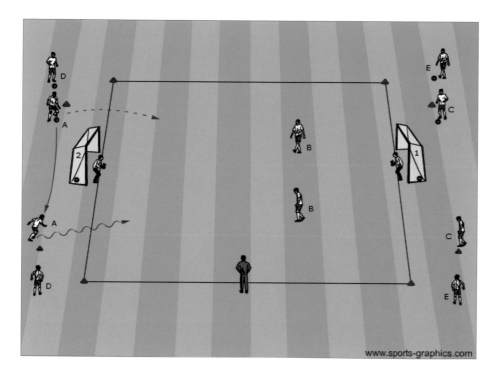

Execution

2-on-2 situations quickly develop in this continuous game, and quick reactions and swift transitions are critical here. Each team of two newly entering the game starts with a square pass from behind the goal (see A). Team A performs the described start and attacks goal 1 against team B. Each 2-on-2 ends with a goal or a shot on goal. If the ball goes into touch, the 2-on-2 continues, and when a goalkeeper catches the ball, he brings it back into the game. If team A scores a goal or misses, team B has to leave the field, and team A defends goal 2 against team C. Team C attacks goal 2. If team B scores a goal or misses, team A has to leave the field, and team B defends goal 1 against team D. Team D then attacks goal 1. The objective is to generate quick shots on goal, which are then rewarded with continued presence on the field.

Variations

- Organize as a competition: Which team of two is the first to score 10 goals?
- Organize as a competition: Which team of two will score the most goals within 10 minutes?
- Double points awarded for finishing after winning the ball.
- Double points awarded for finishing with the weak kicking leg.

1.7.9   4-on-4 (ball in hand)

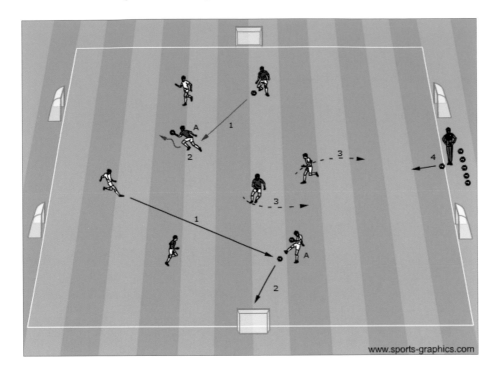

Execution

The RED and WHITE teams play 4-on-4 on the field. Each team has a ball, which is passed by hand. In addition, there are game balls (here two balls) that are passed by foot (see 1). The game's objective is to shoot the ball using the foot into one of the mini goals. Only the player who also holds a ball in his hand at the same time is allowed to take the shot (see 2). As soon as a ball is in the back of a net or out of the game, the coach brings another ball into the game (see 4). The players transition accordingly (see 3).

Concept

Due to the several mini goals, the players must adapt to multiple directions of play. At the same time, the players with a ball in their hand must get into tactically advantageous positions in front of the mini goals (see player A), or the ball in hand must be thrown to one of the players in possession. The basic idea is to direct the players' attention to different aspects (lots of goals, ball at the foot, and ball in hand).

1.7.10 Integrated playing fields

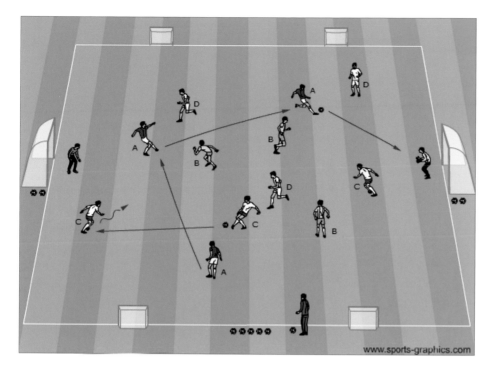

www.sports-graphics.com

Execution

Two out of four teams (see A, B, C, and D) play against each other on one field in two different directions. Team A plays against team B on the two large goals, each guarded by one goalkeeper. Team C plays against team D on the four mini goals. Each team has to defend two mini goals and can attack two mini goals.

Concept

Increased attentiveness is required due to the interfering players who are neither teammates nor opponents. The interfering players can also be used to irritate the opponent or impede opposing running lanes.

Variations

- Vary the player ratio (2-on-2/4-on-4/5-on-5).
- Play without identifying bibs.

1.8   TOURNAMENTS, PLAYING FIELDS, AND RULE VARIATIONS

1.8.1   Tournament (Champions League)

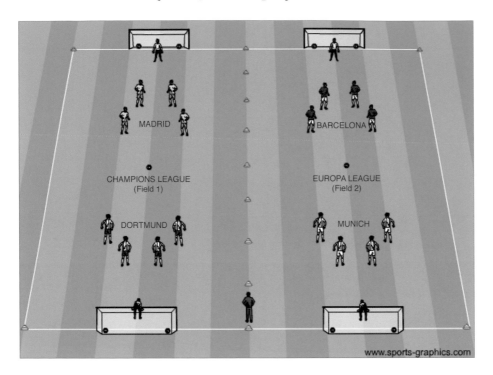

Execution

A permanent goalkeeper guards each goal. Four teams are formed (here Madrid, Dortmund, Barcelona, and Munich). When a ball goes out of bounds, play continues with the ball being rolled or kicked in. If a shot on goal goes really wide, the shooter has to retrieve it, and the game continues with a majority or minority situation until the player retrieving the ball is back in the game. This ensures brief waiting periods.

Concept

Playing fields are arranged in an ascending order (here Champions League field and Europa League field). After one round, the winning team moves up one field, and the losing team moves down one field. The winner on the Champions League field and the loser on the Europa League field remain. Each team's objective is to work up to the Champions League field or to remain there for as long as possible.

Variation

Add additional fields and opportunities for advancement and relegation: In terms of the hierarchy, a third field (Bundesliga) can be added to the right of the Europa League field. This creates additional opportunities for advancement and relegation.

1.8.2   Tournament (4-on-4)

Execution

Each goal is guarded by a permanent goalkeeper. Four teams are formed during each round. New teams are formed for each new round. Teams are always designated as A, B, C, and D. For children, teams can also be named Arsenal, Barcelona, Chelsea, and Dortmund, for example. Teams play each round on the same fields with the same goalkeepers. Team A always plays on the left field against team B, and team C always plays on the right field against team D. Teams are newly formed after each round so that over time each player plays on different teams with different players. Players report the results after each round, and the coach announces team memberships for the upcoming round. Team A and team C always play in identifying bibs. Team B and team D do not require bibs. After each round, the identifying bibs remain with the respective goalkeeper on the field. Refer to the chart on the next page to divide players into four teams and award points after each round.

Concept

Eventually each player has his own points system and ranking. But in each individual round, a player only receives as many points as his actual team does so that the best team player wins in the end.

1.8.3   Tournament (4-on-4)—explanations

Points system

For each player, the points of his respective team are recorded after each round according to the previously achieved results. Points are awarded based on the following valuation:

Win: 20 points plus the number of goals the team scored.

Draw: 10 points plus the number of goals the team scored.

Loss: 5 points plus the number of goals the team scored.

Division of players into four teams

All players present are recorded on the following chart. The team column lists team membership for each round. The points column shows the number of points scored in each individual round. The overall score column shows the final result for each player.

Player	Round 1 Team	Round 1 Points	Round 2 Team	Round 2 Points	Round 3 Team	Round 3 Points	Round 4 Team	Round 4 Points	Round 5 Team	Round 5 Points	Round 6 Team	Round 6 Points	Additional round Team	Additional round Points	Overall score	Place
Marco	A	25	A	10	A	6	A	5	A	23	A	11			80	
Thomas	A	25	B	10	A	6	B	23	A	23	B	11			98	2nd place
Bastian	A	25	C	21	B	22	B	23	A	23	B	11			125	1st place
Lukas	A	25	D	5	B	22	A	5	B	5	B	11			73	
Mats	B	7	A	10	C	12	C	24	C	12	C	9			74	
Jerome	B	7	B	10	C	12	D	7	C	12	D	26			74	
Mesut	B	7	C	21	D	12	D	7	C	12	D	26			85	
Mario	B	7	D	5	D	12	C	24	D	12	D	26			86	
Philip	C	13	A	10	A	6	A	5	B	5	B	11			50	
Andre	C	13	B	10	A	6	B	23	B	5	A	11			68	
Miroslav	C	13	C	21	B	22	B	23	B	5	A	11			95	
Kevin	C	13	D	5	B	22	A	5	A	23	A	11			79	
Julian	D	13	A	10	C	12	C	24	D	12	D	26			97	3rd place
Sammy	D	13	B	10	C	12	D	7	D	12	C	9			63	
Lars	D	13	C	21	D	12	D	7	D	12	C	9			74	
Sven	D	13	D	5	D	12	C	24	C	12	C	9			75	
Additional player																
Additional player																

Results on the adjacent chart

Round 1: Team A (5-2) Team B / Team C (3-3) Team D

Round 2: Team A (0-0) Team B / Team C (1-0) Team D

Round 3: Team A (1-2) Team B / Team C (2-2) Team D

Round 4: Team A (0-3) Team B / Team C (4-2) Team D

Round 5: Team A (3-0) Team B / Team C (2-2) Team D

Round 6: Team A (1-1) Team B / Team C (4-6) Team D

Advantages and further options

Each game as well as the current round can be immediately terminated if individual results are too high or unbalanced. By and by, the individual player will no longer be able to distinguish his current ranking. The final results generated by the tournament structure are often very narrow so that individual goals can be conclusive even if the actual game is lost. There is no specified number of rounds. The tournament can be discontinued after each round or continued at a later date. If new rounds are played on individual practice days the tournament structure can be used for the entire season. The tournament structure is not subject to a specific number of players. A player can also skip individual rounds without losing his individual points.

1.8.4   Tournament (touches)

www.sports-graphics.com

Execution

Each goal is guarded by a permanent goalkeeper. Four teams are formed (here players A, B, C, and D). When a ball goes out of bounds, play continues with the ball being rolled or kicked in. If a shot on goal goes really wide, the shooter has to retrieve it, and the game continues with a majority or minority situation until the player retrieving the ball is back in the game. This ensures brief waiting periods.

Concept

All teams start out with a limited number of touches for each player. The initial limit is four touches. When a team scores a goal, the maximum number of touches goes down to three. With another scored goal, the maximum number goes down to two touches, so in the end only direct play is possible. The team that scored a goal keeps its specified number of touches. A round ends when one team scores another goal during direct play. The opposing team wins the round. This forces the teams to play for quick shots on goal.

Variation

* Game starts with direct or increased passes based on the number of touches after each scored goal.

1.8.5   Tournament (goal hunt)

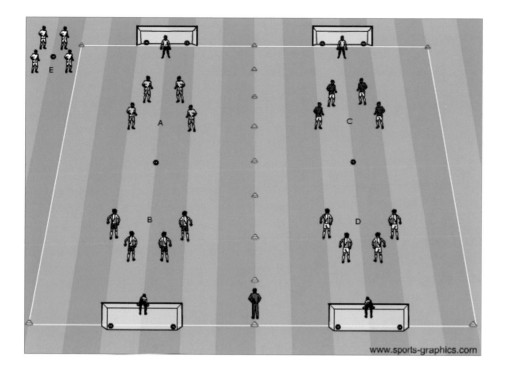

Execution

Each goal is guarded by a permanent goalkeeper. Five teams are formed (here teams A, B, C, D, and E). When a ball goes out of bounds, play continues with the ball being rolled or kicked in. If a shot on goal goes really wide, the shooter has to retrieve it, and the game continues with a majority or minority situation until the player retrieving the ball is back in the game. This ensures brief waiting periods.

Concept

The game's objective is to score two or three goals as quickly as possible. The first team to score two or three goals wins the current round. The team with the fewest goals at the time the decisive goal is scored sits out the next round in favor of the waiting team (here team E). In the event of a draw, the coach decides which team will continue to play or rather sit out. The amount of determination shown against the opposing goal is the critical factor here.

Variation

★   Create a movement task for the team sitting out a round: run/team juggling/individual juggling.

1.8.6   Tournament (winner plays)

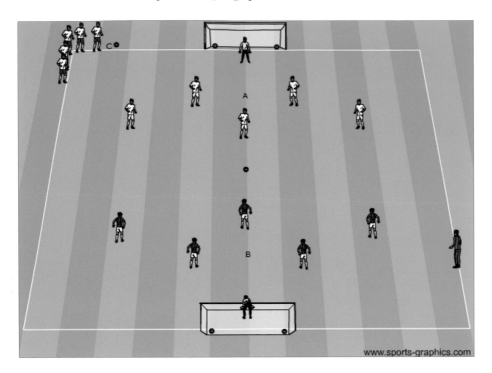

www.sports-graphics.com

Execution

Each goal is guarded by a permanent goalkeeper. Three teams are formed (here teams A, B, and C). When a ball goes out of bounds, play continues with the ball being rolled or kicked in. If a shot on goal goes really wide, the shooter has to retrieve it, and the game continues with a majority or minority situation until the player retrieving the ball is back in the game. This ensures brief waiting periods.

Concept

The game's objective is to score a goal as quickly as possible. The team that scores a goal wins one point and is allowed to remain on the field. The losing team sits out the next round and assumes the waiting position of team C.

Variations

* Create a movement task for the team sitting out a round: run/team juggling/individual juggling.
* Variation at the end of the game: three goals/two goals/direct goal/goal with the weak foot.

1.8.7   Playing field (vertical field in the center)

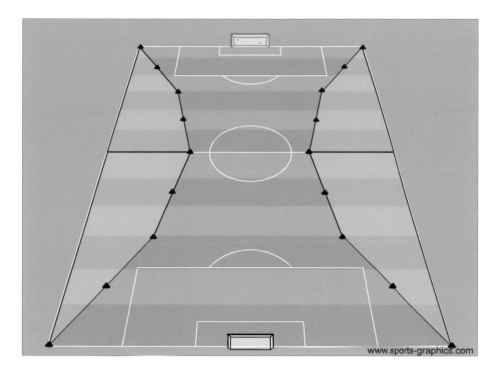

Field zones

The zones marked in YELLOW are out of bounds, and players are not allowed to enter them or play into them. The field narrows in the center and opens up near the goals.

Concept

The playing field makes active, offensive defense against the ball promising. It is sensible and easier for the players of the defending team to push up through the narrow area in the center and then transition to pressing in the opposing half, actively disrupting the game build-up in the opposing half early on. For the attackers, it is important to play through the narrow area in the center as quickly and vertically as possible. After winning the ball and the subsequent transition, it is particularly promising on this type of field when the ball is quickly played deep and vertical through the narrow area in the center because due to the narrowing, the opponent will only be briefly disorganized.

1.8.8   Playing field (vertical field to the goal)

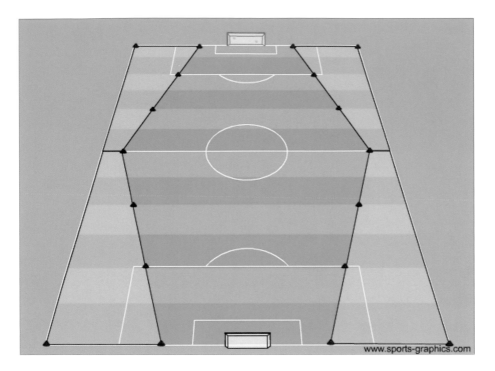

Field zones

The zones marked in YELLOW are out of bounds and players are not allowed to enter them or play into them. The field narrows near the goals and opens up near the center.

Concept

This field forces the team in possession to play purposefully toward the goal. Narrowing the field near the goal makes switching play near the goal difficult and limited. Nearly the entire field width can be used in the midfield so that vertical attacks can be prepared accordingly. The defense is automatically forced to drop back and compress in a funnel shape and constrict the space in front of the own goal. Quick and vertical forward balls after winning the ball are promising. Due to the narrowing in front of the opposing goal, possible gaps in the opposing team present themselves only very briefly.

1.8.9   Playing field (switching play)

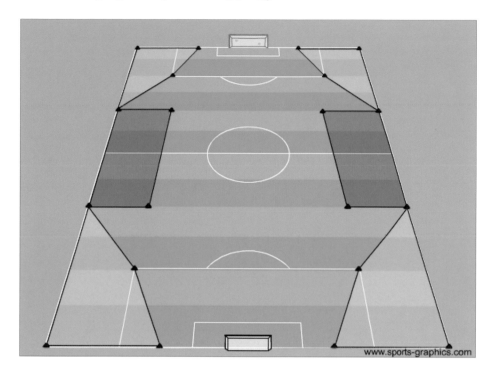

Field zones

The zones marked in YELLOW are out of bounds, and players are not allowed to enter them or play into them. The configuration of the fields near the corner flags narrows the field near the goals. The zones marked in GRAY are rectangular and located outside. These zones must or can be played in.

Concept

Narrowing the field near the goals makes the defense against the ball easier. The distances between the individual team segments automatically narrow, and during transitions, the defense organizes more quickly so that gaps in the defensive unit open only briefly. The fields on the wings marked in GRAY are of interest to the team in possession. Playing into these zones forces switching of play and play through the wing player in the midfield area. To this effect, the defensive unit is forced to shift, and potential gaps can open and be played into.

Guidelines

* The team in possession must play at least two passes in one rectangle.
* Creating goal-scoring chances is also possible without first playing on the rectangles.

1.8.10   Playing field (play through the center)

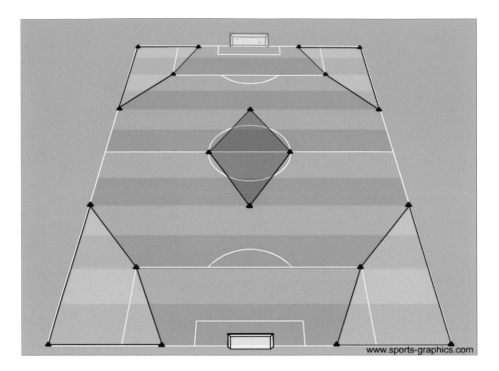

Field zones

The zones marked in YELLOW are out of bounds, and players are not allowed to enter them or play into them. The configuration of the fields near the corner flags narrows the field near the goals. The zone marked in GRAY is a diamond and located in the center of the field. This zone must or can be played in.

Concept

Narrowing the field near the goals makes the defense against the ball easier. The distances between the individual team segments automatically narrow, and during transitions, the defense organizes more quickly so that gaps in the defensive unit open only briefly. The GRAY area in the center forces play through the center and diagonal passes. Requiring play through the diamond prompts the faster attacks and offensive plays needed to put pressure on the defensive unit that is strengthened by the out-of-bound zones.

Guidelines

The diamond has been played in if a pass is played to a teammate across two lines of the diamond. A goal scored after a ball that was played through the diamond counts as double. Only players in possession can enter the diamond. Creating goal-scoring chances is also possible without first playing through the diamond.

1.8.11 Playing field (breadth and depth)

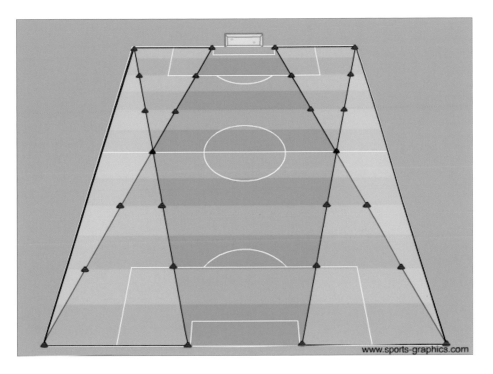

Field zones

The zones marked in YELLOW are out of bounds, and players are not allowed to enter them or play into them. Two zones always overlap and are identified by BLUE and RED markings. The BLUE cones pertain to the BLUE team. The RED cones pertain to the RED team. The RED team plays from top to bottom on the field. The closer they get to the opposing goal, the smaller the zones make the field for the team in possession.

Concept

The zones make it possible to start the game wide near the own goal. Narrowing the field near the opposing goal forces deep attacks. At the same time, defense near the own goal is easier. After winning the ball, the attacking team should quickly take advantage of the opponent's lack of organization and swiftly play toward the opposing goal.

1.8.12   Playing field (target zones)

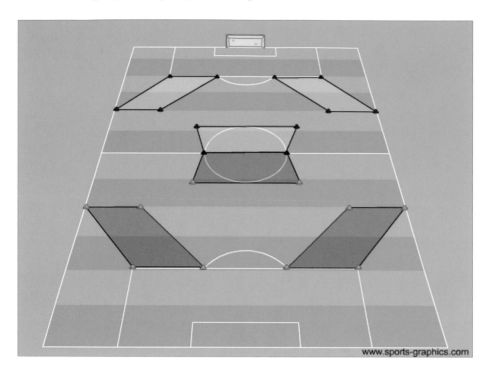

Field zones

The marked zones are target zones, and the team in possession must play in them. The zones marked within the opposing half pertain to the team in possession. Defending the zones within the own half is a priority.

Concept

The target zones are sensitive zones that have a special function during defense and attack. During possession, the central zone offers good opportunities for continued play with various options in all directions. The outer zones near the penalty box are particularly well suited for building pressure against the defense and goal threats.

Guidelines

If a team in possession played in one of the offensive zones by receiving a pass or by dribbling into the zone and scores a goal in the course of the attack, that goal counts as double.

1.8.13 Creative rule variations

Orientation and transition

* Instead of a throw-in or corner or free kick, the game continues with a game opener by the goalkeeper of the team in possession. Keep replacement balls in both goals.
* After a scored goal (and finish), the game continues with a game opener from the goalkeeper of the team that finished. Keep replacement balls in both goals.
* A scored goal only counts if all teammates high five the goal-scorer within five seconds.
* Two teams play against each other, but four teams wear identifying bibs: team A (blue and red bibs) against team B (green and yellow bibs). Players can switch teams after a signal from the coach (specifying two new colors counts as a new team).
* Continuing play after the ball goes into touch can be done using a kick (pass, cross, or shot on goal) or by dribbling onto the field.

Communication and coaching

* Players cannot talk to each other while the ball is in play.
* With each pass, the name of the receiving player must be called out loud.
* With each pass, the command "left" or "right" must be called out. The command specifies the leg with which the receiving player must control the pass.
* With each pass, the command "left" or "right" must be called out. The command specifies the leg with which the receiving player must perform his next action (pass or shot on goal).

Shot on goal and finish

* Goals can only be scored with a direct shot.
* Goals can only be scored with the weaker leg.
* The goal-scorer must have at least three touches prior to the finish.
* Goals can only be scored with headers.
* Each player on a team must have had the ball before a goal is scored.
* Each team designates two goal-scorers. Only these two players are allowed to score.
* Each team designates two goal-scorers. Goals scored by the designated players count as double.
* Goals can only be scored from a specific zone (e.g., penalty box).

Tempo and intensity

* In order for a goal to count, all payers must have crossed the centerline.

* All players must be in the own half, or a goal by the opponent counts as double.

* All players can only use their weaker foot.

* The player in possession cannot run and cannot be attacked.

* Direct passes only.

* No direct passes.

* Each player must complete at least three touches after receiving a pass.

* After a scored goal, each opposing player must immediately complete an extra task (e.g. push-ups). In the meantime, the successful team can continue the game with the own goalkeeper and create an advantage.

2 DRILLS

In training, drills are used primarily for learning, fine-tuning, stabilizing, and automating the most basic forms of movement like passing, controlling the ball, and dribbling. When implementing the drills in chapter 2, there is the option of training the movement patterns required in a game separately. Certain drills do not require opposing pressure, so the training player can fully concentrate on the technical movement sequence. As with all challenging content technique training, particularly very complex and unfamiliar content should be completed while rested.

A very important factor in training with technical emphasis is a high number of repetitions so the movements are ingrained. The desired automatism that helps a player in pressure situations during a game only takes place with the appropriately high number of repetitions. It also makes sense to have the players train with both feet so they have more potential solutions in the form of directional changes.

But training in the form of drills and frequent repetition of the same movement tasks with a similar exercise structure can also be dangerous because monotony can cause deficiencies in the areas of concentration, motivation, and, finally, precision. The coach has the opportunity to counteract that by holding competitions, being creative in his choice of drills, and varying drills to make them more diverse.

Fine-tuning
Ingraining
Using both feet
Repeating
Learning   Applying
Improving
Stabilizing

2.1   PASSING (LOOPS)

2.1.1   Triangle passing (simple passing)

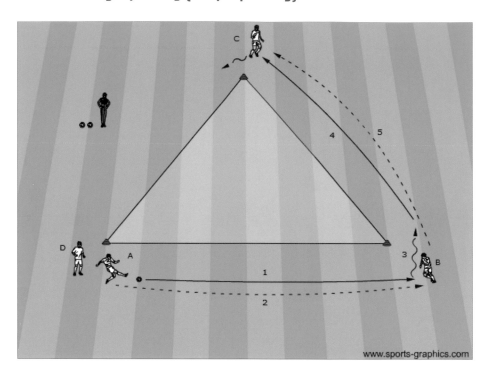

www.sports-graphics.com

Execution

The ball moves in an endless loop along the outside of a triangle. Player A passes the ball to player B (see 1), follows his pass, and takes player B's position (see 2). Player B handles the ball in the direction of play (see 3), passes to player C (see 4), and moves to take player C's position (see 5). Players C and D continue the passing loop.

Coaching

* Forceful passes with pursuit (see position change).
* Target-oriented passing play for the receiver's continuation.
* Starting motion and dropping off before receiving the ball.

Variations

* Change direction of play (both feet).
* Set up drill as a passing square (requires at least five players).
* Specify the passing technique: direct passes.
* Three mandatory touches per player (settle/carry/pass).

2.1.2 Triangle passing (ball control and first touch)

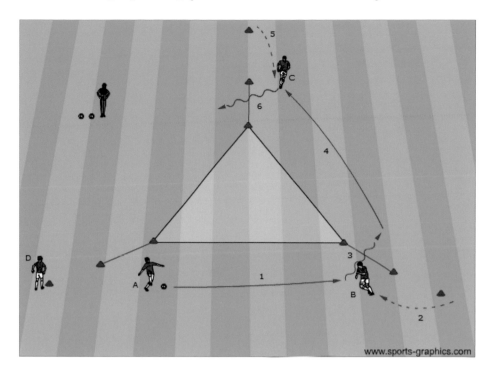

Execution

The ball moves in an endless loop around the triangle. After receiving a pass, each player must play the ball through the cone goals with precision. Player A plays the ball to player B (see 1), follows his pass, and takes player B's position. Player B moves away from the RED cone with good timing (see 2) and with his first touch plays the ball through the blue cone goal at the triangle (see 3). Player B passes to player C (see 4) and takes player C's position. Player C moves away from the cone (see 5) and with his first touch (see 6) plays the ball in the direction of play. Players C and D continue the passing loop.

Coaching

* Well-timed getting open for fluid ball control.
* Starting motion toward the ball immediately before getting open.
* Precise passing to facilitate receiver's optimal ball control through the goal.

Variations

* Change direction of play (both feet).
* Limit touches to no more than two (first-touch control and pass).

2.1.3   Triangle passing (first-touch control and tempo dribbling)

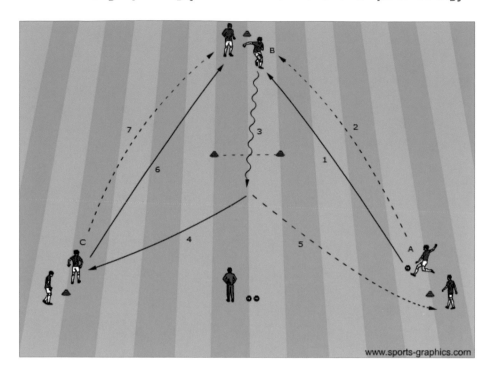

Execution

The ball moves in an endless loop always through position B and the cone goal in the center of the triangle to the two outside positions, A and C. Player A plays to player B (see 1), follows his pass, and takes player B's position (see 2). Player B controls the ball toward the cone goal and dribbles through the cones at a very fast pace (see 3). Afterward, he plays a side pass to player C (see 4) and takes player A's position (see 5). Player C plays the ball to the waiting player in position B (see 6) and then takes player B's position (see 7). The receiver in position B dribbles through the cone goal, but then (subsequently alternating regularly) passes to position A and takes position C.

Coaching

* Precise passing to facilitate receiver's optimal ball control toward the goal.
* Quick ball control/fast dribble.
* Shoulder check prior to passing to the right or left.

Variations

* Specify the passing technique for positions A and C: direct passes.
* Specify the free leg for ball control on position B (left/right).
* Specify number of touches for player B prior to passing (see 3).
* Perform a feint at a level with the cone goal in the center.

2.1.4   Triangle passing (double-double pass)

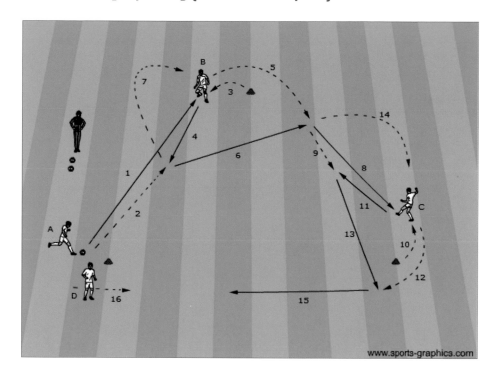

Execution

The ball moves clockwise around the passing triangle in an endless loop. Player A starts the passing loop by passing to player B (see 1) and following his pass (see 2). Player B moves toward him (see 3) and passes directly back to player A (see 4). After his pass, player B immediately moves around his own start cone (see 5) and receives a pass from player A (see 6). Player A takes over player B's position (see 7). Player B passes to player C (see 8) and follows his pass (see 9). Player C comes toward him (see 10), lets the ball bounce back (see 11), and then also moves around his start cone (see 12). Player B plays to player C (see 13) and takes up player C's position (see 14). Player C continues the passing sequence with player D (see 15 and 16).

Coaching

✶   Maintain eye contact to the ball and with the teammate (see 5).

Variations

✶   Change the direction of play (both feet).
✶   Specify the number of touches and completion of a feint after pass 6 (or 13).

2.1.5   Triangle passing (dropping off)

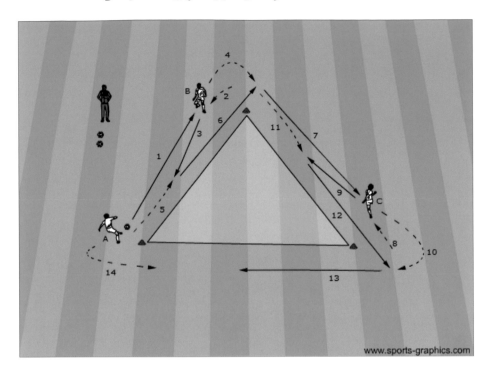

Execution

The ball moves clockwise around the passing triangle in an endless loop. Player A starts the passing loop and plays a pass to player B (see 1). Player B starts toward the pass (see 2) and lets it bounce back (see 3). Immediately after the pass, player B moves around his start cone (see 4) so he can play the return pass (see 6) by the approaching player A (see 5) direct and with an open body position to player C (see 7). The passing order continues from player C to player A (see 8 to 14). This passing exercise requires only three players. No position changes are needed.

Coaching

⋆   Maintain eye contact to the ball and with the teammate (see 4).

Variations

⋆   Change the direction of play (both feet).
⋆   Specify the free leg for the pass receiver with command by the passer.

2.1.6   Passing square (Ping-Pong straight)

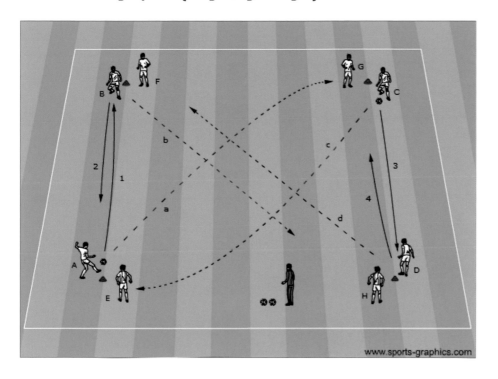

www.sports-graphics.com

Execution

All players simultaneously move the two balls between the marking cones using straight passes. After each pass, the player moves to the diagonally opposed position. Player A passes to player B (see 1) and then takes player G's position (see a). Player B passes to player E (see 2) and takes player H's position (see b). Player C passes to player D (see 3) and takes the position of player E (see c). Player D passes to player G (see 4) and takes the position of player F (see d).

Coaching

★ Starting movements and receiving player runs to meet the pass.

Variations

★ Specify the number of touches: direct play/play with 2 or 3 touches.
★ Specify the receiving leg (left/right) and passing leg (left/right).
★ Perform various running exercises during the diagonal run.
★ Perform a feint immediately before each pass.

2.1.7   Passing (square Ping-Pong diagonal)

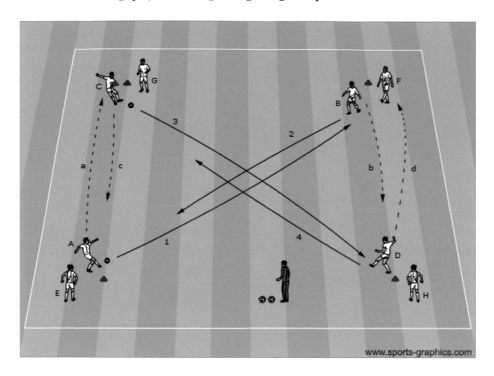

Execution

All four players simultaneously move the two balls between the marking cones using diagonal passes. After each pass, the player moves to the directly opposed position. Player A passes to player B (see 1) and takes player G's position (see a). Player B passes to player E (see 2) and takes player H's position (see b). Player C passes to player D (see 3) and takes the position of player E (see c). Player D passes to player G (see 4) and takes the position of player F (see d).

Coaching

★   Starting movements and receiving player runs to meet the pass.

Variations

★   Specify the number of touches: direct play/play with 2 or 3 touches.

★   Specify the receiving leg (left/right) and passing leg (left/right).

★   Perform various running exercises during the diagonal run.

★   Perform a feint immediately before each pass.

2.1.8   Passing square (Ping-Pong alternate)

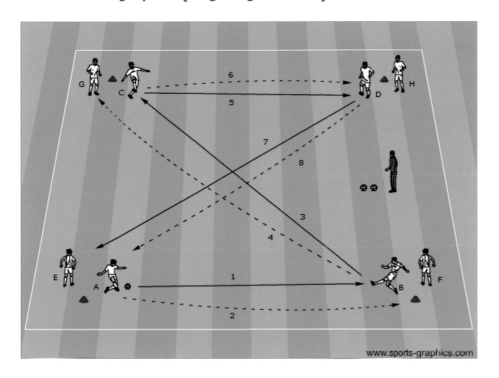

Execution

Player A passes to player B (see 1), follows his pass, and takes over the position of player F (see 2). Player B plays a diagonal ball to player C (see 3), follows his pass, and takes over the position of player G (see 4). Player C passes to player D (see 5), follows his pass, and takes over the position of player H (see 6). Player D plays a diagonal ball to the starting position to player E (see 7), follows his pass, and takes over the position of player E (see 8).

Coaching

★   Starting movements and receiving player runs to meet the pass.

Variations

★   Specify the number of touches: direct play/play with 2 or 3 touches.

★   Specify the receiving leg (left/right) and passing leg (left/right).

★   Perform various running exercises during the diagonal run.

★   Perform a feint immediately before each pass.

2.1.9   Passing square (double pass)

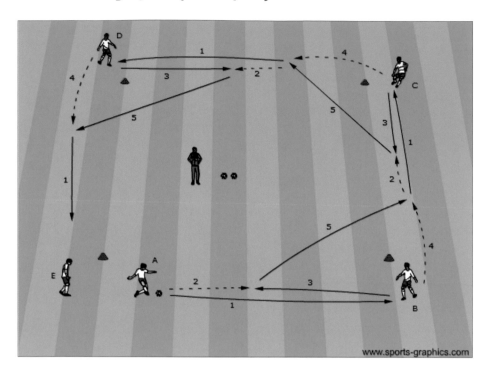

Execution

Player A plays to player B (see 1), follows his pass (see 2), and receives the return pass from player B (see 3). Player B moves around the cone (see 4) and again receives the pass from player A (see 5). Player B plays the ball to player C (see 1), follows his pass (see 2), and receives the return ball from player C (see 3). Player C moves around the cone (see 4) and again receives the pass from player B (see 5). The sequence continues as described.

Coaching

- ★ Maintain constant eye contact between passer/receiver (see 4).
- ★ Optimal timing and coordinated hardness of passes for fluid ball circulation.
- ★ Starting movements/running feint before every initial action at the cone.

Variations

- ★ Change the direction of play (both feet).
- ★ Specify the number of touches: direct passes for all actions.

2.1.10 Passing square (third man running)

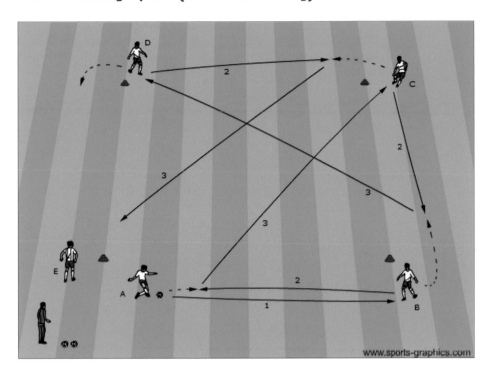

www.sports-graphics.com

Execution

Player A plays the ball to player B (see 1). Player B lets the ball bounce back (see 2) and moves off toward player C. Player A plays a diagonal ball to player C (see 3). Player C lets the ball bounce off toward the approaching player B (see 2) and then moves toward player D. Player B plays the ball diagonally to player D (see 3). Player D lets the ball bounce off toward the approaching player C (see 2). Player C continues the passing sequence to player E (see E).

Coaching

* Optimal timing and coordinated, hard passes for fluid ball circulation.
* Starting movements/running feint before every initial action at the cone.

Variations

* Change the direction of play (both feet).
* Specify the number of touches: direct passes for all actions.

2.1.11   Passing square (looking for position)

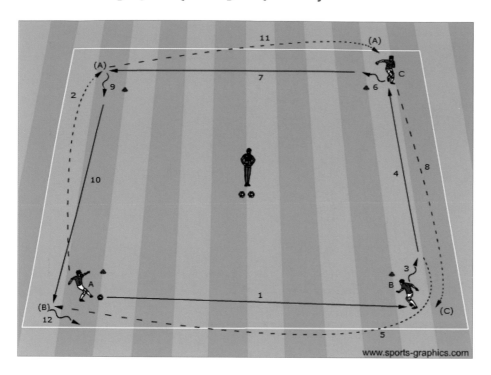

Execution

The three players circulate one ball around the marked square (here counterclockwise). Each player controls the ball with the first touch and passes it to the next position with the second touch. In doing so, one position is unmanned and must be newly manned by one of the players. Each player makes a position change after his own pass. Player A passes to player B (see 1) and immediately occupies the next position in the passing order (see 2). Player B controls the ball (see 3), passes to player C (see 4), and occupies the next unmanned position in the passing order (see 5). Player C controls the ball (see 6), passes to player A (see 7 and A), and occupies the next unmanned position in the passing order (see 8). Player A controls the ball in his new position (see 9), passes to player B (see 10), and occupies the position of C (see 11). Player C controls the ball in his new position (see 12) and continues the passing sequence as described. After his own pass, each player must always occupy the next unmanned position in the passing order.

Variations

★   Perform a feint/body feint right before every pass.

★   Change the direction of play (both feet).

2.1.12   Passing square (play through the center)

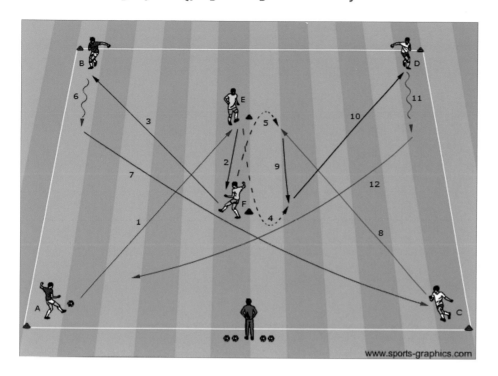

www.sports-graphics.com

Execution

The six players circulate one ball within the passing square. Players are divided into pairs (see A/B, C/D, and E/F). Player A begins, playing a pass to player E (see 1). Player E lets the ball bounce off to player F (see 2). Player F plays a direct pass to player B (see 3). After their passes, players E and F immediately switch positions (see 4 and 5). Player B controls the ball (see 6) so he can play a diagonal pass to player C (see 7). Players A and B switch positions. Player C now starts the same sequence on the other side. Player C passes to player F (See 8). Player F passes to player E (see 9), and player E passes to player D (see 10). Player D controls the ball (see 11) and passes it back to the starting position (see 12), where player B now starts the next sequence.

Coaching

Prior to the first pass (see 1 and 8), the central players should create depth and stand far apart (see 4 and 5). They decrease the distance to each other with the pass so they are then able to play a very short pass to each other (see 2 and 9), directly followed by a long pass (see 3 and 10).

Variation

* Change the direction of play (both feet).

2.1.13   Diamond passing (double pass)

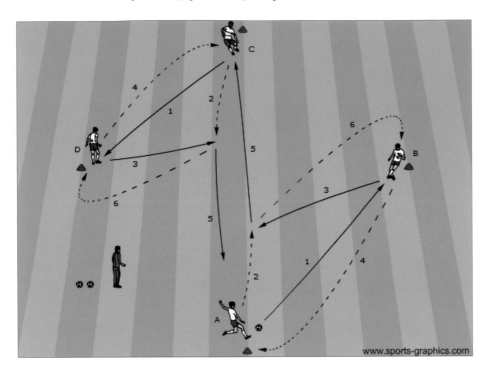

Execution

Player A plays the ball to player B (see 1) and moves off toward the center (see 2). Player B passes to player A in the center (see 3). Player A passes directly to player C (see 5). Player A and player B switch positions (see 4 and 6). Player C plays to player D (see 1), follows his pass into the center (see 2), and receives the pass from player D (see 3). Player C plays the ball to position A where player B is already waiting to continue the passing loop. Players C and D also switch positions after the action (see 4 and 6).

Coaching

* Drop off into the center with courage and pace (see 2).
* Optimal timing for the pass to the center (see 3).
* Quick position changes (see 4 and 6).

Variations

* Change the direction of play (both feet).
* Specify the number of touches: direct passes for all actions.

2.1.14   Diamond passing (double pass and pursuit)

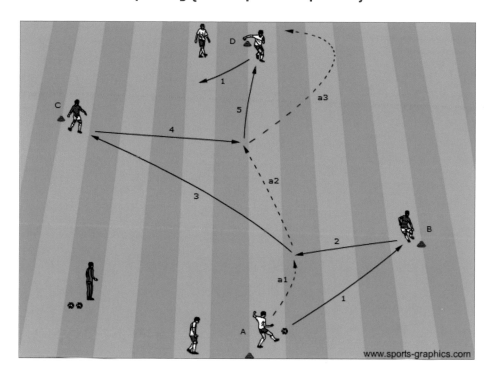

Execution

Player A plays to player B (see 1), follows his pass to the center (see a1), and receives the pass from player B (see 2). Player A plays a diagonal ball to player C (see 3) and also follows his second pass to the center (see a2). Player C lets the ball bounce off into the center (see 4), and player A finishes his action with a pass to player D (see 5) before taking over the position of D (see a3). Player D now continues the passing loop first through player C, then through player D, and finally to the position A. Players A and B keep their positions and serve as permanent passing stations. Switch the players in positions A and B regularly.

Coaching

* Follow the ball into the center with courage and purpose.
* Starting movements/running feint before receiving each pass in positions B and C.
* Optimal timing and coordinated, hard passes for fluid ball circulation.

Variations

* Change the direction of play (both feet).
* Specify the number of touches: direct passes for all actions.

2.1.15 Diamond passing (overlapping)

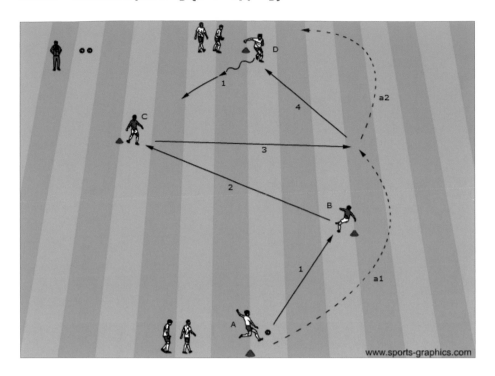

Execution

Player A plays the ball to player B (see 1) and overtakes the player in position B (see a1). Player B plays a diagonal ball to player C (see 2). Player C plays the ball into the running path of player A (see 3). Player A finishes his action with a pass to player D (see 4) and switches to position D (see a2). Player D continues the passing loop with players C and B to position A (see 1). Positions B and C serve as permanent neutral players. Regularly switch players B and C.

Coaching

Overlapping should always be done at top speed. The overlapping player (see a1) always chooses a running path closely behind the player he is overlapping (see B). The cone does not serve as a guide during overlapping. The overlapping player must always orient himself by the player he is overlapping. It is, therefore, possible to have a running path between the player and the cone if, for example, the first pass is played farther into the center (see 1) and the player to be overlapped (see B) leaves his position in the direction of the center.

Variations

* Change the direction of play (both feet).
* Specify the number of touches: direct passes for all actions.

2.1.16 Diamond passing (overlap and third man running)

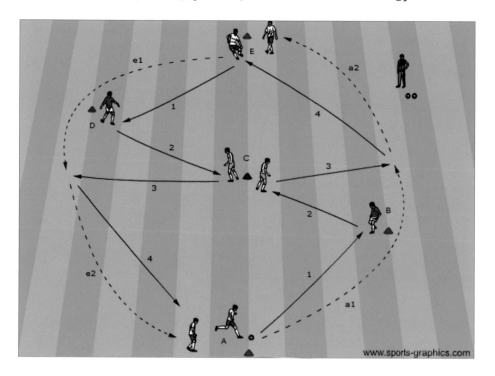

Execution

Player A plays to player B (see 1) and overtakes player B (see a1). Player B plays to player C (see 2). Player C plays into the running path of player A (see 3). Player A finishes his action with a pass to player E (see 4) and a switch to position E (see a2).

Coaching

The guidelines outlined in drill 2.1.5 apply to overlapping: top speed and a running path close behind the player being overlapped. During play with the third man running, players B and C must delay the game if necessary (see 2 and 3) if player A is still in the process of overlapping (see a1).

Variations

* Single occupancy of position C.
* Change the direction of play (both feet).
* Specify the number of touches: direct passes for all actions.

2.1.17   Passing rectangle—overlap and play deep (1)

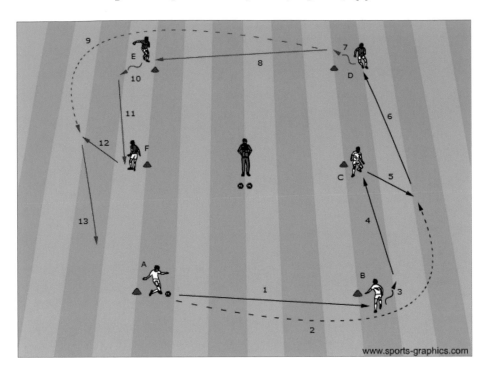

Execution

Player A passes to player B (see 1) and overtakes him (see 2). Player B controls the ball in the direction of play (see 3) and passes to player C (see 4). Player C passes into the running path of player A (see 5). Player A plays deep to player D (see 6). Player A occupies the position of player C; player C occupies the position of player B; and player B occupies the starting position of player A. Player D continues the passing sequence in the direction of play, controls the ball (see 7), passes to player E (see 8), and overtakes him (see 9). Player E controls the ball in the direction of play (see 10) and passes to player F (see 11). Player F passes into the running path of player D (see 12). Player D passes to the starting position to player B (see 13). Player D occupies the position of player F; player F occupies the position of player E; and player E occupies the position of player D. Player B starts the new passing sequence from the starting position through player C to player A.

Variations

* Change the direction of play (both feet).
* Specify the number of touches: direct play/play with 2 or 3 touches.
* Perform a feint/body feint prior to specified passes (e.g., prior to pass 1, 4, or 6).

2.1.18   Passing rectangle—overlap and play deep (2)

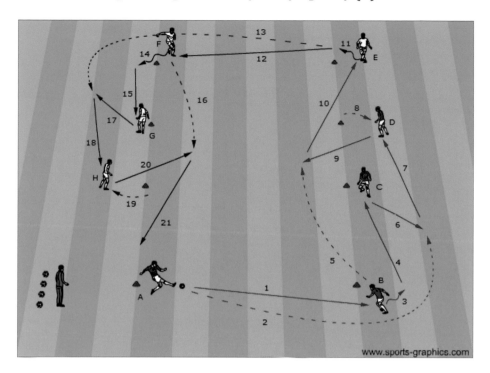

www.sports-graphics.com

Execution

Player A passes to player B (see 1) and overtakes him (see 2). Player B controls the ball in the direction of play (see 3), passes to player C (see 4), and moves off into the center (see 5). Player C passes into the running path of player A (see 6). Player A passes to player D (see 7). Player D moves away from the start cone (see 8) and passes into the center to player B (see 9). Player B plays a deep pass to player E (see 10). Player A takes over the position of player C; player C takes over the position of player D; and player D takes over the position of player A. Player E continues the passing sequence through players F, G, and H to the starting position to player D.

Coaching

* Starting movement/optimal timing for dropping off from the start cone.
* Assume an open body position according to the subsequent passing direction.

Variations

* Change the direction of play (both feet).
* Perform a feint/body feint prior to specified passes (e.g., prior to pass 1 or 4).

2.1.19   Passing hexagon (double pass and third man running)

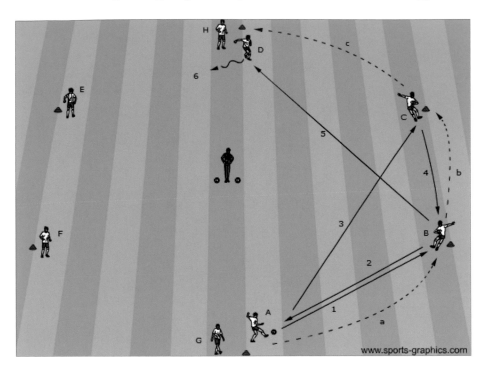

Execution

Player A plays the ball to player B (see 1). Player B lets it bounce off (see 2), and player A plays the ball deep to player C (see 3) before taking position B (see a). Player C passes to player B (see 4). Player B plays a diagonal ball to player D (see 5). Player B changes to position C (see b), and player C changes to position D/H (see c). Player D continues the passing loop through players E and F in the direction of player C (see 6).

Coaching

* Forceful passes (see 3 and 5).
* Starting movements/running feint before every initial action at the cone.

Variations

* Execute with two balls (simultaneous start on positions A and D).
* Change the direction of play (both feet).
* Specify the number of touches: direct passes for all actions.

2.1.20   Passing hexagon (looking for position)

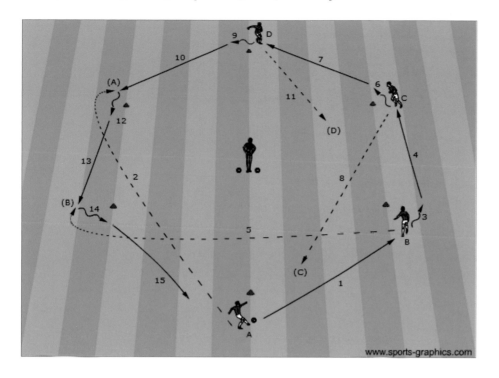

www.sports-graphics.com

Execution

The four players pass one ball around the hexagon marked with six cones (here counterclockwise). Each player controls the ball with the first touch and passes to the next position with the second touch. Two positions are unmanned and always must be manned by a new player. Each player changes positions after his own pass. Player A passes to player B (see 1) and immediately occupies the next unmanned position in the passing order (see 2). Player B controls the ball (see 3), passes it to player C (see 4), and occupies the next unmanned position in the passing order (see 5). Player C controls the ball (see 6), passes it to player D (see 7), and runs to an unmanned position (see 8). Player D controls the ball (see 9), passes it to player A (see A), and occupies an unmanned position (see D). Player A controls the ball in his new position (see 12) and passes it to player B (see 13 and B). Player B controls the ball (see 14) and passes it to player C (see 15). After his own pass, each player must take over the next unmanned position in the passing order.

Variations

* Perform a feint/body feint immediately before each pass.
* Change the direction of play (both feet).

2.1.21   Passing star (competition)

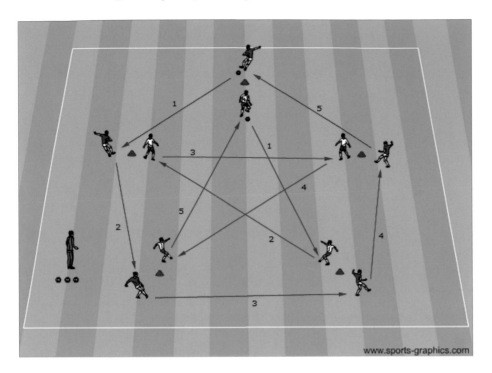

Execution

Use five cones to mark a pentagon. One cone is a different color and serves as the start and finish (see the BLUE cone). Both teams begin their passing sequences in front of this cone. The BLUE team plays inside the markers and rotates the ball as shown in a star pattern (see 1 to 5). The RED team plays around the outside of the markers (here counterclockwise; see 1 to 5). The goal is to let the own ball rotate as fast as possible. Each player must run around his own marking cone after playing a pass. Each time the ball is back at the start or finish (see the BLUE cone), that team is awarded a point. The teams play against each other. Tasks switch after two minutes, and the points from both rounds are combined.

Variations

- ★   Specify the number of touches: no direct passes.
- ★   Specify the number of touches: 2 or 3 mandatory touches.
- ★   Complete the drill with the weak playing leg.
- ★   Change the direction of play (both feet).

2.1.22 Double passing square

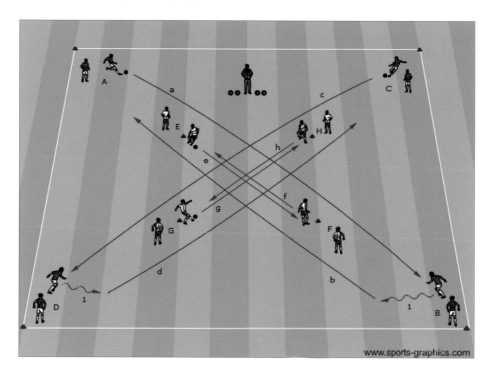

www.sports-graphics.com

Execution

All players let four balls circulate in a central square (see BLUE marking cones) and an outside square (see RED marking cones). Two balls are moved around the center using short passes (see BLUE team), and two balls are moved by the outside players (see RED team) using long passes. The players in the center act as moving obstacles to the long passes of the outside players. The outside players must recognize and use the resulting spaces with skillful ball control and courageous passing in order to pass the ball to the intended position. On the outside field, position A passes to position B (see a); position B passes back to position A (see b); position C passes to position D (see c); and position D passes back to position C (see d). On the center field, position E passes to position F (see e); position F passes back to position E (see f); position G passes to position H (see g); and position H passes back to position G (see h).

Variations (running lanes)

* Complete without changing positions.
* Complete with position changes in the center (E/F and G/H switch).
* Complete with position changes after each pass (A/E, B/F, C/H, and D/G switch).
* Complete with position changes after each pass (A/B, C/D, E/F, and G/H switch).

2.1.23 Double passing loop

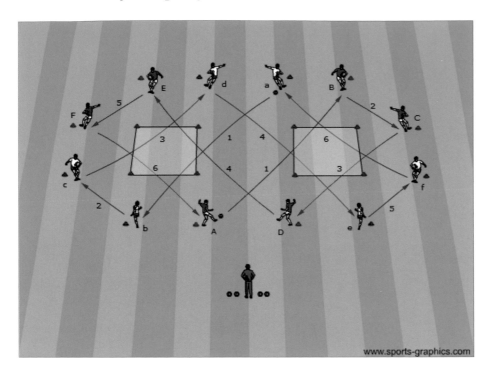

Execution

The RED team (see players A to F) and the BLUE team (see players a to f) each have six players circulating a ball. The majority of passes must be played across two lines in the central zone, resulting in diagonal passes. Player A passes to player B (see 1); player B passes to player C (see 2); player C passes to player D (see 3); player D passes to player E (see 4); player E passes to player F (see 5); and player F passes to player A at the starting position (see 6). Players remain in their positions after passing.

Variations

* Specify the number of touches: direct passing with all actions.
* Specify the number of touches: 2 o 3 mandatory touches.
* Organize as a competition: Which team will be the quickest to pass through all the fields?

2.1.24 Passing loops (organized as a competition)

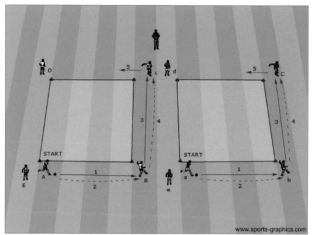 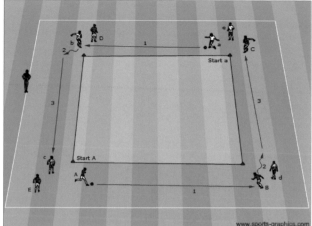

Execution

The endless passing loops can be organized into competitions so that the passing groups compete against each other. A group's objective is to get through the passing sequences faster than the opposing team. Turning the drill into a competition increases the motivation of the players, so the required passes are played quicker and with more precision. The competition can be set up so two groups play on one field (see figure on right), or the groups play separately on two fields (see figure on left). The groups always start their passing loops at a start cone. Competition goals can be set so a certain number of rounds must be played or as many rounds as possible within a specified time period. A round is complete when the ball moves past the start cone again.

Passing competition on one field (see figure on right)

Competition goal: Catching up with and passing up the opposing ball with the own ball.

Passing competition on two fields (see figure on left)

Competition goals: Which team is the first to complete 20 rounds?

Which team completes the most rounds in two minutes?

2.2   PASSING GAME (PASSING CIRCLES)

2.2.1   Passing circle (basic passing game)

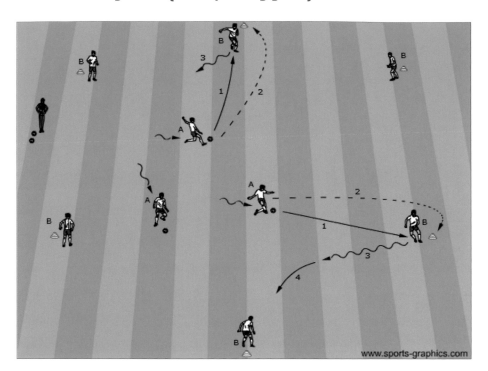

Execution

Players B are positioned at the outside cones and signal their readiness to receive the ball. Players A in the center each have a ball, dribble freely around the field, and look for an outside player who isn't involved in another action. Player A plays the ball to the outside to player B (see 1) and after the pass takes the outside position (see 2). Player B controls the ball, dribbles to the center (see 3), and now becomes the center player, again looking for an outside player.

Coaching

* Players B in the outside positions perform starting motions toward the other player.
* Players A and B maintain constant eye contact.
* Coaching and communication: Call the name of the receiving player.

Variations

* Execute a feint/body feint right before each pass.
* Specify the receiving leg (left/right) and the passing leg (left/right).
* Vary the passing distance (see 1).

2.2.2 Passing circle (double pass)

Execution

Players B are positioned at the outside cones and signal their readiness to receive the ball. Players A in the center each have a ball and dribble freely around the field, looking for an outside player who isn't involved in another action. Player A passes to player B (see 1). Immediately after the pass, player A asks for the ball back with a definite running path (see 2). Player B plays the ball into the running path of player A. Player A controls the ball and looks for a new outside player (see 4). After a short while, the inside players A and the outside players B trade places.

Coaching

* Complete a double pass with gaining of space/depth (see D).
* Players B in the outside positions perform starting motions toward the other player.
* Players A and B maintain constant eye contact.

Variations

* Specify the receiving leg (left/right) and passing leg (left/right).
* Specify the number of touches between actions (see 4).

2.2.3   Passing circle (double-double pass)

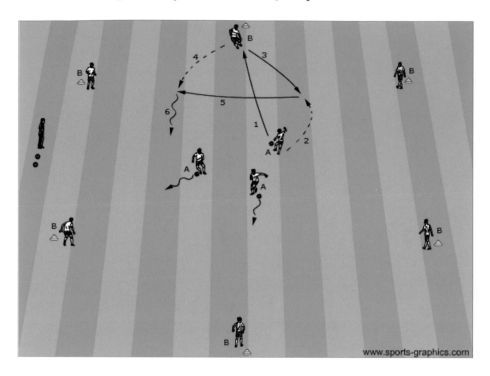

Execution

Players B are positioned at the outside cones and signal their readiness to receive the ball. Players A in the center each have a ball and dribble freely around the field, looking for an outside player who isn't involved in another action. Player A passes to player B (see 1), indicates his running path (see 2), and then gets the ball back as a double pass from player B (see 3). Player B starts away from the cone, gaining space (see 4), and receives a pass from player A (see 5). Players A and B switch positions. After controlling the ball, player B begins a new action with another outside player (see 6).

Coaching

★   Drop off/get open and gain space/depth (see 2 and 4).

Variations

★   Specify the number of touches: direct passes (see 1, 3, and 5).

★   Specify the receiving leg (left/right) and passing leg (left/right).

★   Vary the passing distance (see 1).

2.2.4 Passing circle (overlapping)

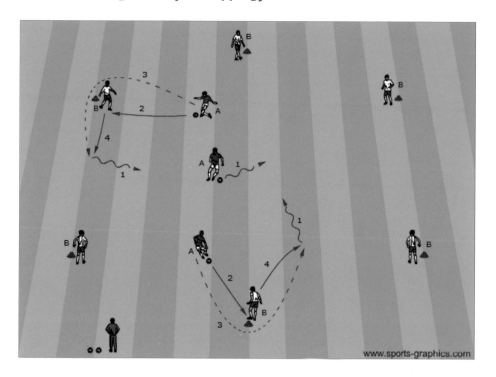

Execution

Players B are positioned at the outside cones and signal their readiness to receive the ball. Players A in the center each have a ball and dribble freely around the field, looking for an outside player who isn't involved in another action. Player A passes to player B (see 2) and overtakes closely behind the outside player (see 3). Player B passes into the running path of player A (see 4). Player A controls the ball, dribbles to the center, and heads toward another outside player. After a short while, the inside players A switch places with the outside players B.

Coaching

* Use the dribble in the center as a recovery phase (see 1).
* Overlap at top speed (see 3).
* Optimal timing and possible hesitation for fluid ball control by player A.

Variation

* Abort overlap and direction into running path of player A.

2.2.5   Passing circle (instep shot and header)

Execution

Each of the outside players holds a ball in his hand. The six players in the center do not have a ball but continuously ask for passes from one of the open outside players. The outside players throw their passes. Players A throw their balls to waist height so players C are able to play an instep volley directly back to the hands of the outside player (see 1 and 2). Players B throw the balls high for a return pass header (see 3 and 4). After a short while, the inside players C switch with the outside players A and B.

Coaching

* Precise throws: underhand throw/throw-in.
* Shorten the passing distances (see 1 and 3).

Variations

* Specify the passing technique: instep/inside foot/dropkick/chest reception (see 1 and 2).
* Specify the passing technique: headers from a standing position (see 3 and 4).

2.2.6   Passing circle (third man running)

Execution

Three players in the center are in possession (see A), and three other players in the center are without a ball. Six players with a ball position outside (see C). The players in possession team up in groups of two (see A and B). Player A passes to C (see 1); player C passes to player B (see 2). Player A takes the position of player C (see 5). Player B controls the ball toward the center (see 3). Player C gets involved, runs to the center (see 4), and forms a new pair with player B (see 3 and 4). Outside and inside players switch regularly.

Coaching

* Orientation to the partner for optimal timing (see A and B).
* Ask for sufficiently large distances between players A and B.
* Coaching and communication during the search for an outside player.

Variation

* Specify the number of touches: direct passes (see 1 and 2).

2.2.7   Expanded passing circle (overlap and third man running)

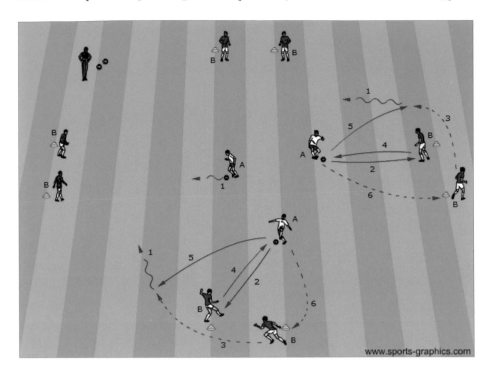

Execution

The players on the field (see A) are in possession and look for an outside player pair (see B) that is not involved in an action. Player A passes to one of the two outside players B (see 2). This player B plays a direct return pass (see 4) and remains in his position. With the pass by A (see 2) the player B who did not receive the pass moves away by overlapping the outside player who did receive the pass (see 3). Player A takes the position of the overlapping player. Player B controls the ball from A (see 5) and dribbles into the center to pass to a new outside pair (see 1).

Coaching

* Maintain constant eye contact.

Variations

* Specify the number of touches: direct passes with all actions.
* Vary the passing combination or add additional passes.

2.2.8   Combination passing circle and open passing game (interfering player)

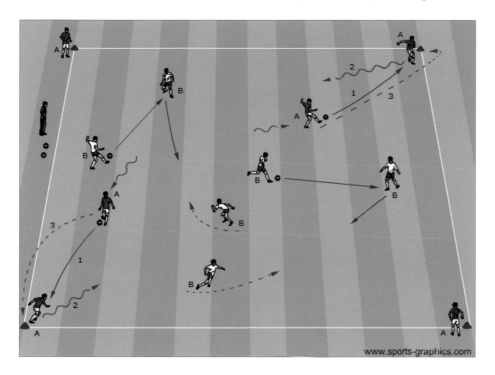

www.sports-graphics.com

Execution

Players A complete a separate drill independent of the players B. Two of the players A are in the center and in possession. They look for an open outside player and pass to him (see 1). The outside player A dribbles onto the field and again looks for an open outside player (see 2). The passer takes over the outside position (see 3). The players B in the center also serve as interfering players as well as complete a separate drill with each other. The six A players pass two balls in their own ranks while moving freely around the entire field. After a short while, the two groups switch tasks.

Coaching

* Situation-specific search for a quick path to the next outside player.

Variations

* Players A complete a double-double pass.
* Specify 2 or 3 mandatory touches for players B.

2.2.9 Passing circle (passing and looking for position)

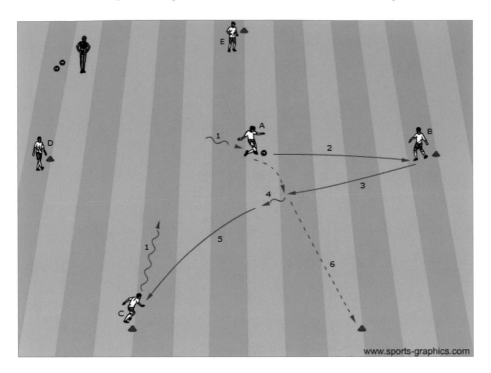

Execution

The outside of the passing circle is marked with five cones. One outside cone is not manned. The player in the center (see A) dribbles freely on the field and looks for an outside player to pass to (see 1). Player A passes to outside player B (see 2). Player B plays a direct return pass (see 3). Player A controls the ball and passes to another outside player (here player C) and switches to the unmanned outside cone (see 6). The outside player C controls the ball into the center (see 1) and becomes the inside player.

Coaching

The inside player should try to finish the action as quickly as possible with smart runs between passes 2 and 4 and keep the dribble (see 4) brief, or avoid it all together and pass directly.

Variations

* Add another unmanned outside cone.
* Add another player with a ball in the center.

2.2.10 Passing circle (6er behavior)

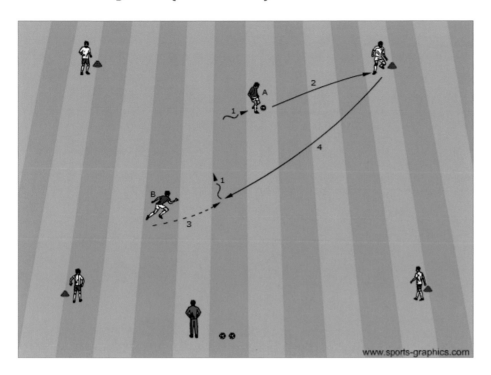

Execution

Four permanent neutral players are positioned outside. The two inside players A and B stay in the center for a while and eventually switch with two outside players. Players A and B should always be positioned diagonally to each other. Player A chooses an outside neutral player (see 1), and player B already reacts to the anticipated pass to the outside (see 3). Player A passes the ball to an outside player (see 2). The outside player plays a direct pass to the other inside player (here player B; see 4). Player B then looks for another receiver. Player A reacts to player B's behavior and before the new pass to the outside is even played moves into a diagonal position to B.

Coaching

* Pass 2 should be short, but pass 4 should be long.
* Inside players are positioned diagonally to each other.

Variations

* Specify the passing technique: direct passes (see 2 and 4).
* Specify additional involvement of an outside player:
  The first outside player to receive a pass plays it directly to a second outside player. The second outside player then passes the ball to player B (see 4).

2.3   OPEN PASSING

2.3.1   Open passing (commands)

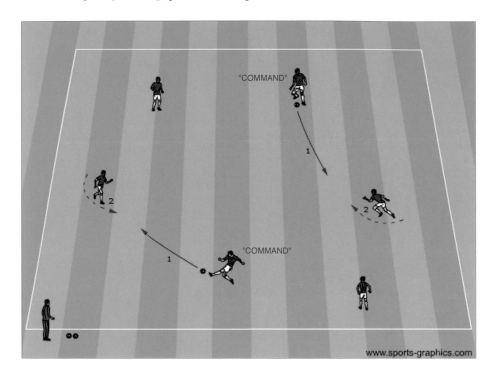

Execution

Players pass openly with multiple balls. The passers freely decide which players to pass to. Each pass is accompanied by a command.

Commands

#Name 1	Call out the own name.
#Name 2	Call out the name of a receiver.
#Name 3	Call out the name of a player the pass receiver should play to.
#Leg controlling the ball	Call out the receiver's ball-controlling leg ("left" or "right").
#Passing leg	Call out the receiver's passing leg ("left" or "right").
#Bounce	Call out the passing leg ("bounce left" or "bounce right") for a direct return pass from the receiver.
#Turn	Call out direction ("left" or "right") for a 180-degree turn by the receiver.
#Opposing pressure	Call out the direction ("left" or "right") the imaginary opponent is coming from: Control the ball in the opposite direction.

2.3.2   Open passing (groups of three)

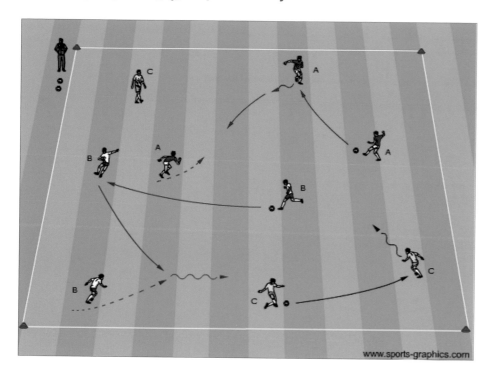

Execution

Players are divided into groups of three. Each group circulates a ball in the own ranks. Each group must choose its own running and passing lanes so they can avoid the other groups. After playing a pass, that player must find a new position on the field so the groups mix with one another and new passing lanes are found in between the interfering players.

Coaching

★   Use the entire field and position change after every pass.

Variations

★   Add additional teams.
★   Specify 2 or 3 mandatory touches.
★   Specify the receiving leg (left/right) and passing leg (left/right).

2.3.3   Open passing (groups of three plus handball)

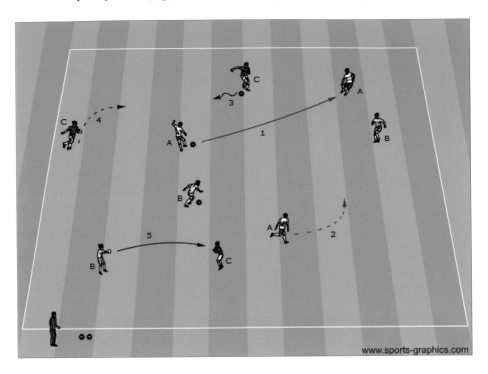

Execution

Players are divided into groups of three. Each group circulates a ball in the own ranks. Each group must choose its own running and passing lanes so they can avoid the other groups. After playing a pass, that player finds a new position on the field so the groups mix with one another and new passing lanes are found in between the interfering players. An additional ball in the game must be passed and caught by hand. This ball can be passed independent of group affiliation (see 5).

Coaching

⋆   Use the entire field and position change after every pass.

⋆   Assistance by calling out names of receivers.

Variations

⋆   Add additional teams.

⋆   Briefly bounce the ball (e.g., three touches on the ground) directly after catching the ball.

⋆   Quick tempo dribble (e.g., three touches) after receiving the ball.

2.3.4   Open passing (color game)

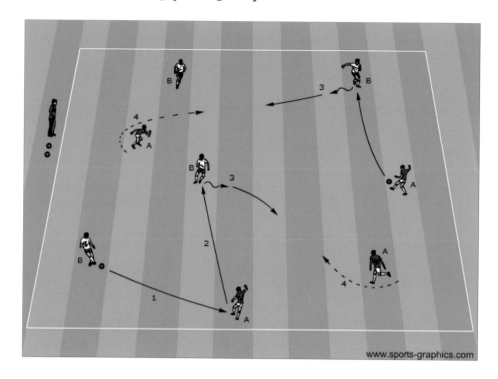

Execution

Multiple players are on the field and identified by either a RED or a BLUE bib and are thus assigned to different groups. The players circulate two balls. The ball must always be passed to a player on the other team. If a player from the BLUE team is in possession, he must pass the ball to a player on the RED team (see 1). The player from the RED team then passes to a BLUE player (see 2) who continues the passing order as specified (see 3).

Coaching

* Ask players to use both feet to receive and pass the ball.
* Recognize the necessary passing stations and get open accordingly.
* Coaching and communication while searching for a receiver.

Variations

* Add more game balls.
* Add more teams (e.g., GREEN team).

2.3.5 Open passing—sequence (1)

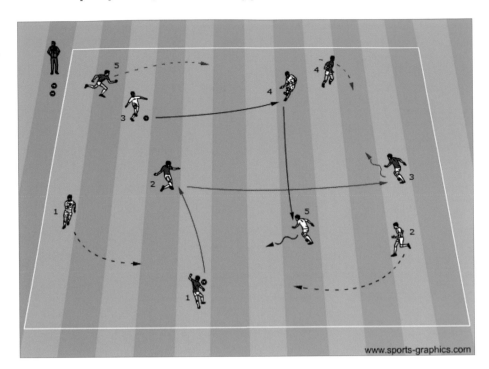

Execution

Players are divided into two groups (e.g., RED and WHITE teams). Each group circulates one ball without crossing or interfering with the other group's running and passing lanes. The ball follows a specified order in which the players have been numbered accordingly (here from 1 to 5).

Coaching

* Timing of the next player's attempt at getting open.
* Coaching and communication during the search for a receiver.

Variations

* Add more game balls.
* Add more teams (e.g., GREEN team).
* Change the passing order after a signal from the coach (e.g., 5-4-3-2-1).
* Change the passing order after a signal from the coach (e.g., 1-3-5-2-4).
* Specify the number of touches: direct passes/2 or 3 mandatory touches.

2.3.6 Open passing—sequence (2)

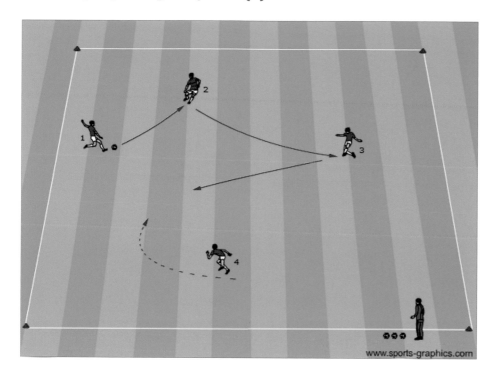

Execution

All players are divided into small groups (here a group of four players). The players are numbered 1 through 4. Passing play takes place in numerical order.

Variations (passing order)

* Player 1 passes to player 2; player 2 passes to player 3; player 3 passes to player 4; and player 4 passes to player 1.

* Player 1 passes to player 2; player 2 passes directly back to player 1; player 1 does a tempo dribble and lays off to player 2; player 2 passes to player 3; player 3 passes directly back to player 2; and player 2 does a tempo dribble and lays off to player 3.

* Player 1 passes to player 2; player 2 passes directly to player 3; player 3 does a tempo dribble and lays off to player 2; player 2 passes to player 3; player 3 passes directly to player 4; and player 4 does a tempo dribble and lays off to player 3.

* Specify the passing technique: every third pass is a volley.

Variations (technique)

* Ask for passes played into the running path (see player 4).
* Specify the number of touches: 2 or 3 mandatory touches/no direct passes.
* Perform a feint right after controlling the ball with the first touch.
* Perform a body feint before or after controlling the ball with the first touch.

2.3.7   Open passing in groups of two—cone goals (1)

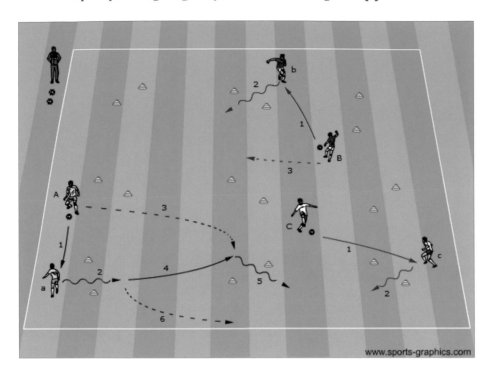

Execution

Players are divided into groups of two (e.g., A and a). Each group has a ball. Players must play passes to each other (see 1) and, after receiving the ball, must dribble through one of the cone goals (see 2). As soon as the pass has been made, the passer must move toward the next cone goal (see 3 and 6). He then receives another pass (see 4) and dribbles through the cone goal (see 5). The individual groups must keep an eye on the behavior of the other groups and avoid any interfering players accordingly.

Coaching

* Coordinate while approaching the cone goal.
* Coaching and communication within each group of two.

Variations

* Precise passing and getting open through the cone goal with the first touch (see 2).
* Organize as a competition: Which team is the first to dribble through 20 cone goals?
* Organize as a competition: Which team dribbles through the most goals in two minutes?

2.3.8   Open passing in groups of two—cone goals (2)

Execution

Players are divided into groups of two (e.g., A and a). Each group has a ball. Players must play passes to each other (see 1). The pass must be played with precision through one of the cone goals. Right after each pass, the passer targets another cone goal and gets open accordingly (see 2). The pass receiver reacts and controls the ball in that direction of play (see 3) to subsequently play the next pass through the targeted cone goal (see 4).

Coaching

* Coordinate running lanes while approaching the cone goal.
* Coaching and communication within each group of two.

Variations

* Specify the number of touches between actions (see 3).
* Specify the receiving leg (left/right) and passing leg (left/right).

2.3.9   Open passing in groups of three (cone goals)

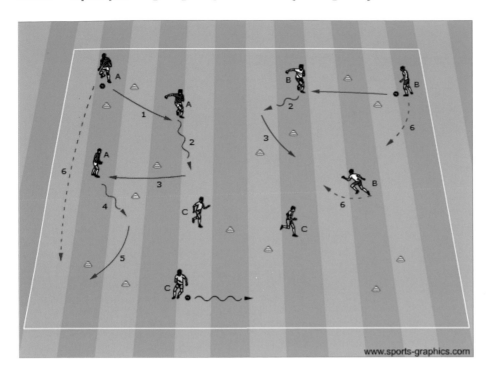

www.sports-graphics.com

Execution

Players are divided into groups of three. Each group has a ball. Players must pass the ball to each other (see 1). Passes to each other must all be played through the cone goals. Double passes are not allowed.

Coaching

* Coordinate running lanes while approaching the cone goal.
* Coaching and communication within each group of three.
* Coordinate optimal timing and hardness of passes for fluid ball circulation.

Variations

* Specify the number of touches between actions (see 2).
* Specify the receiving leg (left/right) and passing leg (left/right).

2.3.10 Open passing in groups of three (around triangles)

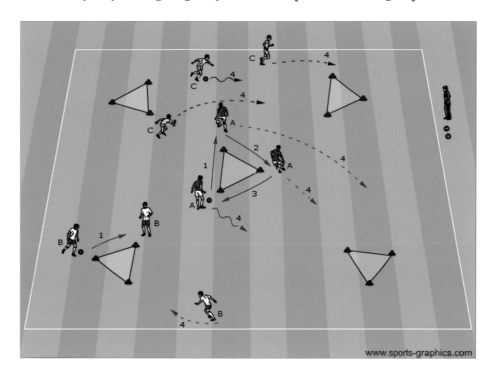

www.sports-graphics.com

Execution

Players are divided into groups of three. Each group has a ball. Players must pass the ball to each other. Each group must pass the ball completely around a triangle (see 1, 2, and 3). After the ball has been passed completely around one triangle, another triangle is targeted (see 4).

Coaching

* Coordinate running lanes while approaching the cone goal.
* Coaching and communication within each group of three.

Variations

* Specify the direction of play around the triangles (left/right).
* Organize as a competition: Which group is the first to play around 10 triangles?
* Complete an additional pass on the way to the next triangle (see 4).
* Specify the number of touches for passes around the triangle: direct passes/2 or 3 touches.

2.3.11   Open passing in groups of four (play on triangles)

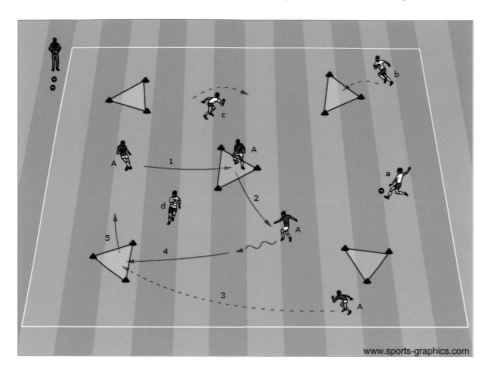

www.sports-graphics.com

Execution

Players are divided into groups of four. Each group has a ball. Players must pass the ball to each other. The passes must be played so one player receives the ball in each triangle (see 1) and then plays a direct pass out of the triangle to a third player (see 2). Once a triangle has been played in, players quickly target a new triangle.

Coaching

* Timing when approaching triangles: fluid running lanes without standing phases.
* Coordinate approach of cone goal.
* Coaching and communication.

Variations

* Specify the receiving leg (left/right) and passing leg (left/right).
* Organize as a competition: Which group is the first to play in 10 triangles?
* Complete an additional pass on the way to the next triangle (see 5).
* Specify the number of touches in the passing order at the triangle: direct passes/2 or 3 touches.

2.3.12 Open passing (catcher)

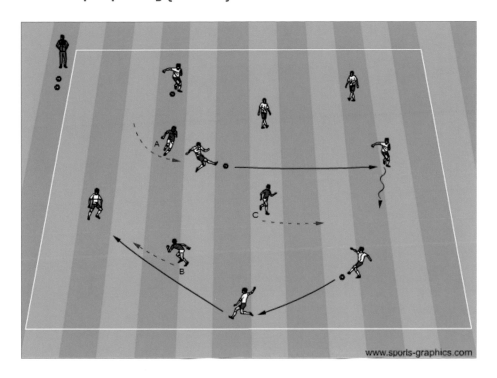

Execution

Multiple players pass multiple balls to each other on the field in the own ranks. Additional players hold bibs in their hands. The players holding the bibs are catchers whose job it is to tag a player in possession (see A, B, and C). As soon as a catcher succeeds, he hands his bib to the player he tagged, and the two players switch positions and roles.

Coaching

★ Sensible orientation of players in possession (shoulder check).

Variations

★ Add more players or game balls.
★ Specify 2 or 3 mandatory touches.

2.4   DRIBBLING

2.4.1   Individual dribbling

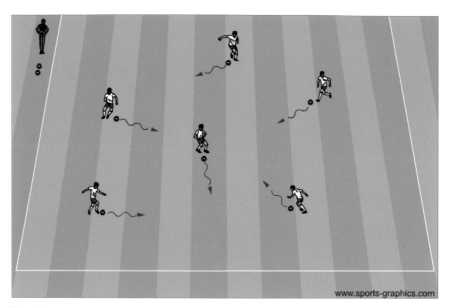

Execution

Each player dribbles on the field and performs the following types of dribbling as specified by the coach:

* Basic dribble with the right foot; basic dribble with the left foot.

* Caress the ball sideways with the sole of the right foot; caress the ball sideways with the sole of the left foot.

* Caress the ball forward with the sole of the right foot/forward left foot/backward right/backward left.

* Caress the ball forward with the sole, alternating feet/backward alternating feet.

* Caress the ball, using the sole and alternating feet.

* Pendulum motion forward with of inside foot; pendulum motion backward with inside of foot.

* Pendulum motion forward with inside of foot and alternate clapping hands in front and behind the back.

* Pendulum motion backward with inside of foot and alternate clapping hands in front and behind the back.

* Alternate outside foot and inside foot with right foot (one touch each).

* Alternate outside foot and inside foot with left foot (one touch each).

* Alternate outside foot and inside foot with right foot (two touches each).

* Alternate outside foot and inside foot with left foot (two touches each).

* Outside/inside foot right; outside/inside foot left.

* Alternate caressing the ball with the sole right and then left with the inside foot; alternate caressing the ball with the sole left and then right with the inside foot.

Variations

* Add neutral players (e.g., goalkeepers) as a passing option for all players.

* A single player imitates the group: Perform a dribbling variation or feint.

* Organize as a competition: Which player is the first to reach the sideline?

    (Groups of two are numbered: Call a pair of players ➡ start in 1-on-1-contest).

2.4.2   Shadow dribbling

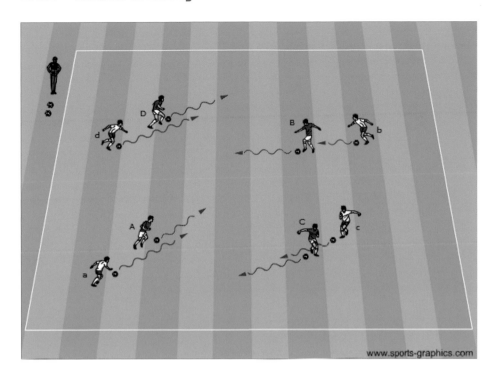

www.sports-graphics.com

Execution

Players are divided into pairs (see e.g. A and a). Each player has a ball. The first player from each team (see A) dribbles in front, the second player (see a) follows behind. The second player (see a) tries to copy the first player's dribble path and movements (feints) (see A).

Coaching

The first player tries to complete various changes in direction and creative feints while keeping the ball close to the body. The second player acts as his shadow and by taking his eyes off his ball, has to constantly watch the front player's movements, react quickly and immediately imitate him.

Variation

★   Specify certain feints (body feint/step-over/feint shot).

2.4.3   Linear dribbling

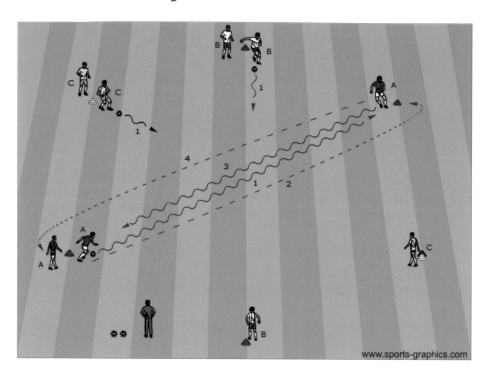

Execution

Players are divided into several groups of at least three players each and position themselves opposite each other and the colored cones, as shown in the illustration. The first player in each group has a ball. Another player is positioned behind that player. The player in possession dribbles straight through the center to the player from his group waiting on the opposite side (see 1), transfers the ball to him and takes over his position (see 2). The player who received the ball dribbles to the starting position (see 3), transfers the ball and takes over the starting position (see 4). All three groups practice simultaneously with the same exercise structure.

Coaching

Players must watch out for the other players, particularly in the center, in order to find an open dribbling lane. This requires changes in pace and constantly looking up. It is important that the players are told to take a direct route to the other side and not to avoid the center.

Variations

* Always perform a feint near the center.
* Specify certain feints (body feint/step-over/feint shot).

2.4.4   Linear dribbling (feints)

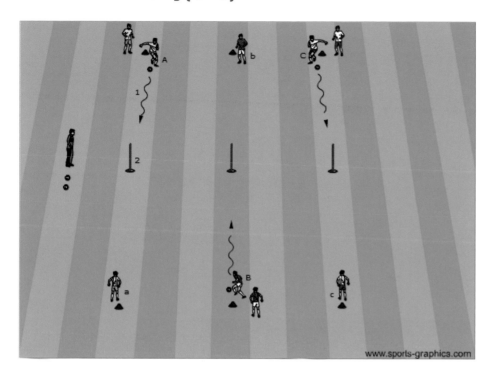

Execution

Players are divided into several groups of at least three players each. The first player in each group has a ball (see A) and dribbles to his partner on the other side (see 1), hands off the ball there and takes over the position of the player who controls the ball (see a/b/c) and continues the dribbling relay. A pole (or cone) in the center represents an opposing player (see 2). Just before he reaches the opponent the player in possession performs a feint.

Coaching

* Optimal timing of the feint for a sensible distance to the opposing player.
* Perform a directional change right after the feint and increase the tempo.

Variations

* Specify certain feints (body feint/step-over/feint shot).
* Replace poles with actual opposing players (partially active/active).

2.4.5   Individual dribbling (field changes)

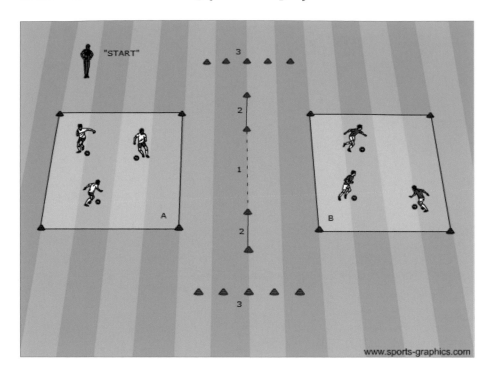

Execution

One group of players is on field A and one group is on field B. Each player has a ball and dribbles freely on the field. At a signal from the coach (here "START") the players must switch fields and dribble onto the opposing field.

Coaching

* Use the entire field.
* Keep the ball close with lots of touches.

Variations

* Change fields through cone goal 1.
* Change fields through cone goals 2.
* Change fields through cone row 3.
* Change fields clockwise through cone goals 2.
* Change fields counterclockwise through cone goals 2.
* Vary/change the starting signal for the field change (visual/audible).
* Organize as a competition: Which group is the first to completely reach the other field?

2.4.6   Individual dribbling (dribble through cone goals)

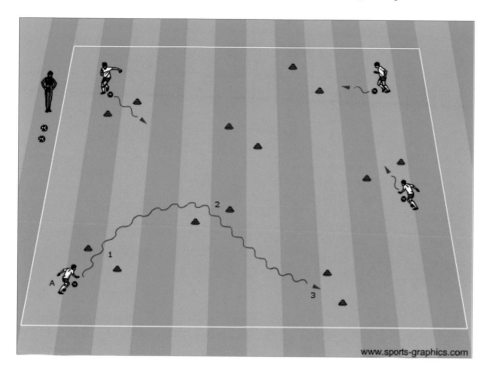

Execution

Several small cone goals are set up on a field. Several players spread out on the field, each with a ball. Each player performs a fluid dribble with smart directional changes without unnecessary loss of time (see 1, 2, and 3). Players can dribble through the cone goals from both sides, and multiple players can do so simultaneously.

Coaching

★ Keep the ball close with lots of touches.

★ Choose a sensible dribble lane.

Variations

★ Specify the dribbling leg (left/right).

★ Specify alternating dribbling leg (left/right/left).

★ Organize as a competition: Which player is the first to dribble through 20 cone goals?

★ Organize as a competition: Which player dribbles through the most goals in two minutes?

2.4.7   Individual dribbling (dribble figure-8s)

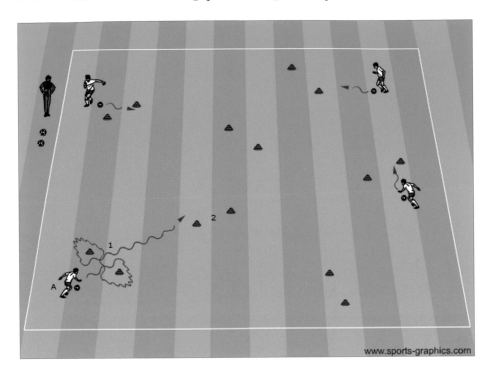

Execution

Several small cone goals are set up on a field. Several players spread out on the field, each with a ball. Each player passes through a cone goal by dribbling a figure-8 around the two cones (see 1).

Coaching

* Keep the ball close with lots of touches.
* Choose a sensible dribble lane.

Variations

* Specify the dribbling leg (left/right).
* Specify alternating dribbling leg (left/right/left).
* Organize as a competition: Which player is the first to dribble through 20 cone goals?
* Organize as a competition: Which player dribbles through the most goals in two minutes?

2.4.8   Dribbling (competition)

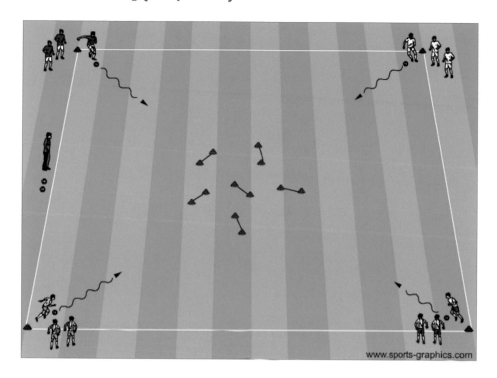

Execution

A team is positioned at each of the four corners of a field. A team must have at least two players. Several small dribbling goals are set up in the center of the field. The first player from each team dribbles onto the field and chooses three cone goals to dribble through and then dribbles back to his team. Next the second player from each team takes the ball and dribbles toward the center.

Coaching

* Players in possession perform starting motions, and receiving players move toward them.
* Precise ball transfer: ball transfer between players.
* Keep the ball close with lots of touches.

Variations

* Vary the dribbling technique in the center (dribble figure-8s).
* Vary the ball transfer: optional return pass to the receiving player.
* Specify the dribbling leg (left/right).
* Specify alternating dribbling leg (left/right/left).
* Organize as a competition: Which team is the first to complete 20 actions?
* Organize as a competition: Which team completes the most actions in two minutes?

2.4.9   Dribbling (fields)

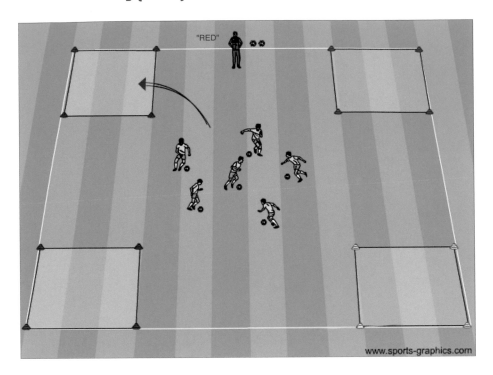

Execution

Each player has a ball and dribbles freely in the center. There are four outside fields marked with different colors. With a signal (here "RED"), the coach specifies the field the players must dribble to. The goal is to react as quickly as possible to the specified color and dribble to the specified field.

Coaching

⭑   Keep the ball close with lots of touches.

Variations

⭑   Vary or change the starting signal for the field change (visual/audible).

⭑   Vary or change the field names (e.g., use numbers).

⭑   Vary or change the field names (e.g., use the names of famous stadiums).

2.4.10 Combination individual and linear dribbling

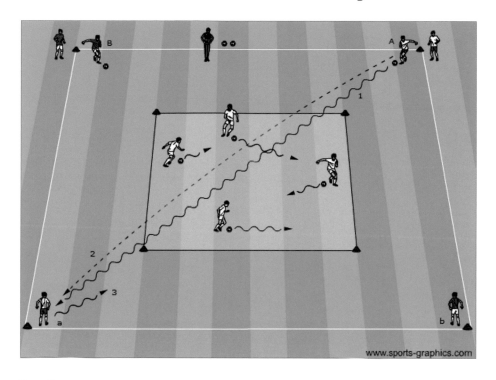

www.sports-graphics.com

Execution

Several players dribble freely in the center field. Two groups are positioned outside the field. Each group has at least three players. The position of the player in possession (see A and B) must always be double-manned. The first player from each group (see A) has the ball and must dribble through the inner field to the opposite side (see 1). There he transfers the ball to the waiting player (see a) and takes over his position (see 2). The player waiting for the ball continues the dribble relay (see 3).

Coaching

* Keep the ball close with lots of touches.

Variations

* Specify a minimum number of touches during the dribble (e.g., 12 touches).
* Specify a dribbling leg (left/right).
* Specify an alternating dribbling leg (left/right/left).
* Vary the technical task in the center: individual juggling/tempo juggling.
* Vary the technical task in the center: passing play with one ball.
* Organize as a competition: Which group is the first to complete 20 dribble paths?

2.5   SHOT ON GOAL

2.5.1   Basic shot on goal

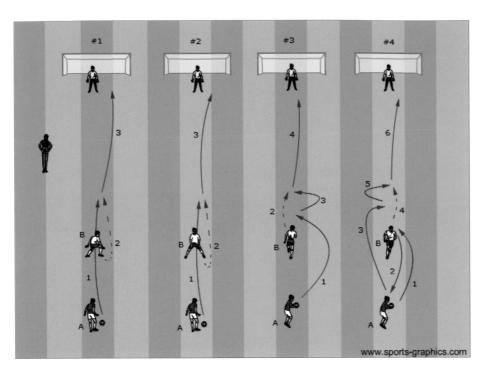

Execution

Following are four different goal-shooting drills (see #1 to #4). Two players (see A and B) center one in front of the other approximately 6.5 feet apart in front of a large goal with goalkeeper.

#1: Player B stands in a straddle position in front of the player in possession A with his eyes on the goal. Player A plays the ball through B's legs (see 1). Player B reacts, goes after the pass (see 2), and takes a quick shot on goal (see 3). Player A takes player B's position. The next player A starts a new action.

#2: Player B stands in a straddle position in front of the player in possession A with his eyes on the goal. Player A plays the ball through B's legs. Player B reacts, turns (see 2), goes after the pass and takes a quick shot on goal (see 3). Player A takes B's position. The next player A starts a new action.

#3: Player A performs a throw-in over player B (see 1). The ball can bounce once (see 3) before player B takes a shot (see 4).

#4: Player A throws the ball to player B (see 1). Player B heads it to player A (see 2). Player A heads it over player B (see 3). The ball can bounce once (see 5) before player B takes a shot (see 6).

2.5.2   Shot on goal (first-touch control)

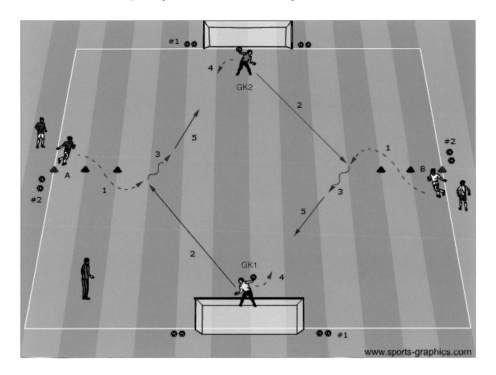

www.sports-graphics.com

Execution

Players A and B simultaneously start on their curved running path through the cone goal located in front of their starting position (see 1). Both goalkeepers throw a well-timed ball into the running paths of players A and B (see 2). Players A and B settle the throws in the direction of the goal (see 3). During this phase, both goalkeepers must shift their focus to the opposing team after their throws to position for the subsequent shot by the opposing player (see 4). Players A and B take shots on goal (see 5).

Variations

* Specify the shooting technique: direct finish.
* Specify the shooting technique: inside foot/instep/left/right/weak foot.
* Perform a feint/body feint right before the shot on goal (see 3).
* Vary goalkeeper passes: roll out/waist-high and high throws (see 2).
* Change direction of play (use both feet).

2.5.3   Shot on goal with passing (1)

Execution

Player A passes to player B (see 1) and overtakes player B (see 2). Player B passes directly to player C. Player C plays directly into the running path of player A (see 4). Player A settles the ball and dribbles toward the marking pole that represents an opposing player (see 5). Just before he reaches the marking pole, player A performs a feint and then takes a shot on goal (see 6). The next action will be played on the other side, starting with a first pass from player A to player C. After a while, the permanent neutral players B and C are switched out. After the shot on goal by player A, the next player in position A starts a new cycle.

Variations

* Player A decides independently whether to pass to player B or C.
* Specify certain feints (body feint/step-over/feint shot).
* Specify the shooting technique: direct finish after the feint (see 5 and 6).

2.5.4   Shot on goal with passing (2)

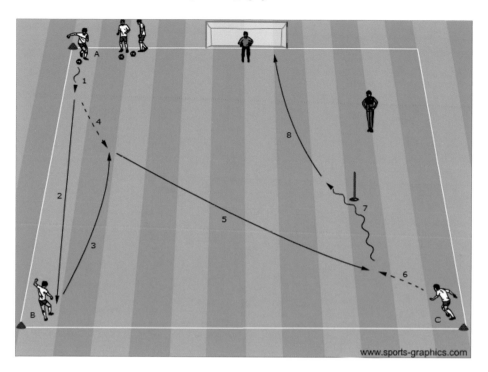

Execution

Player A dribbles briefly (see 1) and plays a pass to player B who is moving away from the cone (see 2). Player A chases his own pass (see 4). Player B lets the ball rebound directly to player A (see 3). Player A plays a direct diagonal pass to C (see 5). Player C moves away from the cone with a starting motion (see 6), settles the pass, and dribbles toward the marking pole that represents an opposing player. Player C performs a feint directly in front of the marking pole (see 7). Next player C finishes on the goal (see 8). After the shot on goal, player C retrieves his own ball and lines up at the position of player A. All players move up one position. Player A becomes player B, and player B becomes player C. A new player starts the next action as player A.

Variations

- Specify 2 or 3 mandatory touches for players A and B.
- Specify the passing technique for players A and B: direct passes.
- Specify certain feints (body feint/step-over/feint shot).
- Specify the shooting technique: direct finish after the feint (see 7 and 8).
- Change the direction of play using a mirrored exercise structure (use both feet).

2.5.5   Shot on goal with passing (3)

Execution

Player A passes to player B (see 1) and follows his pass (see 2). Player B lets the ball rebound directly to Player A (see 3) and then pivots around the marking cone (see 4). Player A passes to player C (see 5). Player C moves away from the marking cone (see 6) and plays a pass to player B (see 7). Player D initially starts toward player C and signals his availability to receive a pass but then pivots toward the goal when player C makes a pass (see 9). Player B plays a direct pass to player D as a goal assist (see 8). Player D takes the shot (see 10). After the shot on goal, each player moves up one position: Player A becomes player B, player B becomes player C, and player C takes over the position of player D.

Variations

* Specify 2 or 3 mandatory touches for players B, C, and D.
* Specify the passing technique for players B, C, and D: direct passes.
* Perform a feint/body feint right before the shot on goal (see 9 and 10).
* Specify the passing technique (e.g., volley) for pass 5.
* Change the direction of play using a mirrored exercise structure (use both feet).

2.5.6 Shot on goal with passing (4)

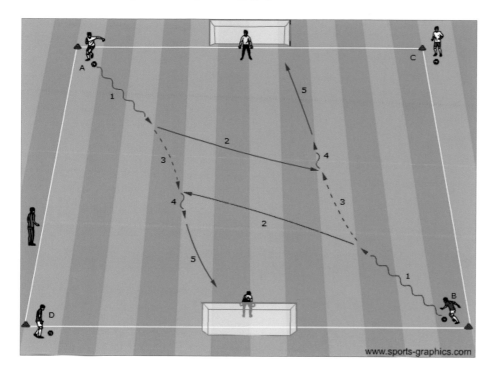

www.sports-graphics.com

Execution

Players A and B start toward each other diagonally across the field, each with a ball (see 1). Maintaining eye contact, both players play their ball, ideally at the same time, into the running path of the other player (see 2). The players keep running (see 3), settle the ball from the partner (see 4), and finish on the goal (see 5). Players D and C start the next cycle.

Variations

* Specify the shooting technique: direct finish after pass 2.
* Specify the shooting technique: inside foot/instep/left/right/weak foot.
* Perform a feint/body feint right before the shot on goal (see 4).
* Specify the passing leg (left/right) and shooting leg (left/right).
* Specify the number of touches during the dribble (see 1).
* Organize as a competition: Which team is the first to score 10 goals?

2.5.7   Shot on goal with passing (5)

Execution

Player A passes to player B (see 1). Player B plays a diagonal direct pass to player C (see 2). Player C passes to player D (see 4). The position in the center is manned by just one player, so player B becomes player b. After his first pass, player B pivots (see 3) and receives the pass from player D (see 5). Now player B plays a diagonal direct pass to Player E. Player E settles the ball toward the goal (see 7) and takes a shot (see 8). Player E retrieves the ball and lines up at position F. Each player moves up one position: Player A becomes player B (b); player B (b) becomes player C; player C becomes player D; and player D becomes player E. Player F starts a new cycle. This ensures that the new passing sequence starts promptly, reducing wait times. It is important that each individual player quickly takes up his new position.

Variations

* Perform a feint/body feint right before the shot on goal (see 7).
* Specify certain feints (body feint/step-over/feint shot).
* Change the direction of play using a mirrored exercise structure (use both feet).
* Specify the shooting technique: direct finish after pass 6.
* Specify the shooting technique: inside foot/instep/left/right/weak foot.
* Organize as a competition: Which player is the first to score 5 or 10 goals?

2.5.8   Shot on goal with passing (6)

Execution

Player A passes to player B (see 1) and runs after his pass (see 2). Player B lets the ball rebound directly to player A (see 3). Player A plays a diagonal direct pass to player C (see 4). Player C settles the ball toward the goal (see 5) and takes a shot (see 6). Player C retrieves the ball he shot and lines up again at position D. Each player moves up one position. Player A becomes player B, and player B becomes player C. After player C finishes, the red players start the same sequence from the other side. After a while, the groups switch sides (use both feet).

Variations

* Specify the shooting technique: direct finish after pass 4.
* Specify the shooting technique: finish with the second touch after receiving the pass.
* Perform a feint/body feint right before the shot on goal (see 5).
* Specify certain feints (body feint/step-over/feint shot).
* Organize as a competition: Which player is the first to score 5 or 10 goals?

2.5.9   Shot on goal with passing (7)

Execution

Player A passes to player B (see 1) and runs after his pass (see 2). Player B lets the ball rebound directly to player A (see 3). Player A plays a diagonal direct pass to player C (see 4). At the same time player B pivots toward the goal (see 4) and receives the pass from player C (see 6). After his pass to player B, player C moves away from the cone and runs parallel   to the goal on an imaginary offside line (see 7). Player B passes the ball into the running path of C (see 8). Player C finishes with a direct shot. Player C retrieves the ball and lines up at position D. Each player moves up one position. Player A becomes player B, and player B becomes player C and player C retrieves the ball he shot and lines up again at position D. After player C finishes, the RED players start the same sequence from the other side. After a while, the groups switch sides (use both feet).

Variations

* Specify the shooting technique: direct finish after pass 8.
* Specify play against the goalkeeper: defeat the goalkeeper in a dribble.
* Organize as a competition: Which player is the first to score 5 or 10 goals?

2.5.10 Shooting competition (dribbling)

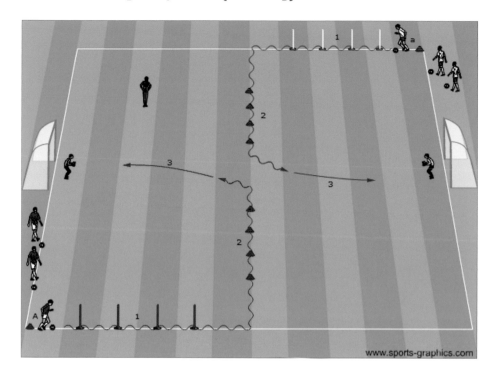

Execution

After a signal from the coach, a player starts from each of the two marking cones with a ball (see A and a). First the players dribble around the four marking poles in a slalom (see 1). Then they dribble to the center to the next row of cones and dribble around these in a slalom (see 2). After the second row of cones, both players turn toward their respective goals and take a shot (see 3). After the shot, they retrieve their ball and line up again with their group. As soon as player A has completed the first slalom (see 1), the next player starts a new action.

Variations (Slalom)

* Slalom run with ball in hand (forward and backward).
* Slalom run with ball in hand in side step (forward and backward).
* Slalom run with ball in hand in one-leg hop (left/right).
* Slalom run with the in hand in closed-leg jumps (forward and backward).
* Slalom run at a dribble with the ball at the foot (left and right).
* Slalom run at a dribble with the ball at the foot, alternating the dribbling leg (left and right).

Variation

* Organize as a competition: Which player is the first to score 5 or 10 goals?

2.5.11   Shooting competition (squaring)

Execution

Players A and B dribble toward the center and each other (see 1). The players dribble past each other. Shortly after passing each other, the players turn left toward the goal (see 2). The turn should be explosive with an increase in speed. The players dribble toward the action fields (see 3). The players take a shot on goal from the action field. After player A's finishes, two new players start the next action. After a while, groups should turn in the other direction (use both feet).

Variations

* Organize as a 1-on-1-competition: Which player is first to score a goal?
* Organize as a 1-on-1-competition: Which player finishes first?
* Organize as a competition: Which player is the first to score 5 or 10 goals?
* Perform a feint in the action field (body feint/step-over/feint shot).
* Specify the shooting leg (left/right).
* Specify the shooting technique: inside foot/instep/left/right/weak foot.

2.5.12 Shooting competition—passing (1)

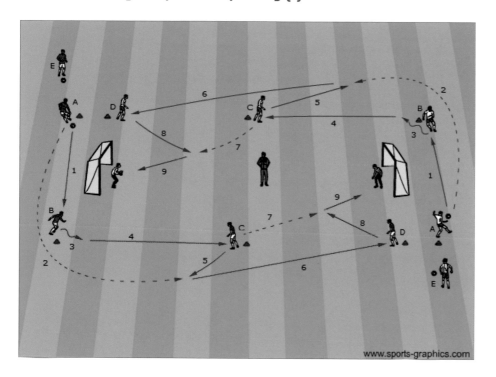

www.sports-graphics.com

Execution

Player A passes to player B (see 1). Player A overtakes player B (see 2). Player B settles the ball in the direction of play (see 3) and passes to player C (see 4). Player C plays directly into the running path of A (see 5). Player A plays a deep direct pass to player D (see 6). Player C turns around (see 7) and receives a direct pass from player D (see 8). Player C takes a shot on goal (see 9). After the shot, each player moves up one position. Player A becomes player B; player B becomes player C; and player C becomes player D. Player D retrieves the ball and lines up at position E. Player E starts the next action.

Variations

* Specify the shooting technique for player C: inside foot/instep/direct finish.
* Specify the shooting technique for player C: direct finish.
* Specify the shooting technique: finish with the second touch after receiving the pass (see 9).
* Perform a feint/body feint immediately before the shot on goal (see 9).
* Specify the passing technique (e.g., volley) for pass 1 (see 1).
* Specify the passing technique (e.g., volley) for pass 8 (see 8).
* Organize as a competition: Which team is the first to score 10 goals?
* Organize as a competition: Which team sores the most goals in five minutes?

2.5.13   Shooting competition—passing (2)

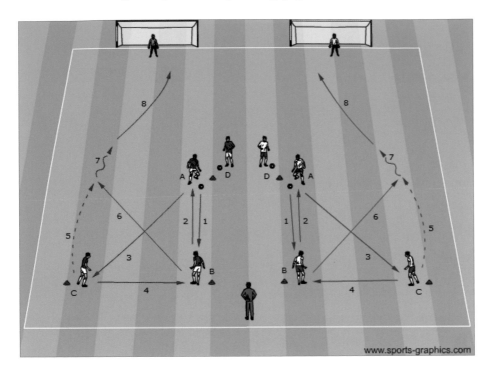

Execution

The RED and BLUE teams compete against each other by trying to play a passing combination in the direction of the large goal as quickly as possible and finishing first. The coach gives both teams a starting signal. Player A passes to player B (see 1). Player B plays a direct pass to player A (see 2). Player A plays a diagonal pass to player C (see 3). Player C passes to player B (see 4) and starts toward the goal (see 5). Player B passes into player C's running path (see 6). Player C dribbles (see 7) and takes a shot on goal (see 8).

Variations

- Specify the shooting technique: finish with the second touch after receiving the pass (see 7).
- Perform a feint/body feint immediately before the shot on goal (see 7).
- Organize as a competition: Which team is the first to score 10 goals?
- The first goal scores double.
- Only the first goal is awarded points.

2.5.14 Shooting sequence with two finishes

Execution

In the course of a sequence, one player (here attacker B) always completes two actions in the form of shots on goal. Player A briefly dribbles (see 1); at the same time, player B moves away from his marking cone with a starting motion (see 2). Player A plays a diagonal pass to player B (see 3). Player B controls the ball (see 4) and takes a shot on goal (see 5). While the shot is being taken, the wing player C already dribbles toward the baseline (see 6). Player B transitions right after his first shot on goal and positions himself for the second ball (see 7). Wing player C plays a pass into the penalty box (see 8), and attacker B converts the pass to a direct kick on goal (see 9). In addition to attacker B, the goalkeeper must also quickly transition in between his actions (see 10). Players D, E, and F complete the next drill sequence. Each player moves up one position. Player A becomes attacker B, attacker B gets a ball and becomes wing player C; and wing player C gets a ball and lines up at position A. After a while, the groups switch so players play as much with the left as the right (use both feet).

Variations

* Specify the shooting technique for players B and E: direct finish (see 9).
* Complete an additional task when the ball doesn't go in the net (e.g., push-ups).
* Specify the passing technique (e.g., volley) for pass 6 (see 1).

2.5.15 Shooting sequence with two finishes (plus 2-on-2 and 3-on-3)

www.sports-graphics.com

Execution

Players A start the action and simultaneously play their balls to each other (see 1). Both settle their balls (see 2) and play a volley to players B and C (see 3) into the marked target field. Players B and C control their balls and finish on the goals (see 5). After their shots, players B and C transition, turn back toward the marked field, and wait there for their next action. With the first touch from an outside player (either B or C), players D pass to each other (see 6) and then start against the large goal in a 2-on-2 with the attackers A (see 7). When players A win the ball or finish, the coach brings a new ball into the game for a 3-on-3 (see 8). To do so, he passes to the outside to either player B or C (here player B). Player B starts toward the coach's pass (see 9), settles the ball toward the goal (see 10), and together with players A plays against the player D and player C, who is moving to the center (see 11).

Variation

When players A win the ball, they can pass to their outside player (here B) and start a 3-on-3 without a pass from the coach. After the defending team wins the ball (here players D and C), they counter-attack in a 3-on-3 on the mini goals positioned at the centerline.

2.5.16 Shooting sequence with three finishes (1)

Execution

Players A and B simultaneously pass their balls to each other. Player A settles the ball toward the goal (see 2) and finishes (see 3). Player B settles the pass toward the center (see 4) and plays a pass to player C (see 5). After their actions, players A and B transition and stand staggered at the penalty box to receive a cross pass (see 6). Player C settles the pass toward the goal and plays a cross pass to player A or B (see 8). Player A or B takes a direct shot on goal (here player B; see 9). Player D dribbles toward the baseline (see 10). After the first shot on goal, players A and B stand staggered at a level with the penalty spot to again receive a cross (see 11). Player D plays the cross (see 12), and player A or B takes a direct shot on goal (here player A; see 13.)

Variations

* Perform a feint/body feint right before the shot on goal (see 2).
* Specify the passing technique (e.g., volley) for pass 5 (see 5).
* Running paths of players A and B must cross (see 6 and 11).
* Stagger positions of players A and B in the back and near the goal (see 6 and 11).

2.5.17 Shooting sequence with three finishes (2)

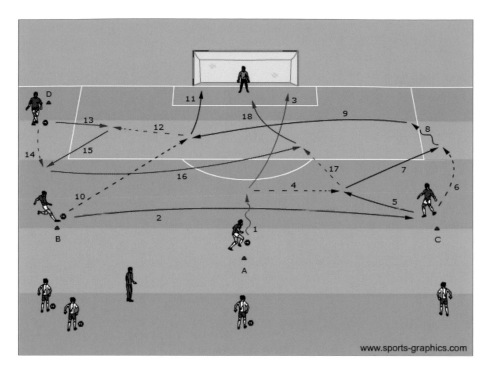

Execution

Player A starts the shooting sequence by briefly dribbling toward the penalty area (see 1). At the same time player B plays a volley to player C (see 2). Player A finishes on the goal (see 3), immediately transitions, and signals that he is open for a pass from player C (see 4). Player C passes to player A (see 5) and moves off for a cross to the outside (see 6). Player A passes into the running path of player C (see 7). Player C settles the ball (see 8) and plays a cross into the center to player B (see 9). Player B comes from the back and moves toward the ball (see 10), converts the cross (see 11), and transitions for a pass from player D (see 12). Player D passes to player B (see 13), moves off into the half-space (see 14), and receives the pass from player B (see 15). Player D crosses to player A (see 16). Player A moves from the back toward the pass (see 17) and converts the cross (see 18). Afterward, the next group starts the described sequence over again.

Coaching

* Timing for approaching the crosses by decelerating/dropping back (see 10 and 17).

Variations

* Additional positioning of player C in the penalty box to convert the cross (see 16).
* Perform a feint/body feint right before the shot on goal (see 1).

2.5.18 Shooting sequence with three finishes (3)

www.sports-graphics.com

Execution

Player A starts the shooting sequence by briefly dribbling (see 1) and then takes a shot on goal (see 2). Player A transitions for a pass from player B (see 3). Player B passes to player A (see 4) and follows his pass (see 5). Player A sets up for player B (see 6). Player B takes a shot on goal (see 7) and transitions for a pass from player C (see 8). Player C passes to player B (see 9) and follows his pass (see 10). Player B provides the assist for player C (see 11). Player C takes a direct shot on goal (see 12).

Coaching

✷ Coaching and communication: Call the name of the pass receiver.

Variations

✷ Perform a feint/body feint right before each shot on goal.
✷ Organize as a competition with scoring:
  One point: Which team can score two goals in one round?
  Two points: Which team can score three goals in one round?

2.5.19 Shooting sequence with five finishes

Execution

During each round, one player (here attacker D) always completes five actions in the form of shots on goal. Player A with three balls and players B and C with one ball each play the passes or crosses. Player D starts the sequence and, after a brief starting motion, asks for the first ball from neutral player A. Neutral player A passes the first ball through the small cone goal to player D (see 1). Player D settles the ball toward the large goal (see 2) and takes a shot on goal (see 3). At the same time, player B dribbles to the baseline (see 4) and plays a cross into the center (see 5). After his first shot on goal, attacker D transitions and directly converts the second ball. Next he asks for the third ball from player A and again receives a pass through the cone goal (see 6). The second pass from neutral player A is also settled and turned into a shot on goal. Next attacker D receives the fourth ball from player C, and after volleying the cross (see 8), he asks for the fifth ball from neutral player A (see 9). Each of the passes to A is quickly controlled and turned into a finish (see 2 and 3). The crosses from outside are played as direct shots (see 5 and 8).

Variations

* Specify the shooting technique: direct finish after passes 5 and 8.
* Specify the shooting leg (first ball: right leg; second ball: right leg; third ball: left leg; fourth ball: left leg; fifth ball: player's choice).

2.5.20 Shot on goal (duels)

Execution

A total of four players (see A, B, C, and D) spread out on the four starting positions. Player D plays four balls one after the other into the drill sequence (see 1, 2, 3, and 4). Player D passes ball 1 to player A. Player A settles it, turns toward the goal, and finishes. As player A takes the shot, player D brings ball 2 into the game and passes it either to player B or C. The receiving player settles the ball toward the goal and tries to score a goal during a 1-on-1 against player A. After the finish or turnover, player D brings ball 3 into the game and passes it to the remaining waiting player. The receiving player calls the name of one of the players who played the 1-on-1 and plays 2-on-1 on the large goal with that player. After the finish or turnover, player D dribbles toward the goal with ball 4, calls a name, and plays 2-on-2 on the large goal with that player. Players regularly change positions.

Variations

* Vary or change the coach's signal (e.g., call the players by position).
* Specify the passing technique for player D: Use the weak leg.
* Organize as a competition: Which player scores the most goals?

2.6   FEINTS AND JUGGLING

2.6.1   Basic feints (1)

www.sports-graphics.com

Execution (RED team)

Players A and B start at the same time with a ball at the foot and dribble toward each other (see 1). In the center, both perform a feint in close proximity of each other (see 2). As soon as the center is open again, players C and D start the next action. Players A and B stand at the opposite side for the subsequent action (see 3).

Execution (BLUE team)

Players A and B start at the same time with a ball at the foot and dribble toward each other (see 1). In the center, both perform a feint in close proximity of each other (see 2) and then play a pass to the opposite position (see 3). Players C and D settle the passes and dribble toward each other ideally at the same time for the subsequent action. Players A and B follow their passes (see 4) and then line up at the opposite position.

Feints

* Basic body feint (feint left/dribble right).
* Basic/double/triple step-over.
* Caress the ball (control the ball with the sole of the foot in dribbling direction).
* Feint pass and feint shot.

2.6.2   Basic feints (2)

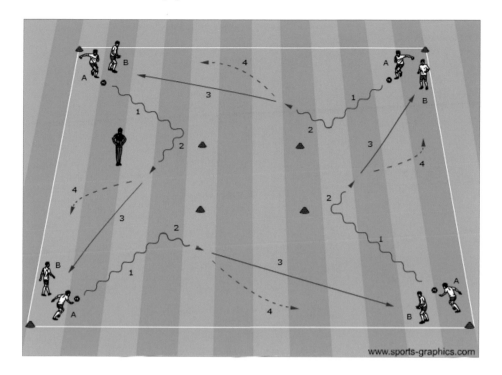

www.sports-graphics.com

Execution

Players start from the four corners preferably at the same time, each with a ball at his foot (see all players A). The players A dribble into the center toward the RED cones (see 1). Just before they reach the cones, they complete a specified feint (see 2). After the feint, they pass the ball to the waiting player in the direction of play (see B). After the pass, the players A position at the next cone (see 4). The players B receive the pass and, after a brief starting motion, dribble to the center to continue the exercise.

Coaching

★   Feints must be executed with precision and accuracy.

★   Optimal timing of the feint for a sensible distance to the cone.

Variations

★   Change the direction of play (use both feet).

★   Specify the dribbling leg (left/right).

★   Players choose feint variations.

2.6.3   Basic feints (3)

Execution

On the field are multiple players with a number of balls at a 2:1 ratio (here six players and three balls). Players can move freely around the field and choose pass receivers without specification or order. One of the players with a ball (see A) calls the name of an open player (see B). Player A passes the ball to player B (see 1) and follows his pass (see 2). Player B dribbles the ball in the passer's direction (see 3) and just before reaching him executes a feint (see 4). Afterward player B looks for a player to pass to and again follows his pass as a passive defender.

Coaching

⋆   Feints must be executed with precision and accuracy.

⋆   Optimal timing of the feint for a sensible distance to the opponent.

Variations

⋆   Vary defensive behavior in 1-on-1 (passive/partially active/active).

⋆   Organize as a competition: Is the player with the ball able to dribble off the field after his feint without the passer touching the ball or tagging him?

2.6.4 Feint competition (team)

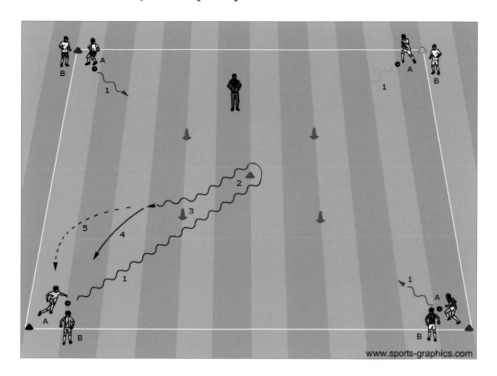

www.sports-graphics.com

Execution

Depending on the total number, players are divided into multiple teams of at least two players each. Every team practices with a ball and starts from their own outside marking cones (here teams RED, WHITE, BLUE, and GRAY). At a signal from the coach, the first player from each team (see A) dribbles toward the cones in the center (see 1). On the way to the center, all players first dribble around the central cone (see 2) and then go back toward their own group. On the way back, they perform a specified feint in front of the cone (see 3) followed by a pass back to the group (see 4). Player A goes back to the starting position, and the waiting player B immediately starts the new action.

Coaching

* Perform a directional change and increase the tempo after the feint (see 3).
* Quick follow-up action (pass after the feint).
* Decrease the number of touches after the feint and pass (see 3 and 4).

Variations

* Organize as a competition: Which team is the first to play 20 passes?
* Specify and vary passing leg, dribbling leg, and feints.
* Perform a feint in front of the first cone on the way out.

2.6.5   Feint competition (individual)

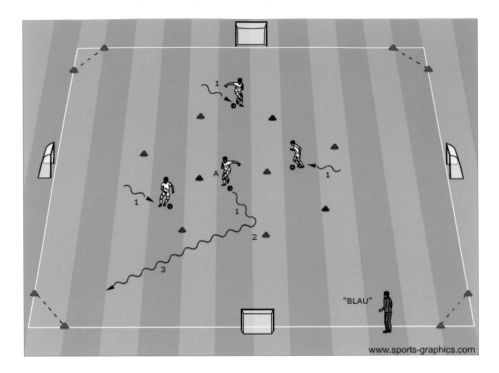

Execution

Each player dribbles his own ball near the center and around the different colored cones (see 1). At a signal from the coach (here "BLUE"), all players must dribble toward the cones of that color and, just before reaching the cone, must perform a specified feint (see 2). The goal of the exercise is to dribble as quickly as possible to one of the dribble goals set up in the corners after the feint (see 3).

Variations

* Designate cones by holding up a cone of the same color.
* Designate cones by whistling (one whistle = RED, two whistles = BLUE).
* Designate cones by calling out numbers (1 = RED, 2 = BLUE).
* Designate cones using alternating signals (color/number/whistle).
* Finish or pass on a mini goal after the feint.
* Finish on a mini goal on the opposite side after dribbling through a corner goal.
* Organize as a competition: Who is the first player to collect five points?

2.6.6   Feints (1-on-1)

Execution

Player A dribbles toward the marking cone positioned directly in front of him, but before reaching it performs a feint (see 1). Immediately after, player A plays a pass to player B. Player A keeps running to position B. Player B dribbles toward the next cone and also performs a feint (see 3) before passing to the waiting player C (see 4). After a pass, player B takes over position C. With the pass from B, players C and D are allowed to leave their marking cones for a 1-on-1. Player C dribbles toward the goal (see 5) and tries to beat the now active defender (see player D and 6) in a 1-on-1 and take a shot on goal. If player D wins the ball, he can counterattack the two mini goals. After the 1-on-1, player C takes over D's defending position. Player D lines up again at position E with the ball while player E starts a new round.

Coaching

★   Offensive action by the attacker in 1-on-1 without cutback.

Variation

★   Specify a certain feint in 1-on-1.

2.6.7 Feints (shot on goal)

Execution

During each round, player A always completes two actions that include controlling the ball, a feint, and subsequent shot on goal. Player A moves off in an arced run around a cone (see 1) and receives a pass from player B (see 2). Player A does an offensive dribble toward the action field (see 3). Player A performs a specified feint in the action field (see 4) and takes a shot on goal (see 5). Next he transitions and does another arced run while asking for the second ball from player B (see 6). He again does an offensive dribble, performs a feint in the action field, and finishes on the goal. Next player B becomes the attacker and player C the neutral player.

Coaching

* Arced run for an open body position and courageous and offensive ball control.
* Perform the action at top speed (precise feint and quick finish).

Variations

* Add more actions and passes.
* Specify an explicit order of particular feints in 1-on-1.
* Organize as a competition: Which group is the first to score 20 goals?
* Add more stations against more goals (see G2 and G3).

2.6.8 Juggling (1)

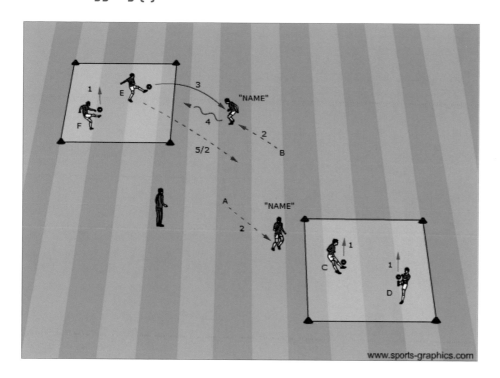

www.sports-graphics.com

Execution

Players C, D, E, and F juggle on the marked fields (see 1). Players A and B start from the center and run toward a juggling field (see 2). When they arrive at the field, they call the name of a juggling player. The juggling player who was called (see E) must play a pass to the asking player without letting the ball touch the ground (see 3). Player B continues to juggle without interruption and juggles onto the field (see 4). Player E now leaves the field without a ball in direction of the center in order to run to the other field and ask for a ball there (see 5).

Variations

*   Specify strictly alternating the playing leg (left/right) while juggling.
*   Every fifth touch is made with the head.
*   Execute running paths without a ball using the versatile running ABCs.
*   Create a movement task for each juggling error.
*   Organize as a competition: How long does it take for a player to make three errors?
*   Organize as a competition with groups of two: Which group will be the first to make three errors?

2.6.9   Juggling (2)

Execution #1 (juggling relay)

Player A juggles the ball to the cone opposite him (see 1) and passes the ball to player B (see 2). Player A takes over player B's position (see 3). Player B continues to juggle toward player C without interruption.

Execution #2 (juggling relay with obstacles)

Player A juggles and passes the ball to player B without interruption (see juggling relay #1). Two hurdles (or cone rows) serve as obstacles. On the way out, player A must juggle in a small arc (see 1) and the pass to player B must be played over the second hurdle (see 2).

Execution #3 (juggling soccer-tennis)

Several mini goals (or cone rows) serve as a net. Players A and B play against players C and D. The goal is to play the ball back and forth over the net as many times as possible (see 1). The ball can touch the ground once after the pass (see 2). Each player must complete at least two touches before he can pass the ball on. Every player on a team must have had the ball at least once during possession (see 4).

2.6.10 Juggling (3)

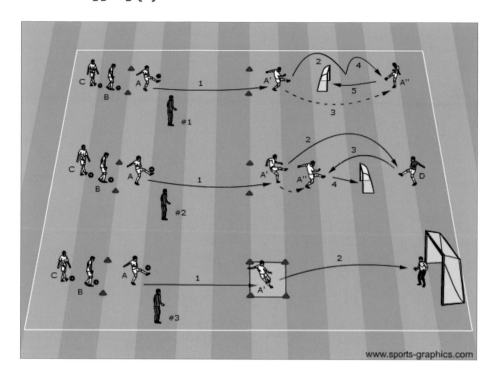

www.sports-graphics.com

Execution #1 (juggling with shot on goal)

Player A juggles up to the RED cone goal (see 1). Only after that is he allowed to continue his task and play the ball high over the mini goal (see 2). Afterward, he must quickly run around the cone goal (see 3). The ball can touch the ground only once before his volley shot on goal (see 4). Player B starts the next action with a pass from player A (see 2).

Execution #2 (juggling with direct shot on goal)

Player A juggles up to the RED cone goal (see 1). Only after that is he allowed to continue his task together with neutral player D, who is positioned behind the goal. Player A plays a high pass over the cone goal to player D (see 2). Player D plays a direct return pass over the mini goal (see 3). Player A follows his pass and takes a direct shot (variation dropkick) on the mini goal (see 4).

Execution #3 (juggling with shot on a large goal)

Player A juggles onto the action field (see 1). Once he has reached the action field without making an error, he can take a volley shot or dropkick on the large goal while moving (see 2).

2.7   1-ON-1

2.7.1   Basic 1-on-1

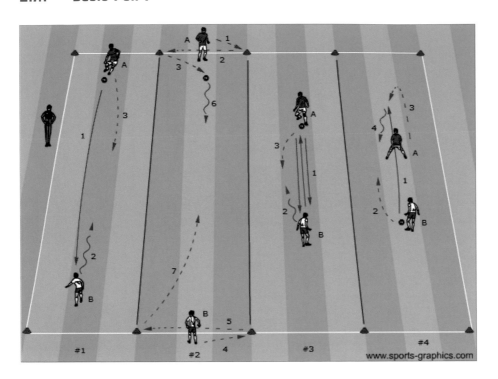

Execution

Following are four different 1-on-1 situations (see # 1 to # 4). In each scenario, two players are positioned opposite each other (see A and B). After various starting motions, the objective is to beat the opponent in a 1-on-1 and break through to the opposite baseline and dribble across it.

#1: Player A plays a long pass to player B (see 1). Player B controls the ball and starts into the 1-on-1 (see 2). Player A follows his pass and takes over the position of defender (see 3). Practice goals: defend high and don't wait; quickly decrease the distance to the player with the ball; defender stands sideways and fast offensive action with lots of feints by the attacker in possession.

#2: Player A starts the action by touching both cones on the own baseline with his hand (see 1 and 2). Next he starts toward the ball on the ground in front of him (see 3), controls it, and starts into the 1-on-1 (see 6). Player B reacts to player A touching the cones and performs a mirrored running path at his own cones before starting into the 1-on-1 (see 4, 5, and 7).

#3: Players A and B play direct passes back and forth (see 1) until one player decides to control one of the balls (here player B; see 2). The other player immediately becomes the defender (see 3).

#4: Player B plays a pass through the straddled legs of player A (see 1) and follows his pass as defender (see 2). Player A turns toward the ball (see 3) and controls it for a 1-on-1 (see 4). He ideally keeps an eye on the defender using a shoulder check.

2.7.2 1-on-1 (transition)

Execution

Player A starts the drill sequence with his first touch. As soon as player A touches the ball, player B reacts and can start his action. Player A dribbles toward the marked shooting line (see 1). Player B immediately starts a slalom dribble around the cones in front of him (see 2). Player A takes a shot on goal from approximately the shot line (see 3), immediately transitions from offense to defense, and becomes the defender in a 1-on-1 against player B (see 4). The goalkeeper also transitions after the first action and concentrates on the second action in the 1-on-1 (see 5). Player a and player b execute the next drill sequence. After each action, players A and B switch positions or sides so that each player spends equal time playing offense and defense.

Variations

* Specify the shooting leg for player A (left/right).
* Specify the number of touches before the shot on goal for player A (see 1).
* Player A performs a feint before the shot on goal.
* Specify the dribbling leg for player B (left/right).
* Add more cones to the slalom course (see 2).
* Add a follow-up action for after player A wins the ball (e.g., pass to coach).
* Organize as a 1-on-1 competition: player A against player B.
* Organize as a competition: Which team is the first to score 10 goals after the 1-on-1?

2.7.3 1-on-1 (decision)

www.sports-graphics.com

Execution

Two attackers (see player B and player b) position close together in the center of the field. A defender is positioned in front of each of the two mini goals (see player C and player c). Two neutral players (see player A and player a) are positioned at the outside marking cones. Players B and b coordinate which of the two will attack which side without letting players C and c know. After a signal from the coach, player A and player a play the balls into the center to players B and b (see 1). As previously arranged, players B and b dribble the ball into their respective direction of play (see 2) and attack the two mini goals in a 1-on-1. Players C and c react to their now obvious opponent and start into the 1-on-1 (see 3). After player C or c wins the ball, he can also attack the mini goals on the opposite side. After the two 1-on-1 situations are resolved, players C and c leave the field, retrieve the two played balls, and line up again at positions D and d. The attackers B and b switch to defense and take over the positions of C and c. The neutral players a and A position as attackers at the positions of B and b. Now the neutral players D and d initiate the new action.

Variation

* Vary the game start by letting players B and b choose who to ask for the ball.

2.7.4   1-on-1—reaction (1)

www.sports-graphics.com

Execution

Players are divided into two groups. First the RED team plays defense, and the BLUE team plays offense. After a while, the groups switch positions. Players A and B play direct passes back and forth (see 1). Player A can choose when to start the 1-on-1. As soon as he uses a second touch (see 2), the defender is allowed to intervene in the 1-on-1 (here player B; see 3). In addition to the start time, player A can also determine the direction of play or the goal to be played on. He can only perform one other change of direction after choosing the first direction of play (here to the right; see 2). After that, the goals are dedicated, and after winning the ball, player B also has the opportunity to score a goal.

Variations

* Specify a required number of passes (see 1) before the 1-on-1.
* Specify the playing leg for player A during the dribble (see 2).
* Vary the passing distance (see 1) or distance to the goals.
* Organize as a 1-on-1-competition: player A against player B.
* Organize as a competition: Which team is the first to score 10 goals after the 1-on-1?

2.7.5   1-on-1—reaction (2)

Execution

Player A is the attacker and starts the action by dribbling through the cone goal in front of him (see 1). Next he has the option of passing to player B or C (here he chooses player B). Player A plays a pass to player B (see 2). At the same time the player who did not receive a pass (here player C) must react and start into the 1-on-1 as a defender (see 3). Player A follows his pass (see 4) and receives a direct return pass from player B (see 5). Player A controls the pass (see 6) and tries to take a shot on the large goal during a 1-on-1. After the defender wins the ball, player C has the opportunity to attack the other two mini goals. After the 1-on-1, player C retrieves the ball and positions at position a. Player A takes over the position of c. Player B remains in his position. Player a starts the next round.

Variations

★ Option for player A after receiving the pass (see 5): one-time involvement of player B.

★ Opportunity for a counter on the mini goals/dribble line for the defender.

★ Organize as a competition: Which player scores the most goals?

2.7.6   1-on-1—reaction (3)

Execution

Player A is the attacker and starts the action by dribbling toward the two cone goals in front of him (see 1). Just before he reaches the two cone goals (see 2), he chooses one and dribbles through it, thereby choosing his opponent for the subsequent 1-on-1-situation. Here player A chooses the BLUE cone goal and activates player C at the BLUE cone. Player C reacts and intervenes as the defender in the 1-on-1. In the 1-on-1, player A tries to finish on the large goal.

Variations

* Perform a feint right in front of the cone goals (see 1).
* Perform a feint right after the cone goals (see 2).
* Specify the shooting leg for player A (left/right).
* Opportunity for a counter on the mini goals/dribble line for the defender.

2.7.7   1-on-1—reaction (4)

Execution

Player A acts as the neutral player and starts with a pass to player B (see 1), who acts as the attacker in the subsequent 1-on-1 situation. Player B plays a direct return pass to player A (see 2). Player B chooses a running lane, either to the right around the RED marking cone, or to the left around the BLUE marking cone. By choosing his running lane, he activates the opposing player marked with the same color for the subsequent 1-on-1 situation. Here player B chooses the running lane around the RED marking cone (see 3), activating the defender D (see 4), and receives the pass played into his running path by player A (see 5). Now the 1-on-1 situation toward the large goal begins. Player A moves up to position B, and player B takes over the position of his defender D. Player D retrieves the ball and lines up at position a. Next player a starts a new round.

Variations

* Perform a feint immediately before the 1-on-1 (see 6).
* Opportunity for a counter on the mini goals/dribble line for the defender.
* Option for player A after receiving the pass (see 6): one-time involvement of player C.

2.7.8   1-on-1—reaction (5)

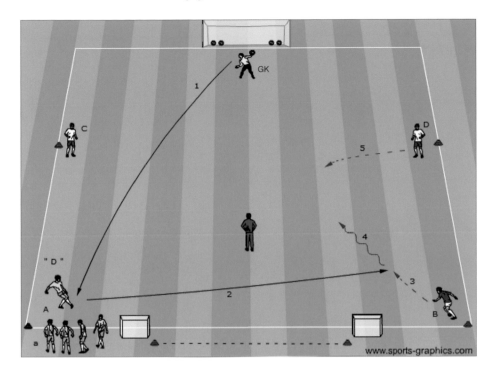

Execution

Player B is the attacker, and players B and C are defenders. Only one defender at a time is active in the 1-on-1 situation. The goalkeeper opens with a throw-out to player A (see 1). Player A plays a direct pass to player B (see 2). At the same time, player A calls either "D" or "C," activating a defender (here player D; see 5). Player B starts toward the pass (see 3) and dribbles (see 4) toward the large goal for a subsequent 1-on-1 situation against the defending player D. Player A moves up to player B's position; player B takes over the position of the active defender (here player D); and player D retrieves the ball and lines up at position a.

Variations

- ★   Player B designates the defender.
- ★   The goalkeeper designates the defender.
- ★   Option for player A after receiving the pass (see 4): one-time involvement of player C.
- ★   Opportunity for a counter on the mini goals/dribble line for the defender.
- ★   Add another goalkeeper to minimize wait times.

2.7.9   1-on-1—reaction (6)

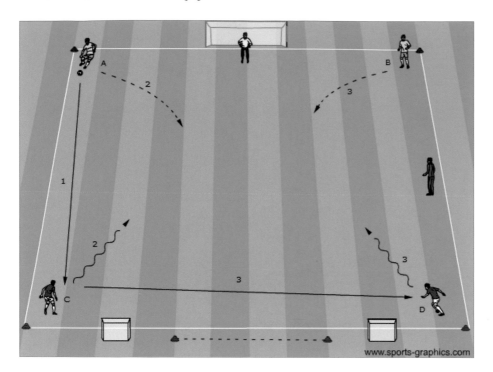

Execution

Players A and B act as defenders; players C and D are attackers. Player A starts the practice sequence and plays a pass to player C (see 1). Player C has a choice and can either dribble toward the large goal (see 2) or play a direct pass to player D (see 3). One of the two defenders is activated, depending on whether player C uses a second touch and starts to dribble (see 2) or passes to player D (see 3). If player C chooses to dribble, player A will start into the 1-on-1 situation (see 2). If player C passes the ball to D, B starts into the 1-on-1 situation (see 3) against attacker D. Attackers and defenders regularly switch positions.

Variations

* A signal from the coach—a pass from A (see 1)—activates all players for a 2-on-2.
* Option for the attacker after receiving a pass (see 2 and 3): Involve the inactive player.
* Opportunity for a counter on the mini goals/dribble line for the defender.
* Organize as a competition: How long will it take the attackers to score five goals?

2.7.10   1-on-1—reaction (7)

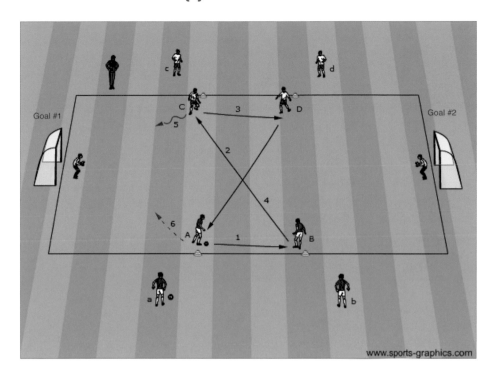

Execution

At first players A, B, C, and D play an endless passing loop. Player A passes to payer B; player B passes to C; player C passes to D; and player D passes to A. Player A continues the passing loop with player B. Each player must play in the passing loop at least once. Afterward, each player in possession has the opportunity to enter into a 1-on-1 situation as the attacker. In doing so, player C always plays against player A, and player B always plays against player D. Here player C decides to dribble toward the goal (see 5). Player A reacts and becomes the defender (see 6). Players A and C are immediately replaced by players a and c so that another passing loop can begin right away.

Variations

* Players A and C always play on goal #1.
* Players B and D always play on goal #2.
* The active attacker can choose between goal #1 and goal #2.
* Vary the passing order.

2.7.11   Frontal 1-on-1

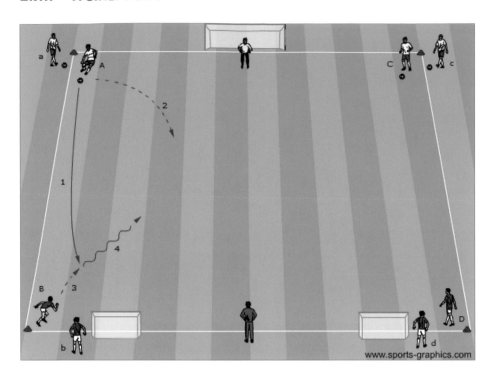

Execution

Player A begins the practice sequence and plays a long pass to player B (see 1). Immediately after he moves to the center of the field (see 2). In the following 1-on-1 situation, player A is the defender and player B the attacker. Player B starts toward the pass (see 3), gets the ball, and dribbles toward the large goal. Player B tries to finish on the large goal from a 1-on-1. After the defender wins the ball, player A has the opportunity to play on one of the two counterattack goals. During the next action, player C starts with player D. After each action, players A and B switch positions.

Variations

* Organize as a competition: Which group is the first to score 10 goals?
* Organize as a competition: How long does it take the attackers to score five goals?

2.7.12 Diagonal 1-on-1 (1)

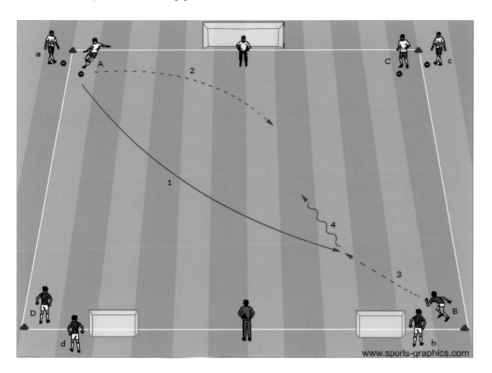

Execution

Player A starts the practice sequence and plays a diagonal pass to player B (see 1). Immediately after, he moves to the center of the field (see 2). In the following 1-on-1 situation, player A is the defender and player B the attacker. Player B starts toward the pass (see 3) and, after receiving it, dribbles toward the large goal (see 4). Player B tries to finish on the large goal from the 1-on-1. After the defender wins the ball, player A has the opportunity to play on one of the two counterattack goals. During the next action, player C starts with player D. After each action, players A and B switch positions.

Variations

* Specify the passing technique (e.g., volley) for pass 1.
* Organize as a competition: Which group is the first to score 10 goals?
* Organize as a competition: How long will it take the attackers to score five goals?

2.7.13 Diagonal 1-on-1 (2)

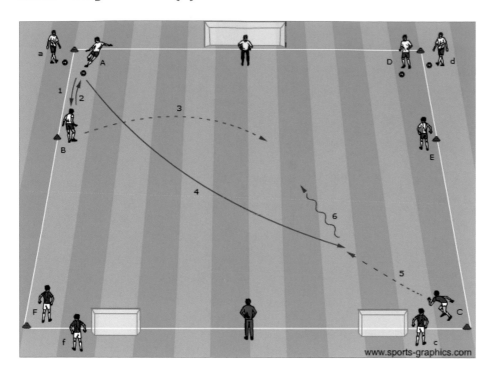

Execution

Player A starts the practice sequence and initially only acts as the passer. Player A plays a pass to player B (see 1). Player B plays a direct return pass to player A and immediately moves to the center of the field (see 3). Player A plays a diagonal pass to player C (see 4). This concludes the action for player A. He lines up at position B for the next action. In the subsequent 1-on-1 situation, player B is the defender, and player C becomes the attacker. Player C starts toward the pass (see 5) and, after receiving it, dribbles toward the large goal (see 6). From the 1-on-1, player C tries to finish on the large goal. After the defender wins the ball, player B has the opportunity to play on one of the two counterattack goals. Player D starts the next action with players E and F. Player B takes over the position of player C. Player C retrieves the ball and lines up again at position a.

Variations

*   Specify the passing technique (e.g., volley) for pass 4.
*   Organize as a competition: Which group is the first to score 10 goals?
*   Organize as a competition: How long will it take the attackers to score five goals?

2.7.14   Diagonal 1-on-1 (3)

www.sports-graphics.com

Execution

Several players are positioned at position B (here two players). Attackers are positioned at the other positions A, C, D, and E. The players at position B switch after a while. Player A plays a pass to player B (see 1) and follows his pass (see 2). Player B plays a direct return pass to player A (see 3), quickly turns, and becomes the defender in the subsequent 1-on-1 situation (see 4). Player A plays a diagonal pass to player C (see 5). Player C dribbles (see 6) and attacks the large goal in a 1-on-1. After the action, player B returns to the defender's position b. Player C retrieves the ball and lines up at position a. Player A moves up to position C. The next action is started by player D and played with players b and E.

Variations

* Add an opportunity for a counter on the mini goals/dribble line for the defender.
* Organize as a competition: Attackers switch to defense after 3 or 5 actions in a row without scoring.

2.7.15   1-on-1 (wing)

Execution

Player A plays a pass to attacker B on the wing (see 1). Player B dribbles toward the penalty box for a 1-on-1 situation against defender C (see 2). Player C stands between two dribble goals (see 3 and 4). In the subsequent 1-on-1-situation, player B has the job of penetrating the large goal across one of the two dribble lines. If player B chooses line 4 and successfully crosses it, he has the opportunity to finish on the large goal without further pressure from the opponent. If player B chooses line 3 and successfully crosses it, player C will remain active as defender and will continue to attempt to interfere with player B's offensive actions. Moreover, crossing dribble line 3 activates neutral player A as an additional attacker for a 2-on-2 situation (see 5). After the action, player C retrieves the ball and lines up at position a. Player B becomes the defender at position C and player A becomes the attacker at position B. The next sequence is played on the other wing with players a, D, and E.

Variations

★   Specify the passing technique (e.g., volley) for pass 1.

★   Add an opportunity for a counter on the mini goals/dribble line for the defender.

★   Organize as a competition: Which player is the first to score five goals?

2.7.16 1-on-1—two goals (1)

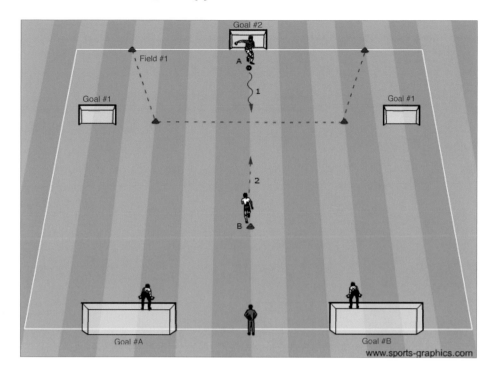

Execution

Player A is in possession and starts from mini goal #2. He dribbles toward player B (see 1). Player A's aim is to finish on one of the two goals #A and #B after a successful 1-on-1 against player B. Player B starts from the marking cone and runs towards the attacker (see 2) to challenge him in a 1-on-1 and win the ball. After player B wins the ball, he can counter against the three mini goals (see goals #1 and #2). A shot into goal #2 scores double points. Winning the ball on field #1 scores triple points.

Coaching

Player B should approach the attacker with an arced run, trying to draw him to his weak foot to challenge him early on and pressure him and then win the ball. After successfully winning the ball, player B can immediately finish on the mini goals. Player A should quickly reduce the distance to the opposing goal and beat the opposing player in a 1-on-1 with a quick feint, including a directional change, and quickly finish.

2.7.17   1-on-1—two goals (2)

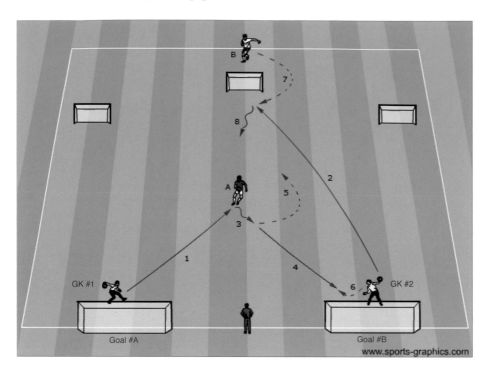

Execution

The 1-on-1 between attacker B and defender A is initiated by an opener from both goalkeepers (see GK #1 and GK #2). Afterward, player A takes a shot on goal. The two goalkeepers each hold a ball. Simultaneously, GK #1 rolls his ball to player A (see 1) and GK #2 throws his ball hard in front of the central mini goal (see 2). Player A controls the pass toward the other goal (see 3), takes a shot on goal (see 4), and immediately transitions toward player B (see 5). After his throw-out to player B, GK #2 also transitions (see 6) and positions so he can parry player A's shot. A 1-on-1 between player B and player A follows. Player B moves toward the goalkeeper's pass (see 7), receives the ball, and dribbles toward the two large goals (see 8 and goals #A and #B). Player B tries to beat player A in a 1-on-1 and can finish on both goals (see goal #A and goal #B). After successfully winning the ball, player A can counterattack on the three mini goals.

Variations

* Regularly alternate passes from the goalkeeper to players A and B.
* Vary the goalkeeper passes (punt/cross/dropkick/pass).
* GK #1 specifies the shooting leg for player A using a command ("left"/"right").

2.7.18 1-on-1—arena (1)

Execution

Players A and B play a 1-on-1 situation in the arena with the goal of reaching one of the two dribble lines or dribble zones (see 4 and 5). After a signal from the coach, the two players start toward the center (see 1). The coach brings the ball into the game (see 2). The coach can modify his passes, and how soft or hard his pass is determines which player should receive the ball (here A).

Variations

* Player A always plays on zone 4.
* Player B always plays on zone 5.
* The player in possession can choose between zone 4 and zone 5.
* Consecutive dribbling through both zones scores double.
* Specify 8, 10, or 12 touches before allowing attack in the zones.
* Organize as a competition: Which player is the first to score five points?
* Organize as a competition: Which is the first team to score 10 points?

2.7.19   1-on-1—arena (2)

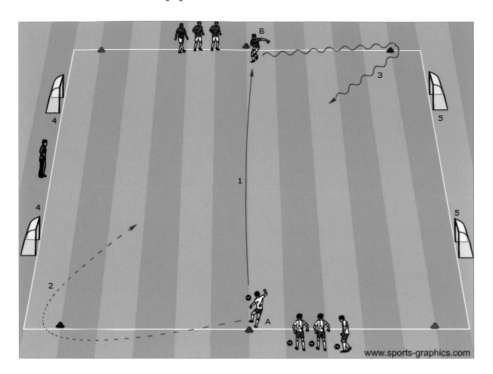

Execution

Players A and B play a 1-on-1 situation in the arena with the goal of scoring on one of the four mini goals. Player A decides with his first running path (see 2) which of the mini goals he will defend. Player A plays a pass to player B (see 1). Immediately after player A runs around one of the cones to his left and right. Here player A chooses the BLACK cone (see 2). Player B reacts to player A's running path and dribbles in the opposite direction to dribble around the cone on the opposite side (see 3). The 1-on-1 situation starts next. As a result of player A's first running path (see 2), player B attacks goals 4, and after potentially winning the ball, player A attacks goals 5.

Variations

* Optional attack on all four mini goals after winning the ball.
* Player B specifies the running path (see 3) and reaction by player A (see 2).

2.7.20 1-on-1—arena (3)

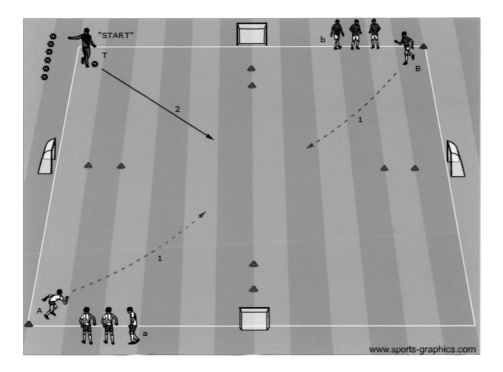

Execution

After a signal from the coach (see "START"), players A and B run into the center of the arena (see 1). The coach plays a ball into the center for a 1-on-1 (see 2). The game's objective is to score on one of the four mini goals. The player in possession is always allowed to attack all four mini goals. A cone goal is set up directly in front of each mini goal. Players must dribble through the cone goal before they can finish.

Variations

* Vary or change the coach's signal (e.g., "2"/prelude to a 2-on-2 situation).
* Limit the number of touches after successfully dribbling through the cone goal.
* Organize as a competition: Which team is the first to score 10 goals?
* Organize as a competition: Which player is the first to score five goals?

2.7.21 1-on-1—arena (4)

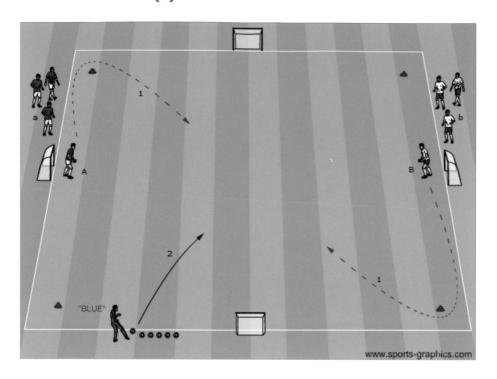

Execution

After a signal from the coach (see "BLUE"), players A and B run into the center of the arena (see 1). First they must run around the cone that matches the color the coach calls (here BLUE). Next the coach plays the ball into the center for the 1-on-1 situation (see 2).

Variations

* Add more colored cones to create different reactions.

* Vary or change the coach's signal (e.g., "2"/prelude to a 2-on-2 situation).

* Specify 3 or 4 mandatory touches for the player in possession.

* Organize as a competition: Coach passes to the faster player.

* Organize as a competition: Which team is the first to score 10 goals?

* Organize as a competition: Which player is the first to score five goals?

2.7.22 1-on-1—arena (5)

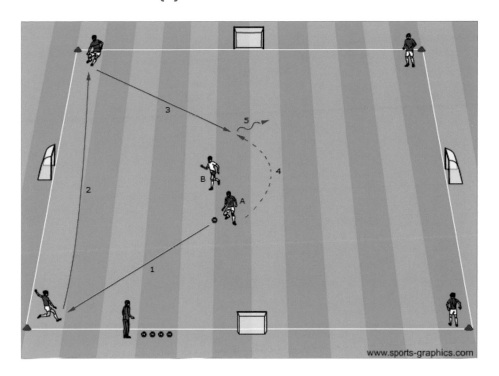

Execution

Four outside players are positioned at the outside marking cones in the arena. In the center are two players playing through a 1-on-1 situation (here player A and B). Player A is the attacker and is allowed to involve the four outside players (see 1) and can also receive passes from them (see 3). Player A plays for possession. The RED team tries to stay in possession for as long as possible without player B being able to win the ball. The outside players can also play direct passes to each other (see 2). Since there is no rule that limits touches, player A can also dribble (see 5). Player B primarily tries to block player A and, if possible, win the ball in a 1-on-1. If player B wins the ball, he can immediately finish on one of the four mini goals. After a while, players A and B switch.

Variations

* After 5 or 6 touches, player A has the option of attacking all four mini goals.
* Specify 3 or 4 mandatory touches for player A after each pass he receives.
* Limit the number of touches for the outside players.

2.8   ACTIVE DEFENSE

2.8.1   Chase and capture (1)

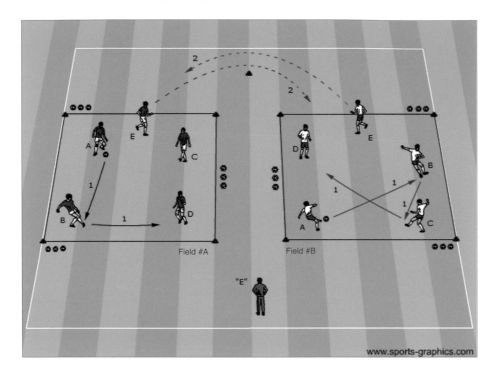

Execution

The players from the RED team (see players A, B, C, and D) pass a ball to each other on field #A (see 1). The players from the BLUE team (see players A to E) also pass each other a ball on field #B (see 1). Players are divided into pairs. The coach calls one player pair as the starting signal (here players E). The players who were called leave the passing relay and simultaneously run around the outside cone (see 2). The balls continue to circulate on the fields. The players E continue their running path onto the opposing field and try to win the ball with a touch in 1-on-4. After the touch, they immediately transition and again run around the outside cone and back onto the field where their own team is playing. If a ball is captured, the team in possession immediately uses a replacement ball and starts a new passing relay.

Variations

* Specify two mandatory touches for the team in possession.
* Specify direct play for the team in possession.
* Organize as a 1-on-1 competition with a points system:

   One point: Which player is the first to win the ball?

   Two points: Which player wins the ball and is the first to return to his own field?

   Three points: Win the ball and return before the opponent wins the ball.

2.8.2 Chase and capture (2)

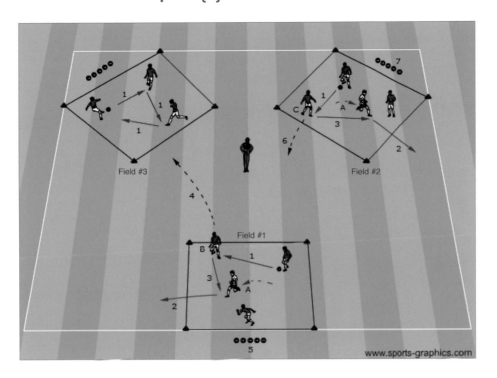

Execution

On each of the three fields, three players start out in possession (see RED players). These players let their ball circulate (see 1). A defending interfering player (see player A) is positioned on each of two fields (here field #1 and field #2). The players A try to get a touch on the ball in their own field as quickly as possible (see 2) and pass it off the field. If one of the players is successful, he immediately switches to offense and participates in play as a player in possession. One of the spare balls is immediately used for this. The player who lost the ball through, for example, a bad pass (see 3) becomes the defender but must move to another open field to win a ball (see players C and B). The players must always run onto the field that doesn't have any defensive players. In the figure, the ball is first won on field #1. As a result, player B switches to the open field #3 (see 4). Next the ball is won on field #2, causing player C to switch to the now open field #1 (see 6).

Variations

★ Limit the number of touches for the player in possession: direct play/two touches.

★ Follow-up action after winning the ball: Dribble off the field (see 2).

2.8.3   Chase and capture (team of two)

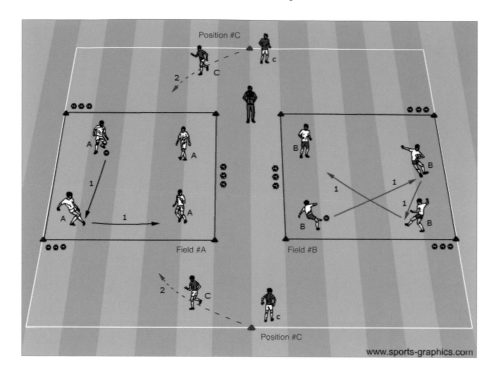

Execution

Players are divided into three teams of four players each and spread out on field #A, field #B and at starting position #C. The players on field #A (see players A) and the players on field #B (see players B) are always in possession and let a ball circulate on their respective field (see 1). The players at starting position #C start onto one of the fields in pairs (here field #A) and try to touch the ball (see player C). Afterward, they all return to their respective starting positions and with a high-five activate the waiting players who immediately start onto the other field (see field #B and player c). After each turnover, the players on fields #A and #B immediately use one of the replacement balls.

Variations

⁎ Limit the number of touches for the player in possession: direct play/two touches.

⁎ Run to the opposite position after successfully winning the ball.

⁎ Exchange high-fives with the chasing pair in the center/joint chase.

⁎ Follow-up action after the first time winning the ball: Win the ball on the opposite field.

2.8.4   Chase and capture (finish)

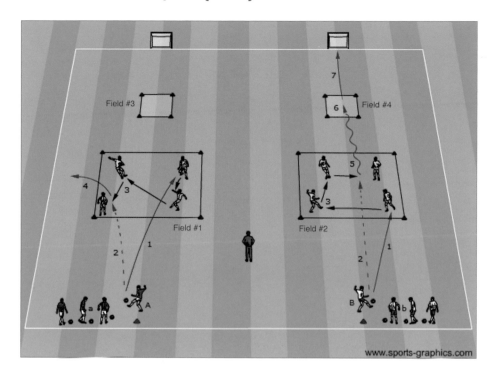

Execution

Players A and B simultaneously pass their ball onto field #1 and #2 (see 1) and immediately follow their passes (see 2). The players on field #1 and #2 control the balls and let them circulate in the own ranks (see 3). Players A and B try to win back the ball they passed as quickly as possible. If the ball leaves the field or is passed off the field, it counts as a turnover (see 4). If the chasing player is able to trap the ball, he can dribble it off the field (see 5) and take a shot on the mini goal on the finishing fields #3 and #4 (here player B in the direction of field #4; see 7).

Variations

★ Limit the number of touches for the player in possession: direct play/two touches.

★ Vary the passes: Lob/throw-in/cross (see 1).

★ Perform a feint/body feint on fields #3 and #4 (see 6).

★ Organize as a 1-on-1-competition: Which player is the first to score a goal?

★ Organize as a team competition: Which team is the first to score 10 goals?

2.8.5   Chase and capture (plus 1-on-1)

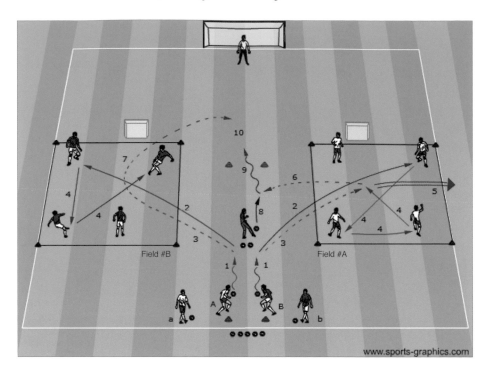

Execution

Players A and B simultaneously dribble briefly (see 1), pass their ball onto fields #A and #B (see 2), and immediately follow their balls (see 3). The players now in possession on fields #A and #B let the ball circulate (see 4). Players A and B try to touch the ball and move it off the field (see 5). As soon as a player succeeds (here player B on field #A), he immediately transitions toward the center and calls for a second ball from the coach (see 6). The call is the starting signal for the still chasing player on field #B, who now also transitions and takes on the position of defender in a 1-on-1. Player B dribbles the ball from the coach through the cone goal (see 9) and tries to score on the large goal in the 1-on-1 (see 10). Player A tries to defend the large goal and, if he wins the ball, can counter on the two mini goals.

Variations

* Organize as a competition with points system:

  One point: Simply winning the ball (see 5).

  Two points: Score on the large goal after 1-on-1.

  Three points: Score on a mini goal after winning the ball in 1-on-1.

2.8.6   Chase and capture (team of three)

Execution

The BLUE team has the larger team with eight players (see players A). Players A circulate two balls simultaneously in the own ranks and try to prevent the opposing RED team from reaching one of the balls. The RED team consists of three players (see players B) and tries to jointly win a ball in a coordinated effort (see 3). When a player B touches the ball, it is taken out of the game, and the coach immediately plays a new ball into the game (see 4), so there are always two balls in the game.

Coaching

The defending RED team must initiate the joint coordinated approach to the ball using clear commands and skillfully approach the player (2) so passing lanes are blocked and the player pressured (see 3).

Variations

- ★ Organize as a competition: Which team of three is the quickest to win eight balls?
- ★ Organize as a competition: Which team of three can win the most balls in two minutes?

3 FITNESS TRAINING

The sports science term **fitness** refers to an organism's physical capacity and is characterized by **speed**, **strength**, **endurance**, and **flexibility**. The differentiation of these important parameters is, on the one hand, genetically determined (e.g., muscle fiber composition or joint range of motion) and, on the other hand, can be influenced by and improved through exercise (e.g., building muscle or increasing flexibility). These parameters are systemic and, even in targeted training for specific factors, are always trained together.

Optimal fitness training focuses on the specific demands while competing. The nature of the game, thus, determines the soccer-specific content, such as running distances, intensities, loading duration, and regeneration phases. The application of generally accepted training methods that are based on sports science, such as the continuous method (endurance), interval method (regeneration), or the repetition method (speed), should always be soccer specific. The named methods aim to train the individual fitness parameters separately and find their narrow and customized interpretation in, for instance, track and field. Because of soccer's complex demands, this chapter introduces exercises and games that train the individual fitness-related factors in a soccer-specific and complex way without losing sight of the specific training emphasis.

Speed
Endurance
Strength
Flexibility
Running style Athleticism
Injury prevention

3.1 SOCCER-SPECIFIC SPEED TRAINING

3.1.1 Speed (repetition method)

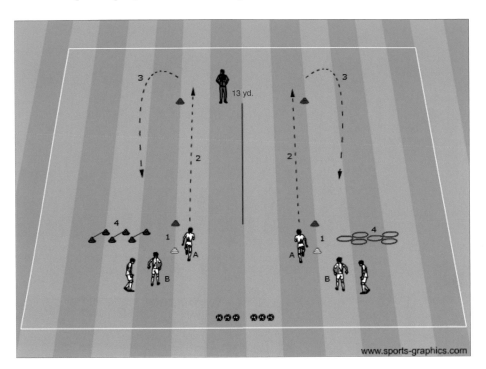

Execution

The speed method is based on a specified sprint distance (see 2). To achieve a training effect, that distance must be completed at maximum intensity. Since few actions in soccer begin from a standing position, we added a short run-up distance (see 1). Every player needs a recovery phase after the intensive sprint (see 3) to regain their form so they can subsequently return to a maximum load. The intensity can be increased with a 1-on-1 sprint duel.

Sample exercise

Sprint distance	13 yards (soccer-specific sprint distance).
Repetitions	Four sprints (one-minute break between sprints).
Break	Serial break for complete recovery (five minutes/e.g., juggling).
Series	Three sets of four sprints (including serial breaks).

Variations

* Vary or change the starting position: standing, sitting, or lying down.
* Vary or change the coach's signal for the start of the game (visual/audible).
* Vary or change the run-up distance with coordination exercises (see 4).

3.1.2   Speed (shuttle race)

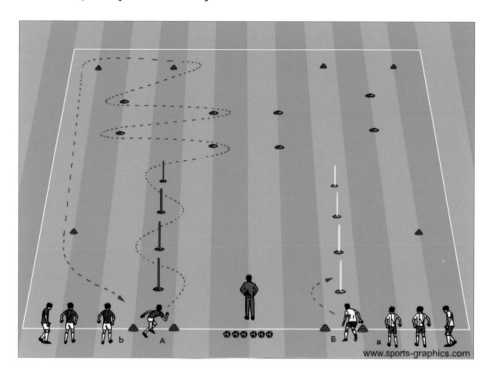

www.sports-graphics.com

Execution

The RED team runs a shuttle race against the BLUE team. After a signal from the coach, players A and B start running the course and return to their teams to activate a new player with a high-five.

Variations

- Organize as a competition: Which team is fastest?
- Organize as a 1-on-1 competition: Winner of the 1-on-1 gets one point.
- Give a movement task for the loser: run/juggle/push-ups.
- Vary the course: narrow slalom/wide slalom/use hurdles.
- Vary the running style: backwards/side-step/add gymnastic elements.
- Vary the exercise execution: Dribble with the ball at the foot.
- Vary the ball exchange: Exchange with a pass.
- Vary the end of the game: All players sit in a row at their own start cone.
- Vary the intensity: Add more teams or players per team.

3.1.3   Speed (reaction and change of direction)

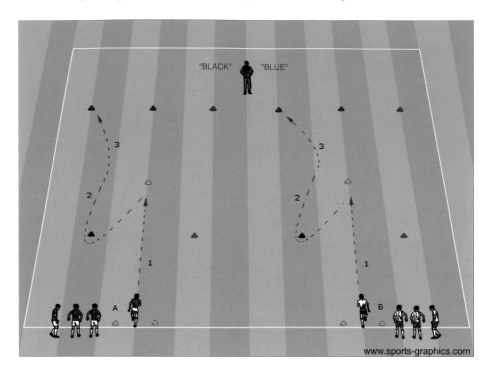

Execution

One player from group A and one player from group B compete against each other in a sprint race. The goal is to reach one of the three finish cones at a level with the coach faster than the opponent. At a signal from the coach, both players take off and sprint straight ahead toward the WHITE cone (see 1). Along the way (see 1), the coach calls out "BLACK" or "RED." The second the signal is given the players have to run around the cone of that color (here "BLACK"). Afterward, both players sprint toward the finish cone. On the way there (see 2), the coach calls out "BLUE," "RED," or "GREEN." The players react and run toward the respective cone (here "BLUE") as the finish (see 3).

Coaching

* Maintain eye contact with the coach.
* Maintain open body position.

Variations

* Vary or change the coach's signal (e.g., no signal: linear sprint).
* Vary or change the coach's signal (e.g., call both colors without a break).
* Organize as a competition: Which team is the first to win 10 sprint duels?

3.1.4   Fast 1-on-1—follow-up action (1)

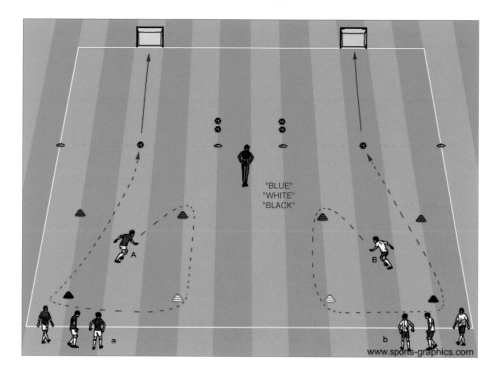

Execution

One player from each team gets ready for 1-on-1 and positions in the center of the action field (see A and B). The action fields are marked with different colored cones and arranged in mirrored reverse order. The coach starts the 1-on-1 by naming three colors. Players must run around the cones in the order of the colors and then shoot the ball positioned on a shooting line into the mini goal.

Coaching

*   Maintain eye contact with the coach.
*   Maintain open body position.

Variations

*   Vary the number of cones called.
*   Specify cones by calling out numbers (1 = RED, 2 = BLUE, etc.).
*   Call nonexistent colors or numbers to increase attentiveness.
*   Vary or change the starting position: standing/sitting/lying down.
*   Vary the movement task: Touch the cone with the foot or the forehead.
*   Specify the shooting leg (left/right).

3.1.5   Fast 1-on-1—follow-up action (2)

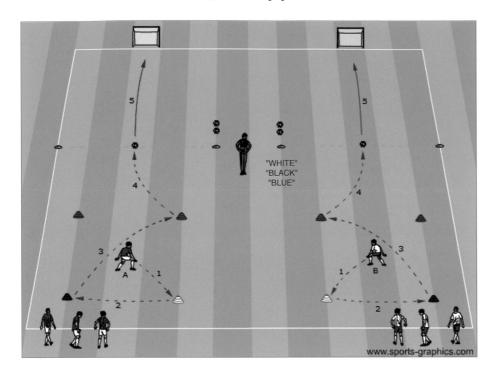

Execution

One player from the RED team and one player from the WHITE team get ready for 1-on-1 and position in the center of the action field (see player A and player B). The action fields are marked with four different colored cones and arranged in mirrored reverse order. The coach starts the 1-on-1 by naming three colors. The players must touch the cones with one hand in the order called and then shoot the ball positioned on a shooting line into the mini goal.

Coaching

- ★ Maintain eye contact with the coach.
- ★ Maintain an open body position.

Variations

- ★ Vary the number of cones to be called.
- ★ Specify cones by calling numbers (1 = RED, 2 = BLUE, etc.).
- ★ Call nonexistent colors or numbers to increase attentiveness.
- ★ Vary or change the starting position: standing/sitting/lying down.
- ★ Vary the movement task: Touch the cone with the foot or the forehead.
- ★ Specify the shooting leg (left/right).

3.1.6   Fast 1-on-1 (dribbling with follow-up action)

Execution

Two players prepare for 1-on-1 and position in the center of the action field (see WHITE and RED), each with a ball. The action fields are marked with different colored cones and arranged in mirrored reverse order. The coach starts the 1-on-1 by naming two colors. The players must dribble around the cones in the specified order before heading for a dribble line. The finish on the mini goal can take place only after crossing the dribble line (see 3).

Variations

* Specify the dribbling leg (left/right).
* Specify the shooting leg (left/right).
* Specify alternating the dribbling leg (left/right/left).
* Scoring: First goal (two points), second goal (one point).

3.1.7   Fast 1-on-1—shot on goal (1)

www.sports-graphics.com

Execution

One player from the RED team and one player from the WHITE team prepare for 1-on-1. The coach starts the 1-on-1 with a signal (audible or visual). Players A and B must dribble as fast as possible through the cone goal (see 3). To do so, they have to dribble along a specified course (see 1 and 2). Only the first player to dribble through the cone goal is allowed to take a direct shot on goal (here player A; see 4). The slower player must take the detour around the single cone (see 5) and after that is allowed to dribble through the cone goal (see 3) and take a shot on goal. Regularly switch sides (use different foot). The pair engaging in 1-on-1 should be similarly fast, otherwise pairs should always be different.

Variations

* Specify the dribbling leg (left/right).
* Specify the shooting leg (left/right).
* Specify alternating the dribbling leg (left/right/left).
* Organize as a competition: Which team is the first to score 10 goals?

3.1.8   Fast 1-on-1—shot on goal (2)

Execution

One player from the RED team and one player from the WHITE team prepare for 1-on-1. The coach starts the 1-on-1 with a signal (audible or visual). Players A and B sprint toward the cones (see 1), square up, and receive a pass from the next team partner (see 2 and players C and D). Players A and B control the ball, dribble around the last cone (see 3), and finish on the large goal (see 4). Next players C and D move to the starting position without a ball. Sides should be changed regularly (use different foot). Pairs engaging in 1-on-1 should be similarly fast, otherwise pairs should always be different.

Variations

* Specify the shooting leg (left/right).
* Specify the receiving leg (left/right) and the passing leg (left/right).
* Perform a feint/body feint right before the shot on goal (see 4).
* Organize as a competition: Which team is the first to score 10 goals?
* Finishes with the weak leg score double.

3.1.9   Fast 1-on-1 (circuits)

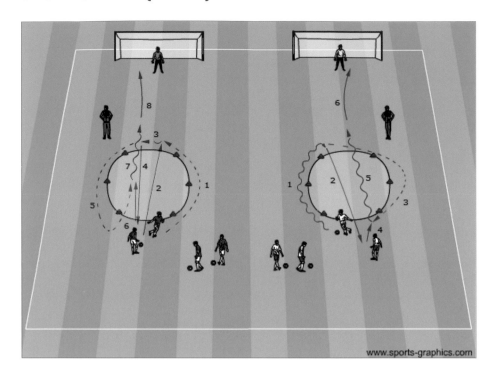

Execution

RED team sample exercise (see exercise sequence on left)
The player runs around the circle at top speed (see 1) and receives a well-timed pass through the circle (see 2). The player briefly controls the ball (see 3), passes the ball back (see 4), and continues the circuit (see 5). He receives a second pass into the circle (see 6), carries the ball toward the goal (see 7), and after leaving the circle is allowed to finish on the large goal (see 8).

BLUE team sample exercise (see exercise sequence on right)
The player dribbles around the circle (see 1), passes the ball through the circle back to his partner (see 2), and continues his circuit (see 3). He receives a second pass (see 4), dribbles the ball into the circle (see 5), and after leaving the circle is allowed to finish on the large goal (see 6).

Variations

* Organize as a competition at two identical stations with points system:
  One point: first goal
  Two points: second goal

3.1.10 Fast 1-on-1 (shot on goal and catch)

Execution

Players are divided into two teams. The two teams are further divided into attackers (see A and B) and defenders (C and D). After a signal from the coach, the attackers start to dribble toward a cone goal (see 1). The attackers' objective is to dribble through the cone goal (see 2) as fast as possible without being touched or tagged by a defender (see 3). The defenders also start with the coach's signal. Attackers can only finish on the goal after they have dribbled through the cone goal without getting tagged. Attackers and defenders switch regularly.

Variations

* Vary the dribbling style (slalom, weak foot, etc.).
* Vary/change the starting position: Standing/sitting/lying down.
* Organize as a competition with a points system: Which team is the first to score 10 points?
  One point for the defender: Touch the attacker before he can finish.
  One point for the attacker: Finish without getting touched by the defender.
  Two points for the attacker: Score without getting touched by the defender.

3.1.11   Fast 1-on-1—duel and shot on goal (1)

Execution

One player from the RED team and one player from the WHITE team prepare for 1-on-1 and position in the center of the action field (see left and right). The action fields are marked with four different colored cones and arranged in mirrored reverse order. The coach starts the 1-on-1 by naming two colors. The players must touch the cones in the specified order (see 1 and 2) before they can start toward the ball played in by the coach. The subsequent player in possession (here RED; see 3) is the attacker and, after dribbling across a finish line (see 4), is allowed to finish on the large goal. The slower player is the defender and tries to prevent the goal, after he wins the ball, can finish on one of the mini goals.

Coaching

* Perform the exercise at top speed.
* Avoid cutting back or decelerating.

Variations

* Organize as a competition with points a system:
  One point for the attacker: Successful shot on the large goal.
  Two points for the defender: Win the ball and score on a mini goal.

3.1.12 Fast 1-on-1—duel and shot on goal (2)

Execution

Players A and B play direct passes to each other (see 1). After a signal from the coach, they start to play 1-on-1. The player in possession at the time of the coach's signal acts as the attacker and tries to score on the large goal (here player A). The attack on the goal (see 2) and the defensive action (see 3) should be carried out at top speed. The respective defending player (here player B) has the opportunity to finish on the mini goals after winning the ball.

Coaching

* Complete the exercise at top speed.
* Avoid cutting back or decelerating.

Variation

* After at least six passes, players can decide independently when to start the game.

3.1.13   Speed (catching game)

Execution

Every player has a bib and tucks it in his pants so it is visible and graspable. The game's objective is for a player to steal the other players' bibs by pulling them out (see 1) without losing his own bib in the process. Every player can be attacked and chased.

Coaching

★   Perform directional changes, accelerations, and running feints.

Variations

★   Organize as a competition: Which player wins the most bibs?

★   Organize as an endless game: The stolen bibs have to be given back immediately.

★   Tuck the bibs into the socks (low center of gravity).

★   Complete the exercise at a dribble.

3.1.14   Speed—sprinting game (1)

Execution

Each player has his own ball depository located in a hoop. At the beginning of the game, the ball is in the depository. Three additional balls are located in the center of the field. The game starts with a signal from the coach. The game's objective is to move three balls into the own depository. To do so, players can collect the balls in the center as well as the balls in the other depositories. Each player can only transport one ball at a time. Adjust the distances between the depositories and observe the break structure to cap the load and maintain maximum speed.

Coaching

The coach can shift the focus to cognitive elements by asking the players to closely observe which player already has two balls in his own depository and to keep the opponent from winning by choosing balls wisely.

Variation

* Organize as a competition: Collect in teams of two with adjusted number of balls.

3.1.15   Speed—sprinting game (2)

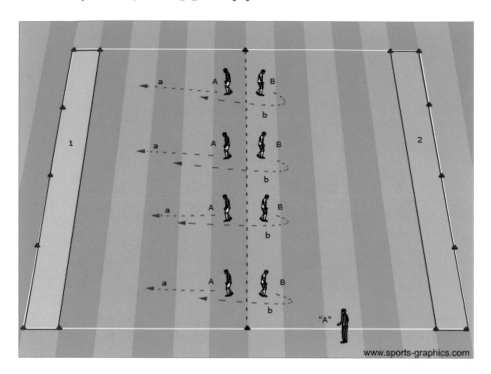

Execution

The RED team and the BLUE team (see A and B) are divided into pairs of approximately equally fast players. Players stand near the dotted centerline with their backs to each other. At a signal from the coach, they start a sprint race in the direction of one of the finish zones (see 2). One player from each pair is the hunter and tries to tag the opponent before he reaches the finish zone. The opponent runs as fast as possible to the end zone without getting tagged. The coach's signal determines the hunter and the runner. Here the coach designates the runner (see A). The coach's signal is also the start signal. Player A immediately sprints away (see a), and player B reacts by turning around and trying to tag the sprinter before he reaches finish zone 1 (see b).

Variations

* Vary or change the starting position (e.g., standing/sitting/lying down).
* Vary or change the coach's signal (e.g., even number: players A become the hunters).
* Vary the coach's signal (e.g., uneven number: players B become the hunters).
* Vary the coach's signal (e.g., designate the players using a math problem).
* Vary the coach's signal (e.g., name the hunters).
* Vary the coach's signal (e.g., call the runners).
* Vary the coach's signal (e.g., use a visual signal).
* Designate the players using changing signals (e.g., color/number/whistle).

3.1.16   Quick reaction and orienting

www.sports-graphics.com

Execution

Each player on the field holds a colored cone or bib in his hand. The cones match the colors of the cones positioned in the corners of the field. Players must constantly exchange the cones with each other (see 1). At a signal from the coach ("whistle"), each player must react and run to the cone in a corner that matches the color of his cone.

Coaching

★ Ask players to exchange the cones quickly and continuously.

Variations

★ Vary the coach's signal:

One whistle: Run to the cone of the same color as the own cone.

Two whistles: Run to the diagonally offset cone of the same color as the own cone.

Three whistles: Run clockwise to the cone next to the one of the own color.

Four whistles: Run counterclockwise to the cone next to the one of the own color.

★ Vary the coach's signal (visual/audible).

★ Perform the exercise at a dribble.

★ Organize as a competition: movement task for the slowest group of runners.

3.1.17   Fast 3-on-7

www.sports-graphics.com

Execution

The WHITE team plays against the RED team on the field. The WHITE team plays for possession and tries to keep the opposing players away from the ball. The RED team's job is to touch the ball as quickly as possible. When a RED player wins the ball, the coach immediately brings a new ball into the game. The tasks change after the RED team wins the ball five times.

Coaching

* Win balls at maximum speed and with quick transitions.
* Enable maximum intensity through adequate recovery times.

Variations

* Limit the number of touches for the team in possession.
* Follow-up action: Finish on the mini goals after successfully winning the ball.
* Follow-up action: Finish on the mini goals after 10 consecutive passes.
* Increase or decrease the number of balls required for a turnover after a goal is scored.

3.2 SOCCER-SPECIFIC ATHLETIC TRAINING (STRENGTH, STRETCHING, STABILIZATION, AND COORDINATION)

3.2.1 Stretching (Balance Pad®)

3.2.2   Strength training (Balance Pad®)

3.2.3   Strength training—posture (1)

3.2.4   Strength training—posture (2)

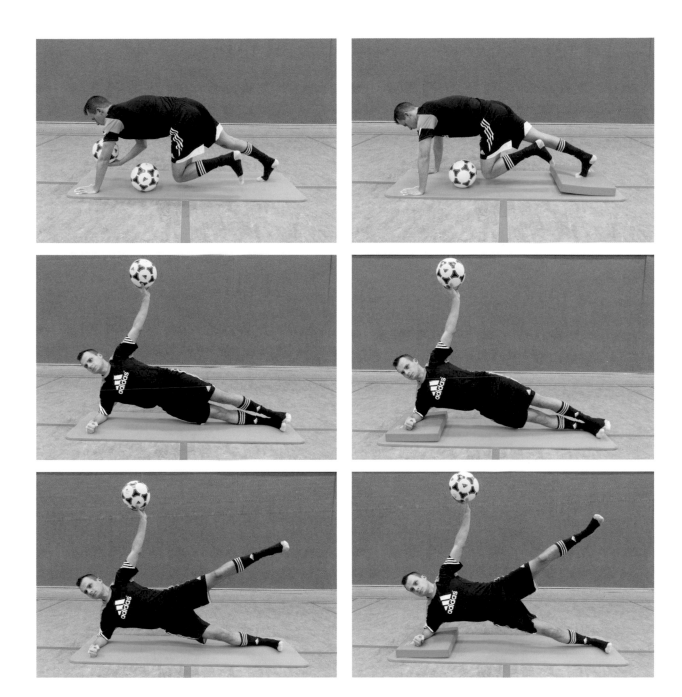

3.2.5   Strength training—posture (3)

3.2.6 Strength training—posture (4)

3.2.7   Strength training—posture (5)

3.2.8   Strength training—posture (6)

3.2.9   Strength training—posture (7)

3.2.10   Strength training—posture (8)

3.2.11   Strength training—Thera-Band® (1)

3.2.12 Strength training—Thera-Band® (2)

3.2.13 Strength training—Pezzi exercise ball (1)

3.2.14   Strength training—Pezzi exercise ball (2)

3.2.15 Strength training—Pezzi exercise ball (3)

3.2.16   Regeneration and massage—Blackroll® (1)

3.2.17   Regeneration and massage—Blackroll® (2)

3.3   SOCCER-SPECIFIC ENDURANCE TRAINING

3.3.1   Endurance course (continuous method)

www.sports-graphics.com

Execution

The continuous method focuses on exertion at a fairly constant intensity over a long period of time without rest. The continuation method is used to improve basic aerobic and anaerobic endurance. Players complete an endurance course consisting of multiple stations (see #1 to #6). While completing the course, players must maintain a medium-intensity level throughout without breaks. The intensity briefly increases at each station. The stations try to reproduce soccer-specific endurance.

Sample exercise

Intensity: Medium intensity with intensive stations.
Duration: 45 minutes without a break.

Tasks at the stations

#1 Tempo dribbling   #2 Movement task on the agility ladder
#3 Movement task: hurdles   #4 Tempo dribbling: slalom
#5 Movement task: poles   #6 Movement task: hoops

3.3.2 Endurance course (passing)

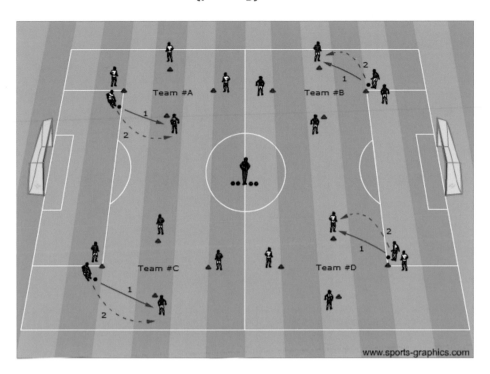

Execution

Players are divided into multiple teams (see Team #A, #B, #C and #D) and are positioned on multiple stations (here four stations of five players each). At each station, players complete a specified passing sequence. Here the players circulate the ball counterclockwise around the cone field (see 1), and after each pass they take over the next position (see 2). After a signal from the coach or specific competition rules, the teams all run around the stations at different intensities. The run around the stations is intended to reproduce soccer-specific endurance.

Circuit (coach's signal)

1: jog clockwise/2: jog counterclockwise

3: intensive run clockwise/4: intensive run counterclockwise

5: tempo run clockwise/6: tempo run counterclockwise

Circuit (competition rules)

2 x 20 passes in the passing sequence and run around all stations and back to the own field.

4 x 10 passes in the passing sequence and run around all stations and back to the own field.

8 x 5 passes in the passing sequence and run around all stations and back to the own field.

3.3.3 Endurance course—shot on goal (1)

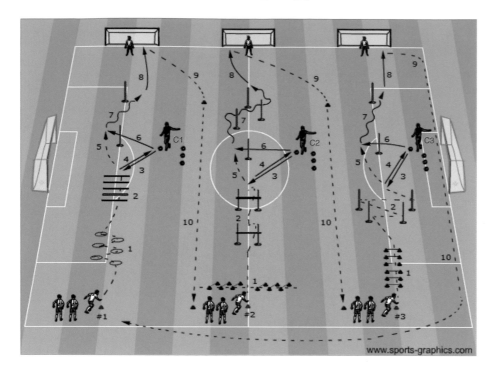

Execution

Players are positioned at multiple starting points (see #1, #2, and #3). Players start without a ball, receive passes from the three coaches (see C1, C2, and C3), which they will turn into shots on goal. After each shot on goal, the players immediately switch to the next station so there is constant exertion.

#1: The player negotiates the hoops with long one-leg jumps (see 1), runs through the poles with short strides (see 2), and then receives a pass from the coach (see 3). He plays a direct return pass (see 4), runs around the marking pole (see 5), receives the second pass from the coach (see 6), controls the ball, and performs a feint at the final marking pole (see 7). He finishes on the goal (see 8), immediately transitions after his shot (see 9), and after an intensive run (see 10), takes over the next position (here position #2).

#2: The player negotiates the agility poles with a specified step sequence (see 1), jumps over the two high hurdles with legs together (see 2), and receives a pass from the coach (see 3). He plays a direct return pass (see 4), runs around the marking pole (see 5), receives the second pass from the coach (see 6), controls the ball, and dribbles through the final marking poles (see 7). He finishes on the goal (see 8), immediately transitions after his shot (see 9), and after an intensive run (see 10), takes over the next position (here position #3).

#3: The player jumps over the coordination hurdles with a specified step sequence (see 1), touches each of the four marking poles during a tempo run (see 2), and receives a pass from the coach (see 3). He plays a direct return pass (see 4), runs around the marking pole (see 5), receives the second pass from the coach (see 6), controls the ball, and performs a feint at the final marking pole (see 7). He finishes on the goal (see 8), immediately transitions after his shot (see 9), and after a moderate run (see 10), takes over the next position (here position #1).

3.3.4   Endurance course—shot on goal (2)

Execution

The players are positioned at two starting positions (see A and B). Two players always start at the same time, each taking a shot on goal and then together carrying out a second action on another goal. After their actions, both players return to their starting positions, so the intensive exertion is followed by a short break, and training takes place in intervals.

Players A and B start at the same time without a ball, run the hurdles with a specified step and jump sequence (see 1), and receive a pass from the coach (see 2). They play direct return passes to the coach (see 3) and run through the hoops with a specified step sequence (see 4). The players receive another pass from the coach (see 5), control the ball toward the goal, dribble through the marking poles (see 6), and finish on the goal (see 7). After the shot on goal, they immediately transition and run toward the other half of the field (see 8). While running, they keep an eye on each other and try to start the subsequent sprint at the same time. They sprint the specified distance (see 9) and negotiate the agility poles with a specified step sequence (see 10). The coach passes a ball to one of the two players (see 11). The receiving player (here player B) passes to his partner (here player A; see 12), who finishes (see 13). After the action, both players transition (see 14), run around the outermost marking cones, and sprint a short distance (see 15) back to the starting position.

3.3.5   4-on-2 (interval runs)

www.sports-graphics.com

Execution

4-on-2 play is taking place on multiple fields (here four fields). The four players (see RED players) are in possession and try to keep the ball in the own ranks with no more than two touches. The two outnumbered players (see BLUE players) try to touch the ball. As soon as one of the players from the outnumbered team succeeds in touching the ball (see player B), that player can switch to the team of four and to possession. The player who caused the bad pass or made the critical error to cause the turnover (see player A) switches to the outnumbered team. But before he can actively participate in the game, he must complete a tempo run around all four fields (see 1). Meanwhile, the game continues with a new ball.

Variations

- Limit the number of touches for the player in possession: direct play/two touches.
- Decrease the sprint distance for the player who lost the ball: sprint around the own field.
- Vary the group size: 5-on-2/3-on-1.

3.3.6   Endurance game (3-on-2 plus 1)

Execution

Form multiple teams of three players each (see teams A, B, and C). The teams play 3-on-2 on the large goals with goalkeepers. After a finish or turnover, the game continues with a new opponent. There are no game breaks, which requires an adequate number of replacement balls. Team A is in possession and attacks the outnumbered team B, trying to score a goal. As soon as team A finishes on the goal and the ball is out of the game or one of the two players on team B wins the ball, team A is eliminated from the game. Team A then takes over team B's position. Team B immediately attacks the opposite goal against team C. If team A scores a goal, the waiting player B (see #1) starts into the next action with a new ball. If a player from team B won the ball, team B, including the waiting player (see #1), attacks with the won ball. Now team B plays 3-on-2 against team C. Meanwhile, team C has another waiting player (see #2). At the same time, team A takes over team B's abandoned position. After the 3-on-2-situation between teams B and C is resolved, the waiting player (see #2) gets involved in the action with or without a ball. This would create 3-on-2 play between teams C and A. The game continues without breaks to provide a continuous load.

3.3.7   Endurance game (4-on-4)

www.sports-graphics.com

Execution

Form three teams (see teams A, B, and C). Two teams always play against each other in 4-on-4 on the two large goals with goalkeepers (here team A against team B). Under the rules of the game, after a shot on goal or scored goal, the game continues with the goalkeeper of the team that finished. To that end, an adequate number of replacement balls is stored in the goals. The third team (see team C) jogs around the outside of the playing field. The ongoing 4-on-4 continues until one team scores and is determined the winner. The team that won can stay on the field. The team that lost switches to jogging around the field. The next game starts right after the end of the first round, and the team that had been running around the field (see team C) switches to the 4-on-4 game on the field. This results in a constantly changing load. The load is higher during the 4-on-4; the jogging team regenerates with a moderate running load.

Variations

★   Organize as a competition in tournament format with four minutes of playing time:
    Which team has scored the most goals after 6, 9, or 12 rounds?

3.3.8   Endurance game (4-on-4 plus 4-on-2)

Execution

Form three teams of four players each (see teams A, B, and C). Mark off two fields (see field #1 and field #2) that extend up to the two penalty boxes. A goalkeeper is positioned in each penalty box (see G1 and G2). The teams start the game on one field (here field #1). Two teams always play together (here team A and team B) to outnumber one team (here team C). Teams A and B try to keep the ball in their ranks for as long as possible. Team C tries to win the ball. If team C succeeds, the superior to inferior number ratio changes. The team that made the critical error to cause the turnover becomes the outnumbered team. After the ball is successfully won, the entire game shifts to the other half of the field (see field #2).

Variations (switching field of play/continuing play after winning the ball)
* Outnumbered team passes to the far goalkeeper (here GK2); continue play on field #2.
* Outnumbered team passes to the near goalkeeper (here G1); switch play using GK1.
* Coach's ball goes to the far goalkeeper and play continues on field #2.
* Coach automatically switches field of play after 20 passes without a turnover.

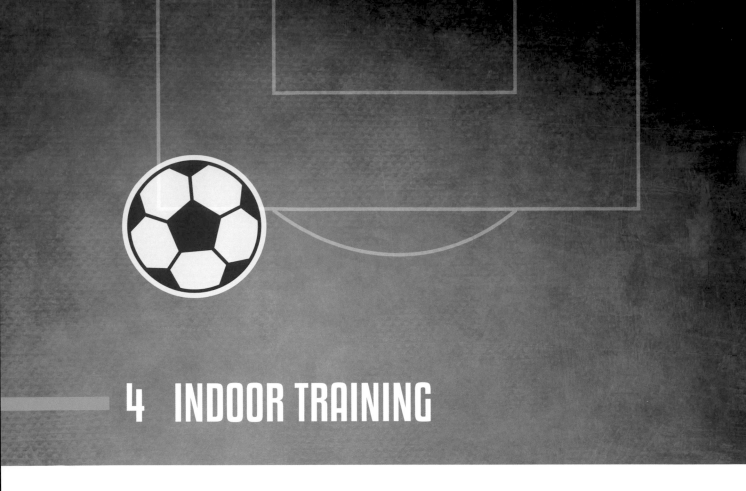

4 INDOOR TRAINING

In this chapter, we will take a separate look at indoor soccer training. On the one hand, training indoors does have its limitations, especially with respect to field and goal sizes. But on the other hand, these factors, in particular, offer opportunities and choices with respect to training design. Next we will introduce drills that take into account indoor training space and the creative use of typical indoor gym equipment, predefined field markings, and typical indoor training aids for versatile training design.

DIGRESSION: FUTSAL

Futsal is FIFA's official version of indoor soccer. The word **Futsal** (futebol de salao) means nothing more than **indoor soccer** and is played with a small and low-bounce ball. Based on a scientific study (Heim, Frick, and Pohl, 2007), a bouncing ball can be received and controlled significantly faster with a futsal ball than a soccer ball or felt ball. Effective playing time with a futsal ball increases significantly, and offensive actions, in particular, are more successful. With the same amount of playing time, players have more time on the ball when playing with the futsal ball, and children, especially, can lose the fear of bouncing balls by using the futsal ball. Moreover, playing with a futsal ball facilitates flat and direct passes.

When comparing the bounce of a traditional soccer ball on turf to that of a futsal ball, the futsal ball actually reproduces the bouncing qualities, particularly the height of the bounce after making contact with the ground once, better than a soccer or felt ball that bounces rather high on a gym floor. The use of the futsal ball for indoor training can result in greater long-term learning progress, especially in children and youth training. The use of the futsal ball for indoor training can, thus, be viewed as a versatile and interesting alternative that permits differentiated training of techniques and movement patterns. Due to the faster playing speed, a game with the futsal ball also requires a large amount of technical and tactical action speed.

Small spaces
Jump ropes Boards
Equipment Futsal

4.1   INDOOR TRAINING

4.1.1   Line drills

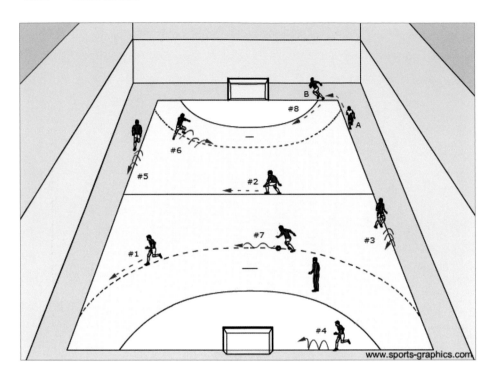

Execution

Players perform various running drills and exercises with the ball. To do so, they use the markings on the gym floor or field lines. Players follow these lines and run, jump, or dribble across the lines according to the specifications of the exercise.

#1: Run or skip forward and backward on the line.

#2: Side step on the line (right shoulder in front/left shoulder in front).

#3: Jump with legs together over or next to the line (forward/backward).

#4: Single-leg jumps on the line (left/right/forward/backward).

#5: Single-leg jumps over or next to the line (left/right/forward/backward).

#6: Long single-leg jumps with a brief stabilizing phase (forward/backward).

#7: Dribble on the lines with the ball at the foot.

#8: Organize as a game of catch: Choose a few catchers who hold a bib in their hands so they can be identified. All players can only run on the lines. If a player is tagged, he becomes a catcher, and the bib is handed over.

Variation

★   At a signal from the coach, complete a 180-degree turn with a directional change.

4.1.2   Movement tasks (hoops)

Execution

Players complete various running drills and exercises using hoops.

#1: Run through the hoops while holding a ball. Players alternate between left foot, right foot, and both feet. Variation: Bounce the ball 1 time inside the hoop or directly in front of or behind the hoop.

#2: Players run around the hoops in a circle, alternating running clockwise and counterclockwise. Variation: Players side step or jump around the hoops.

#3: Players run while holding a ball. They must jump across the hoops with legs together: Which player is the first to jump over 20 hoops?

#4: Players run around the gym bouncing a ball: Which player is the first to bounce the ball into 20 hoops?

#5: Players dribble around the hoops in circles. Players must alternate using the left and right foot as they dribble. Variation: Players must dribble around the hoops using only the inside or outside foot.

#6: Players pass the ball past the hoops and complete a movement task at the hoop before they can once again control the ball and dribble toward the next hoop.

#7: Players are numbered in pairs. The coach calls a number, and each of the respective players finishes on a large goal. Who scores first?

#8: The coach calls one player. That player puts down his ball and turns the pass into a shot on goal.

4.1.3   Movement tasks (benches)

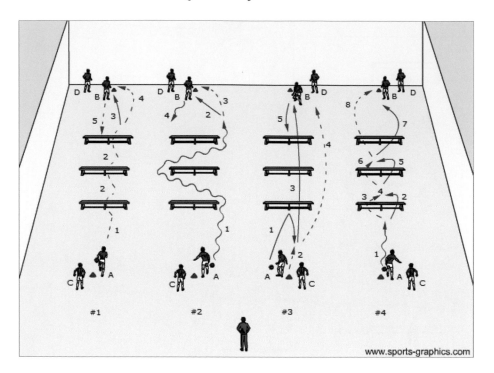

Execution

The following are movement tasks with and without a ball (see #1 to #4).

#1: Player A runs and jumps over the benches with a ball in his hand (see 1 and 2), alternately jumping with the left leg and the right leg (see 2). He hands the ball off to player B (see 3) and lines up again at position D (see 4) before player B starts a new action (see 5).

#2: Player A dribbles around the benches in a slalom (see 1), hands the ball off to player B (see 2), and lines up again at position D (see 3) before player B starts a new action (see 4). Variation: Add dribbling specifications (inside foot, outside foot, dribble with left/right foot).

#3: Player A passes the ball against the first bench (see 1), moves to meet his pass (see 2), and plays a volley to the player at position B (see 3). He runs to position D (see 4), and player B starts the next action (see 5). Variation: Ask players to complete different running and jumping exercises at the benches on the way to the next position (see 4).

#4: Player A does a brief dribble and lobs the ball over the bench (see 2), jumps over the bench (see 3), controls the ball (see 4), lobs the ball over the second bench (see 5), jumps over the second bench (see 6), and plays a lob pass to the player at position B. Player A lines up again at position D (see 8), and player B starts a new action.

4.1.4   Movement tasks (jump ropes)

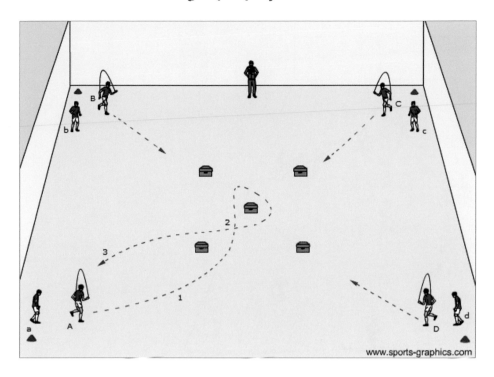

www.sports-graphics.com

Execution

A team with at least two players is posted at each of four starting positions. Each team has a jump rope. In the center are several markers (here vaulting boxes) that serve as obstacles that the players must run around. At a signal from the coach, the first player from each group (see A, B, C, and D) jumps rope to the center (see 1) and completes a specified route around the vaulting boxes (see 2). Afterward, he quickly returns to his group (see 3) and hands the jump rope off to the waiting player (see a, b, c, and d). After the jump rope handoff, the next player starts his action.

Variations

* Vary or change the running path in the center (see 2).
* Vary or change the use of the jump rope: hop on one leg (left/right).
* Vary or change the use of the jump rope: jump with legs together.
* Add a prerequisite for the jump rope handoff: 10 quick jumps at the own start cone.
* Organize as a competition: Which team is the first to complete 10 running paths?

4.1.5   Chain tag

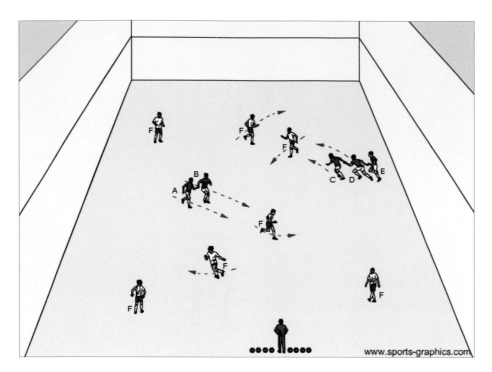

Execution

Depending on the group size, form multiple pairs that will act as catchers and will try to tag the individual players (see player F). The pairs must (see players A/B and C/D) must hold hands. They must coordinate their efforts, act jointly, and cannot let the chain break, meaning they cannot let go. When the pairs have tagged a player, the tagged player becomes a part of the chain (see E).

Variations

* Vary the execution of the exercise: Dribble with the ball at the foot (see player F).
* Vary the execution of the exercise: Bounce the ball with the hand (see player F).
* Reduce the size of the chain to no more than three players (constant division of large chains).
* Add a game ball; player in possession cannot be tagged.
* Organize as a competition to not divide the chains:
  Which pair has the longest chain at the end of the game?

4.1.6   Bridge tag

www.sports-graphics.com

Execution

Depending on the size of the group, choose a certain number of catchers (here two players). The catchers (see player A) try to tag all the players. All other players try to evade capture (see player B). When a player has been tagged, he must immediately stop and stand in a straddle to form a bridge (see player C). Players can be liberated and are allowed to move again after another player crawls through the captive's legs (see player D). While a player is in the process of freeing a teammate (see D) neither of the two players can be tagged.

Variations

* Vary the liberation of captured players: leap-frog/high-five.
* Organize as a team competition: Which group of two catches the players quickest?

Variations (with a ball in the game)

* Captured players are liberated with a pass through the straddled legs.
* A captured player can be liberated by receiving and controlling a pass.
* Players in possession cannot be tagged.

4.1.7 Twin soccer

Execution

Players are divided into pairs. The pairs must hold hands and act together. When a chain breaks, possession changes. Pairs are combined into two teams. Here the RED team plays with six players, or three chains of two against the BLUE team. The pairs pass each other the balls (see 1) and try to score a goal. While a player dribbles (see 2), the ball can also be passed within the pair (see 3).

Variations

★ Eliminate direction of play: Players can play on both large goals.

★ Simplify by playing by hand.

★ Every time the ball is received, it is passed within the pair (see 3).

★ Game continues after the finish: Coach's ball or far goalkeeper opens the game.

4.1.8   Soccer baseball

Execution

Form two teams (here the RED team and the BLUE team). The RED team is in offensive position and can score points; the Blue team is on defense. The goal of the attacking team (here the RED team) is to get back to the group (one point) using the evenly distributed mats in the gym (see 1). The defending team (here BLUE) tries to put the ball in the back of the net as quickly as possible. To do so, the players must position strategically in advance and work together. Here player a chases the ball (see 2) and briefly controls it (see 3). Player C gets in position (see 4) to be able to shoot player a's pass (see 5) on the goal (see 6). During their defense, the RED team tries to score points, meaning each player tries to move one position closer to the target. Right after his shot, player A runs to the next mat (see 7). It is permissible to either run one station farther (see player B and 8) or to advance several positions (see player C and 9), but to do so, the player must touch the mats he crosses with a foot. When the defending team puts the ball in the net, the attacking players must all stand safely on their mats. If a player is still running and has not yet reached his mat, that player is eliminated. Once three players have been eliminated, the other team becomes the attackers.

Variation

* Specify the shooting technique: inside foot/instep/left/right/weak foot.

4.1.9 Shot on goal game (wall target)

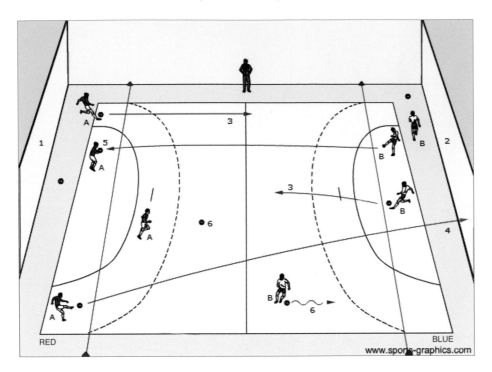

Execution

Form two teams (here the RED team and the BLUE team). Each team has a shooting zone (see RED and BLUE) that is marked by an imaginary line and cones (see 2). The game starts with each player positioning in the own shooting zone with a ball at his foot. The gym wall located behind the zone is the goal (see 1 and 2). The teams try to hit the opposing wall and defend the own wall. Players can only shoot from the own shooting zone (see 3) as well as act as goalkeeper and parry and catch the balls with their hands (see 5). Players are allowed to retrieve the balls lying in their own half while running and dribbling back into the own shooting zone (see 6). A shot that touches the opposing gym wall counts as a goal (see 4).

Variations

* Specify the shooting technique: inside foot/instep/left/right/weak foot.
* Play for time: Who can score the most goals in five minutes?
* Play for points: Which team is the first to score 10 goals?

4.1.10   Shot on goal game (cone target)

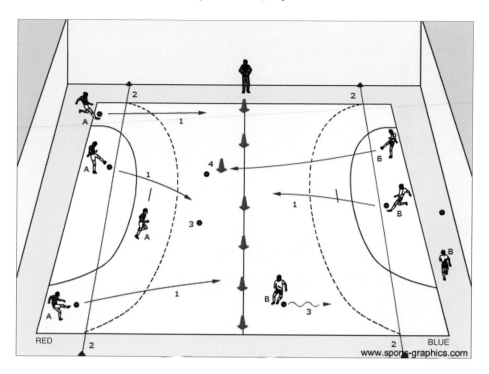

Execution

Form two teams (here the RED team and the BLUE team). Each team has a shooting zone (see RED and BLUE) that is marked by an imaginary line and cones (see 2). The game starts with each player positioning in the own shooting zone with a ball at his foot. Several cones are set up on the centerline. The goal is to hit the cones so they fall into the opposing half (see 4). Players can only shoot at the cones from the own shooting zone (see 1). Players are allowed to retrieve the balls lying in their own half while running and dribbling back into the own shooting zone (see 3). The game is over when all of the cones are in the opposing half.

Variations

★ Specify the shooting technique: inside foot/instep/left/right/weak foot.

★ Vary or change the target objects: Pezzi stability balls/moving boxes.

4.1.11   Shot on goal game (clean half)

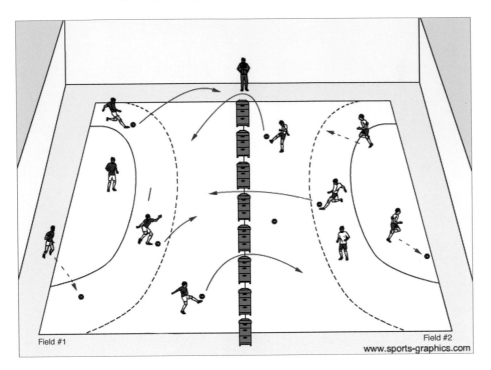

Execution

Use boxes (or benches) to divide the gym into two halves at the centerline (see field #1 and field #2). A team is positioned in each half (see RED and BLUE teams). At the start of the game, each team has four balls in the own half. The game's objective is to get rid of all the balls in the own half and move them to the opposing half. The team that manages to move all the balls into the opposing half wins the game or is awarded one point.

Variations

*   Specify the shooting technique: left/right/weak foot/dropkick/throw.
*   Only select players can shoot over the wall.

4.1.12   Shot on goal game (3 plus 3 vs. 3 plus 3)

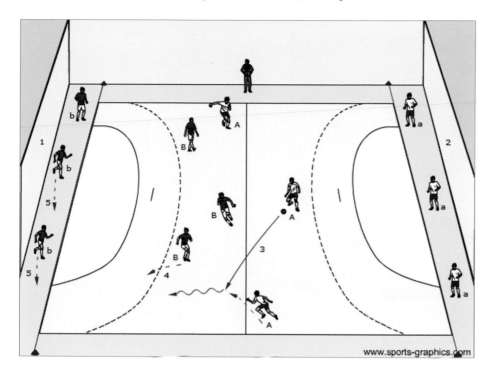

www.sports-graphics.com

Execution

Form two teams (here the RED team and the BLUE team). Each team is subdivided (see players A/a and B/b). On the field, two groups of three players play 3-on-3 (see players A and B). The remaining players are positioned in the end zones (see a and b) and initially participate only as goalkeepers. The gym wall behind the end zones serves as the goal (see 1 and 2). The teams try to get a shot on the opposing wall during 3-on-3 play (see 3) or defend against the shots (see 4). The players a and b positioned in the end zones can defend the shots in their respective end zones (see 5). Positions change after each scored goal. Players A switch with players a, and players B switch with players b.

Variations

* Add an option for the team in possession during 3-on-3: Involve the own goalkeeper.
* Specify the shooting technique: inside foot/left/right/weak foot.
* Specify the shooting technique: direct finish.

4.1.13   Team dodgeball

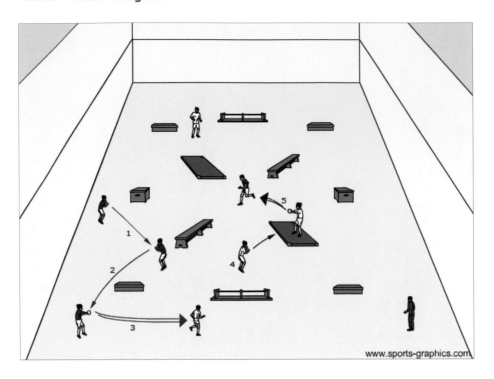

Execution

Form two teams (here the RED team and the BLUE team). Distribute various pieces of equipment around the gym. Depending on the group size, use multiple foam balls for the game (here two balls). The game's objective is to tag an opponent with a ball. A player can take only three steps with a ball in hand. After three steps, he must either throw the ball at an opponent (see 5) or the ball must be passed to a player in the own ranks (see 1 and 2). So it is possible to hunt a player with passes (see 1 and 2) before trying to tag him (see 3). When a player has been tagged, he must stand on a piece of equipment. He can leave that piece of equipment only after tagging another player from that position (see 5). A team wins when all of the opponents have been tagged at the same time and are standing on the gym equipment.

Variations

* Allow unlimited steps with the ball in hand.
* Specify the throwing arm: left/right/weak throwing arm.

4.1.14 Individual dribbling

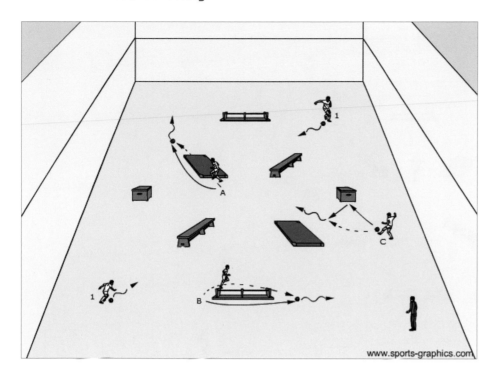

www.sports-graphics.com

Execution

Each player has a ball and dribbles freely around the gym (see 1). Various pieces of gym equipment are distributed around the gym (e.g., mats, benches, vaulting boxes). The players dribble toward the equipment and must perform a movement task.

Player A: Play a pass past a mat; forward roll on the mat; control the ball.

Player B: Play a pass past a bench; balance over the bench; control the ball.

Player C: Play a pass against a vaulting box; control the ball.

Variations (movement tasks on gym equipment)

* Backwards roll on the mat.
* Cartwheel on the mat.
* Juggle over a vaulting box.
* Lob over a bench.

Variations

* Organize as a competition: Which player is the first to play on all the equipment?
* Specify the dribbling leg: left/right/strictly alternate left/right.

4.1.15   Dribbling (movement competition)

Execution

Form four teams (see A, B, C, and D). Each team must consist of at least two players. The teams spread out on the starting positions in the corners of the gym. Various pieces of gym equipment (e.g., mats, benches, vaulting boxes) are set up around the gym. At each piece of equipment, players must complete a certain movement task. At a starting signal, the first player from each team starts and must play on two pieces of equipment (see 1). After he has played on the second piece of equipment, he passes the ball to his partner back at the start cone and lines up again at the own start cone. The second player of the group starts toward the pass and dribbles onto the field to perform the movement tasks at the cone. Which team's players complete all five actions?

Movement tasks and variations

Vaulting box	Pass against the vaulting boxes and control the ball.
Bench	Lob and jump over the bench and control the ball.
Mat	Pass past the mat; forward roll on the mat; control the ball.
Jump rope	Each player has a jump rope and must perform certain movement tasks while running with the jump rope before passing the rope on to the next player on his team.

4.1.16   Dribbling (coordination competition)

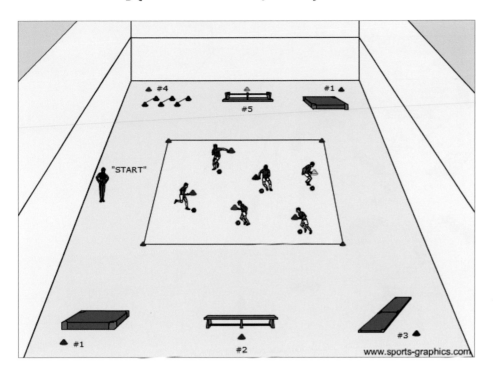

Execution

All players are on the center field, each with a ball. In addition, each player also holds a colored marking cone in his hand. The cones are the same colors as the six stations around the perimeter of the field (see #1 to #5). The players dribble on the field according to different specifications and continuously trade cones. After a starting signal from the coach, each player leaves his ball on the field and runs to his station. He chooses the station that matches the color of the cone in his hand at the time of the coach's signal.

Variations

#1: 20 fast skips on a large soft mat.

#2: 8 side vaults on a bench.

#3: 2 forward rolls and 2 backward rolls on the soft mats.

#4: Specified fitness task on a pole obstacle course.

#5: Balance on a turned over bench.

★   Organize as a competition: Which player is the quickest to return to the field after completing his fitness task and the first to touch the ball he had left there?

4.1.17   Group passing game

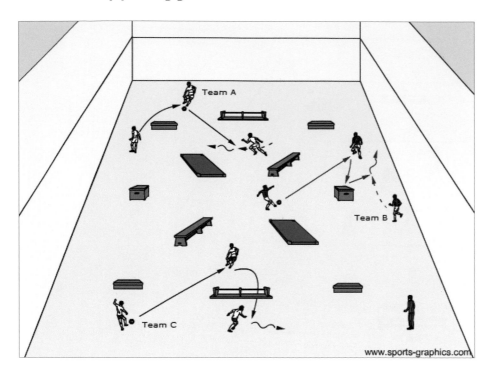

Execution

Various pieces of gym equipment (e.g., mats, benches, vaulting boxes) are set up around the gym. Players are divided into groups of three. Each group of three has a ball and moves freely around the gym while passing the ball. Players must complete various passing combinations that involve the gym equipment.

Team A: Third man running around one of the vaulting boxes.

Team B: Direct pass against a vaulting box; third man controls the rebound from the box.

Team C: Direct lob over a bench to the third man running.

Variations

* Specify the passing leg (left/right).
* Specify the playing leg to control the ball (left/right).
* Organize as a competition: Which team is the first to have played on all pieces of equipment?

4.1.18   Passing loop (benches)

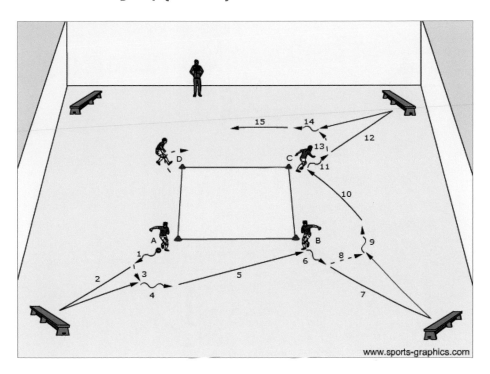

www.sports-graphics.com

Execution

The four players A, B, C, and D play an endless passing loop around the center square and remain in their positions after each action with the ball. Player A starts the passing loop. Player A briefly dribbles toward the bench (see 1), passes against the bench (see 2), starts toward the rebound (see 3), controls the ball in the direction of play (see 4), and passes to player B (see 5). Player B briefly controls the ball toward the bench (see 6), passes against the bench (see 7), starts toward the rebound (see 8), controls the ball in the direction of play (see 9), and passes to player C (see 10). Player C briefly controls the ball toward the bench (see 11), passes against the bench (see 12), starts toward the rebound (see 13), controls the ball in the direction of play (see 14), and continues the passing sequence with player D (see 15).

Variation

Players do not pass directly to the next player in the passing order but rather against the bench (see 5). The next player in the order receives the pass from the bench and controls the rebound from the bench in the direction of play.

4.1.19 Passing (benches)

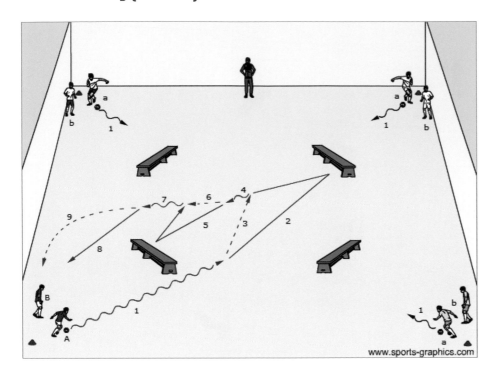

Execution

Form four teams. Each team must have at least two players. The teams position at the starting points in the corners of the gym. The first player from each group starts the action (see A and a). Player A dribbles toward the center (see 1) and passes against the far bench (see 2), follows his pass (see 3), and controls the ball (see 4). Next he passes against the bench near his own starting point (see 5), follows his pass (see 6), and dribbles sideways (see 7) so he can play the ball back to player B at the starting position with ideally his second touch (see 8). After their actions the players always return to their own group. Player B controls the pass and starts a new action.

Variations

★ Vary play against the benches (e.g., play on all four benches).

★ Organize as a competition: Which team is the first to play 10 passes to the starting position?

★ Organize as a competition: Which team can make the most passes to the starting position in five minutes?

4.1.20 Shot on goal (1)

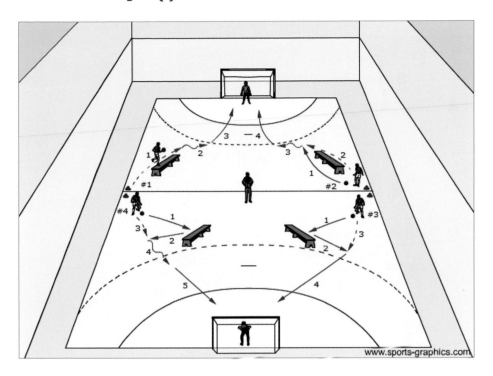

Execution

Following are four different shooting drills (see #1 to #4).

#1: The player in possession holds the ball in his hands and runs across the bench (see 1), kicks the ball ahead, controls it (see 2), and finishes on the large goal (see 3). Variation: Turn the bench over and ask player A to balance across it (see 1). Player A runs and bounces the ball across the bench (see 1). Player A finishes with a volley or a dropkick.

#2: The player in possession passes the ball left or right past the bench (see 1), runs around the bench on the other side (see 2), controls the rolling ball (see 3), and finishes on the large goal (see 4). Variation: The player runs across the bench (see 2).

#3: The player in possession passes the ball against the bench (see 1), follows his pass (see 3), and turns the rebound (see 2) into a direct shot on the large goal (see 4).

#4: The player in possession passes the ball against the bench (see 1), follows his pass (see 3), controls the rebound (see 2 and 4), and finishes on the large goal (see 5). Variation: The player performs a feint prior to the shot on goal (see 4).

4.1.21 Shot on goal (2)

Execution

Following are three different shooting drills (see #1 to #3).

#1: Player A passes the ball through the legs of player B (see 1). Player B immediately turns around (see 2) and receives a pass from player C (see 3). Player B takes a direct shot on the large goal (see 4). Variations: Player B performs a feint prior to his shot on goal. After the pass from A (see 1), player B plays the ball right back to player A before he plays a deep pass to C.

#2: Player A passes the ball through the legs of player B (see 1) against the bench. Player B immediately turns around (see 2) and controls the rebound (see 3). After a short dribble, player B finishes on the large goal (see 5). Variation: Player A calls "right" or "left" with his pass and determines the side on which player B must dribble past the bench.

#3: Player A passes the ball against the bench in the center (see 1). Player B controls the rebound (see 2 and 3) and finishes on the goal (see 4). Variations: After his pass, player A starts as the defender in a 1-on-1 situation. Player A's passing leg (see 1) determines whether player B will have to dribble past the bench on the right or left side. Before taking his shot on goal, player B must perform a feint (see 3). Player A follows his deep pass and receives a square pass from player B. Player A finishes on the large goal.

4.1.22   Shot on goal (3)

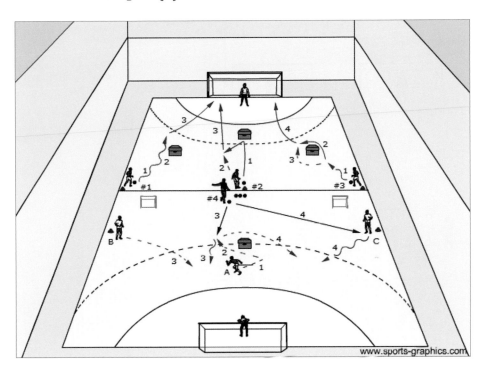

Execution

Following are four different shooting drills (see #1 to #4).

#1: The player in possession briefly dribbles (see 2), performs a feint in front of the vaulting box (see 2), and finishes on the large goal (see 3). Variation: Instead of a feint, the player must dribble once around the vaulting box in a circle (left/right).

#2: The player in possession passes against the vaulting box (see 1), follows his pass (see 2), and takes a direct shot on the large goal (see 3). Variation: Before taking his shot on goal, the player controls the ball and performs a feint.

#3: The player in possession dribbles toward the vaulting box (see 1), lobs the ball over the box (see 2), runs around the box (see 3), and takes a direct shot on the large goal (see 4). Variation: The player climbs over the vaulting box while juggling.

#4: Player A positions deep in front of the vaulting box. After performing a running feint (see 1) he asks for the pass from the coach (see 2). The coach either passes to player A or to one of the wing players. If the coach passes to A, a 1-on-1 situation between A and the wing player closest to the ball ensues (here player B; see 3). If the coach passes to a wing player (see 4), player A defends in a 1-on-1 (see C).

4.1.23 Shot on goal (4)

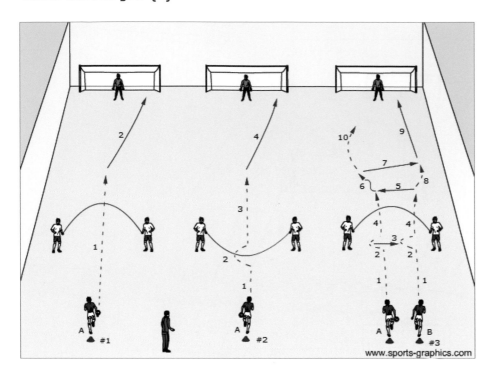

www.sports-graphics.com

Execution

Below are three different shooting drills (see #1 to #3). Two players or coaches turn a long jump rope in which the active players must perform a movement task prior to their shot on goal.

#1: Player A runs through the turning rope with the ball in hand without touching the rope (see 1). Next he sets up and executes his shot on goal (see 2). Variation: Shot on goal as a volley or dropkick.

#2: Player A runs to the turning rope with the ball in hand (see 1) and there performs a number of prespecified jumps (see 2), then continues to run or rather exits the rope (see 3), and sets up and executes his shot on goal (see 4). Variation: Vary the number and type of jumps (e.g. single leg jumps) (see 2).

#3: Players A and B simultaneously run to the turning rope (see 1). Player A holds a ball. The players jump parallel and together (see 2). Meanwhile player A throws the ball to player B (see 3). Next both players exit the rope (see 4). Player B rolls the ball to player A (see 5). Player A briefly controls the ball (see 6) and passes it to player B (see 7). Player B moves towards the ball (see 8) and finishes on the large goal (see 9). Player A plays a possible rebound (see 10).

4.1.24 Shot on goal (roundabout)

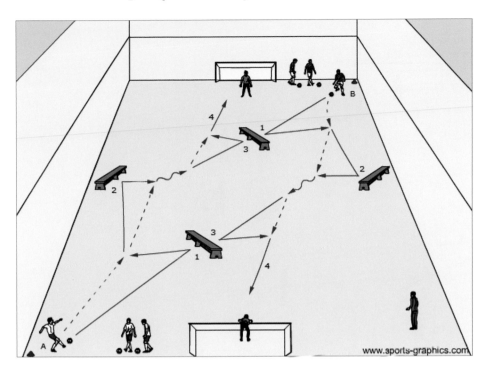

Execution

All players are divided into two groups and position at the two starting positions in the corners of the gym, each player with a ball.   The first two players start simultaneously from the starting positions (see players A and B). Both players complete the same sequence or passing combination against the benches before finishing on the large goal. The pass against the first bench (see 1) is followed by a direct pass against the second bench (see 2). Players briefly control the rebounding ball and pass it against the third bench (see 3). They finish with a direct shot on the large goal (see 4). The next players can start their actions during the pass against the third bench (see 3). After each action, the players line up at the opposite position.

Variations

* Specify the passing leg (left/right).
* Perform a feint/body feint right before each pass against a bench.
* Specify control of rebounding balls: two mandatory touches.
* Add a movement task after a bad shot: short sprint/push-ups/sit-ups.
* Organize as a 1-on-1 competition: Which player is the first to score a goal?
* Organize as a competition: Which team is the first to score 10 goals?

4.1.25 Variable 1-on-1

www.sports-graphics.com

Execution

The attacking player A plays 1-on-1 either against player B or player C and tries to score on the large goal. Player A briefly dribbles (see 1) and passes against the boards (see 2). Player A follows his pass (see 3) and controls the rebound off the boards (see 4) toward the goal (see 5). The defender positioned behind the bench (here player B) immediately reacts with the pass against the boards (see 6), jumps over the bench (see 7), and tries to stop player A from finishing and to win the ball in a 1-on-1 (see 8). After successfully winning the ball, player B can counter on the mini goals. While player A dribbles (see 1) he can and should feint so the two defenders (B and C) won't know until the last second which one will start into the 1-on-1 from the boards.

Variations

* Activate the far defender (here player C).
* Activate the far defender as a teammate for 2-on-2 (here player C).
* Activate both defenders using a signal from the coach during the dribble.
* Option after winning the ball: Involve player C for 1-on-2 on the mini goals.

4.1.26 Diagonal 1-on-1 or 3-on-2

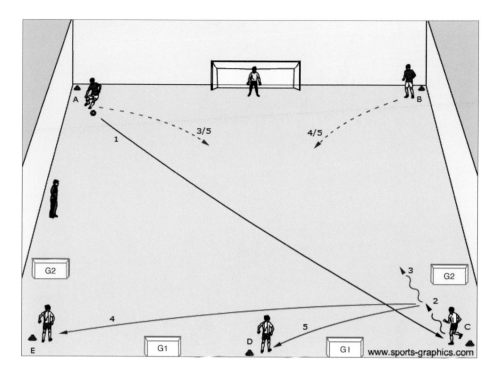

Execution

The player in position A starts each action with the ball at his foot and always plays a diagonal pass to player C (see 1). Player C controls the pass (see 2) and with his second touch chooses one of three follow-up actions. If player C chooses to dribble, he will play 1-on-1 against player A (see 3). If player C chooses to play a long pass to player E, a 1-on-1 situation ensues between players E and B (see 4). If player C chooses to play a pass to player D, a 2-on 3 situation follows. Players A and B defend against players C, D, and E. If a 1-on-1 situation occurs, the player from the RED team (see A and B) can counter on the mini goals G1 after winning the ball. If a 3-on-2 situation ensues, the defending RED team (see A and B) can counter on all four mini goals (see G1 and G2).

Variations

- ★ Specify the passing technique (e.g., volley) for pass 1.
- ★ Specify the passing technique for passes 4 and 5: direct passes.
- ★ Player C performs a feint/body feint before passes 4 and 5.

4.1.27   2-on-2 plus 4-on-4

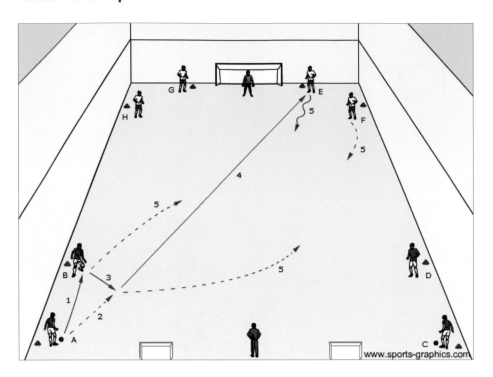

Execution

Player A plays a short pass to player B (see 1) and follows his pass (see 2). Player B plays a direct pass into the running path of player A (see 3). Player A plays a long diagonal pass to player E (see 4). A 2-on-2 situation starts with the pass from player A to player E (see 4). In possession, players E and F play on the mini goals. Players A and B defend and after winning the ball can attack the large goal (see 5). After finishing on the goal, C and D start the previously described passing sequence. Player C plays to player G. The players in the center allow this pass, and a 4-on-4 situation follows. Players E, F, G, and H play in possession against players A, B, C, and D.

Concept

After A, B, E, and F finish their 2-on-2, they must quickly transition to the 4-on-4 situation. Players must organize as a team and get into tactically useful positions.

Variation

* Rotate the players (change positions offense/defense).

4.1.28   From 1-on-0 to 4-on-3

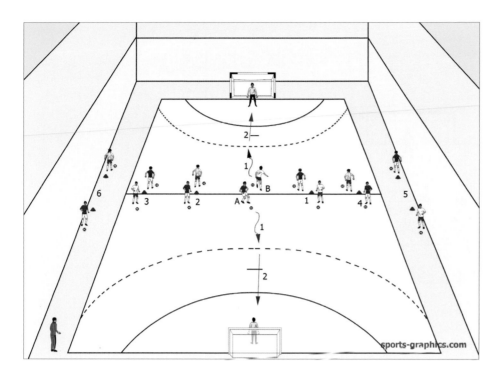

Execution

Players A and B each start the action with their ball, briefly dribble (see 1), and finish on the large goal (see 2). After the finish, both players (see A and B) become defenders and wait for an attacker for 1-on-1 play. The remaining players are divided into pairs of one BLUE and one RED player each and are evenly spaced. The pairs are assigned numbers (see 1 to 5). After the shot on goal by players A and B, the coach calls a number. Those players now start as attackers in 1-on-1 play. After the second ball is off the field, the coach calls another number and with that the next pair for 2-on-1 play, designating the next attackers until there is 4-on-3 play on both goals.

Concept

After the 1-on-1, the players on the field don't know whether they will be attackers or defenders in the subsequent action. Fast transitions, orientation, and sensible position play must be as quick as possible.

Variation

* Follow-up action after winning the ball: Create an opportunity for a counter on the centerline as the dribble line.

4.1.29   4-on-3 plus 2

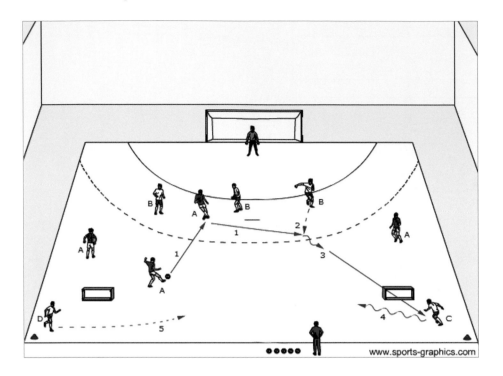

Execution

The RED team (see A) starts in possession and plays against the BLUE team (see B). The RED team initially attacks and tries to score on the large goal from a 4-on-3 superior number situation (see 1). The defending team tries to prevent the goal and win the ball (see 2). After winning the ball, the BLUE team tries to pass it through one of the open boxes (see 3). After winning the ball and a pass through the open box, the players positioned behind the box (see C and D) can get involved in the game (see 4 and 5). The direction of play changes at the same time. The BLUE team now attacks the large goal in a 5-on-4 superior number situation against the defending RED team.

Concept

After losing the ball, the attacking superior number immediately tries to counterpress. After winning the ball, the defense quickly tries to play deep. After a successful pass through an open box, it is important that all players quickly transition.

Variation

* Game continues in 4-on-4; the far player (see D) cannot get involved.

4.1.30 Double 3-on-3

Execution

Players are divided into four teams of three or four players each. It is not necessary nor desirable for the teams to wear bibs. Two teams play against each other with one ball on the same field. Here team A plays against team B, and team C plays against team D. The goalkeepers (see GK) serve as neutral players for the team in possession and can play the ball by foot as well as by hand. Each goalkeeper is a teammate for all four teams when in possession.

Concept

The lack of bibs or color identification in association with the same field for two games trains perception or action speed.

Variations

* Organize as a 1-on-1 competition with points system:
   One point: Passes to all three goalkeepers without a turnover.
   Two points: Pass to a goalkeeper and pass or shoot against a vaulting box.
   Three points: Passes to all three goalkeepers and pass or shoot against a vaulting box.

4.1.31   Game—against the boards (1)

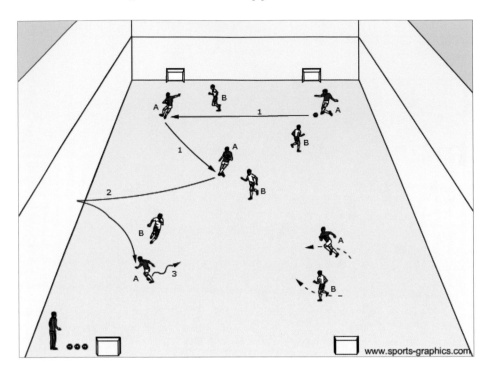

Execution

The RED team (see A) and the BLUE team (see B) initially play 4-on-4 for possession (see 1). The game's objective is to pass to a teammate using the boards (see 2). The rebound off the boards should be used as a pass to the third man.

Concept

After the pass off the boards, the pass receiver must run into the targeted space. This requires optimal timing for getting open so the game can continue in a sensible manner (dribbling, pass, or shot on goal).

Variations

⁕   Specify action after receiving pass off the boards: 2 or 3 mandatory touches (see 3).

⁕   Specify action after receiving pass off the boards: direct pass (see 3).

⁕   Option for transition on the mini goals after two successful passes using the boards.

⁕   Option for transition on the mini goals for the defense after winning the ball.

⁕   Simplify or expand by adding neutral players.

⁕   Provoke a transition with a ball from the coach.

4.1.32 Game—against the boards (2)

Execution

The RED team (see A) and the BLUE team (see B) initially play 4-on-4 for possession (see 1). The game's objective is to score on the mini goals. To score, the ball must be played off the boards and into the goal (see 2). If the ball bounces off the boards and misses the goal, the game continues. After a successful finish, the coach immediately brings a new ball into the game.

Variations

* Specify the shooting technique (see 2): inside foot/instep/direct finish.
* Specify the shooting technique (see 2): left/right/weak foot.
* Vary or change the distances between boards and mini goals.
* Specify play on mini goals: 3 or 4 passes in the own ranks.
* Simplify by playing the game by hand.

4.1.33 Game (diamond)

Execution

Use four cones to mark a diamond in the center of the field. Players cannot enter the diamond. Players must dribble into the diamond with the ball; if they don't have the ball, the go around the diamond. Each team has two wing positions in their respective offensive third—also marked with a cone (see a and b). Team A plays 3-on-3 against team B on the field. Goals can be scored regularly from the 3-on-3. In addition, each team can involve one wing player in the game, but only when playing on the diamond. A direct pass is played through the diamond to one of the wing players (see 2). In addition, the player in possession can dribble into the diamond and from there activate a wing player with a pass. The receiving wing player can now participate in the game in 4-on-3 until the finish. After that, he returns to his wing position, and the game continues as 3-on-3.

Concept

* Courageous, fast-paced, offensive play through the center.

Variation

* A goal from a wing player with his second touch scores double.

4.1.34   Game (deep neutral players)

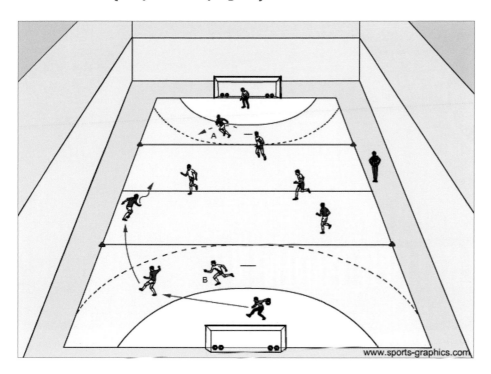

Execution

The RED team and the BLUE team play 4-on-4 against each other on the entire field and on both large goals. Each team must position a forward deep in front within the marked zone and in the direction of play. This player can intervene whenever the ball is in his zone. Here player B (BLUE team forward) interferes with the RED team's game buildup, but is not allowed to give chase while on defense and leave his zone. Player B (RED team forward) tries to get open in the marked zone so he can receive a pass through a gap while his teammates are in possession.

Concept

The forward's job against the ball is to interfere early and to actively run to the opponent in possession. On offense, the continuously manned forward position creates space. At the same time, this position facilitates quick, offensive transitions during possession and calls for the forward to look for the gaps and continuously get open to receive passes there.

Variations

* Specify for play on the large goal: 2 or 3 mandatory touches by the forward (see player A).
* Specify for play on the large goal: Pass to a player who is moving up.

5 GOALKEEPER TRAINING

A modern goalkeeper's requirement profile is extensive. Along with the traditional goalkeeping techniques (trap, punch, throw, dive, roll, and fall), the game also requires a goalkeeper who thinks for himself and joins in the game. It is, therefore, not a bad idea for the goalkeeper to participate in elements of team training along with his specific goalkeeper training in order to work on his soccer-playing and team-playing skills. In this chapter on goalkeeper training, we introduce drills that are primarily intended as a framework specifically for goalkeeper training within which goalkeepers can work individually on their special techniques.

Jump

Trap Reach

Roll Join in play

Transition Fall

Parry Throw

5.1   GOALKEEPER TRAINING

5.1.1   Warm-up (1)

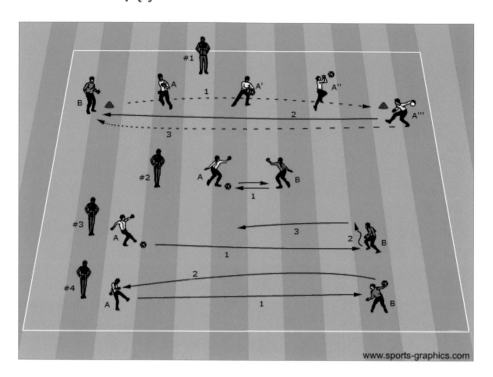

#1 Running ABCs

Goalkeeper A starts and runs to the second cone while performing various movement tasks (see 1), turns, and rolls the ball (alternating left and right) back to goalkeeper B (see 2). Movement tasks: skipping backward (see A) and letting the ball circle around the hips; side stepping and letting the ball circle around the hips (see A'); throwing the ball in the air and catch it like a jump shot (see A''').

#2 Legwork and short passes

Goalkeepers A and B stand facing each other and pass the ball back and forth (see 1). To pass, they continuously make tiny quick steps on the balls of their feet. Movement tasks: making direct passes (left/right); passing with the sole of the foot; receiving the ball with the left foot (right) and passing with the right (left); receiving with the outside foot (left/right) and passing with the inside foot (left/right).

#3 Receiving long passes with the side of the foot

Goalkeepers A and B play long passes back and forth (see 1). Each ball is controlled sideways away from the goal (see 2) and passed back to the partner (see 3). Movement tasks: controlling the pass alternately with the inside foot (left/right) and the outside foot (left/right).

#4 Transition

The goalkeepers play the ball back and forth. At the same time, they repeat the following techniques: volley (see 1), throw-out (see 2), and dropkick. Variation: Integrate additional tasks into the sequence.

5.1.2   Warm-up (2)

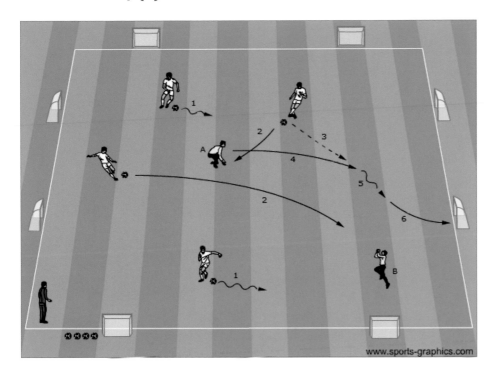

www.sports-graphics.com

Execution

The field players (see WHITE team) each have their own ball and dribble freely around the field. The goalkeepers (see A and B) also move freely around the field. By calling the name of the player in possession, the goalkeepers ask for either short, hard shots (see A) or high, long volleys (see B).

Coaching

* Monitor and correct goalkeeping techniques.
* Safeguard low shots with hands in front of bent knees.
* Single-leg jump/protect body with bent knee.
* Catch balls at the highest point possible.

Variation

After the pass from the field player (see 2), the passing player immediately breaks away (see 3). The goalkeeper (see A) rolls or throws a well-timed ball into the teammate's running path (see 4). The field player controls the pass (see 5) and finishes on a mini goal (see 6).

5.1.3   Warm-up (3)

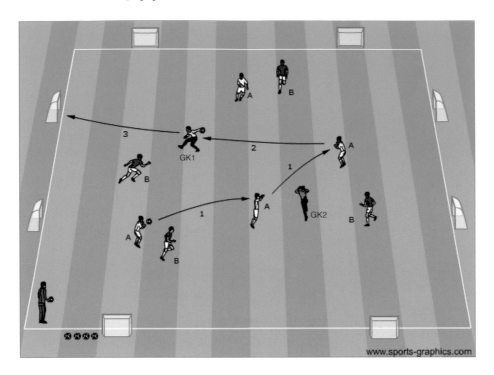

Execution

The WHITE team (see A) plays with GK1 against the RED team (see B) playing with GK2. The teams pass each other the ball by hand as often as possible (see 1) without an opposing player catching the ball or the ball touching the ground (change of possession). The goal is to play eight passes in a row for one point. A team can score a second point with an additional eight passes, and so on. As an alternative, the team's goalkeeper can score with throw-out or by rolling the ball into a mini goal for two points. After the finish on a mini goal, the coach brings a new ball into the game.

Variations

* Vary the passing and shooting technique: Play the ball with the feet.
* Vary play with the ball at the feet: mandatory/optional use of hands by goalkeeper.

5.1.4   Legwork (follow-up action)

Execution

Following are four different drills. At each station, the goalkeeper begins at the RED start cone. He starts with a specified movement task (see 1) and then receives a low (see #1 and #2) or waist-high (see #3 and #4) shot from the coach or a second goalkeeper (see 2).

Coaching

The movement tasks should be executed quickly and accurately. The goalkeeper should make only brief contact with the ground. It is better to work on the balls of the feet and practice with a low center of gravity.

Variations

#1: Specify the technique for jumping over the hurdles (single-leg/two-leg jumps).

#2: Specify the technique for jumping over the hurdles (quick/reactive push-off).

#3: Specify the step sequence on the agility ladder.

#4: Specify the step sequence and jumping technique at the hoops.

5.1.5   Legwork—low balls (1)

Execution

Goalkeeper A stands on the goal line with his back to the field. At a signal from the coach ("START"), he squats down and then jumps up explosively and touches the crossbar with this hands (see 1). Immediately afterward, he takes a big side step to the post and touches it (see 2). Next he turns (see 3) and receives a low ball in the lower corner from goalkeeper B or the coach (see A"). After five shots, the two goalkeepers switch tasks. After several practice rounds, the running direction changes (see 2).

Variations

- Vary or change the starting position: stand/sit/lie down/squat.
- Vary or change the running style: hobble/two-leg jumps (see 2).
- Vary or change the passes from player B: waist height and high shots.
- Add transition actions using additional shots.

5.1.6   Legwork—low balls (2)

Execution

Goalkeeper A stands on the goal line and starts with a brief sprint toward the first hurdle. He jumps over the hurdle and back again with legs together (see 1). Afterward, he takes a deep side step to the other hurdle (eyes on the field at goalkeeper B) and jumps over it (see 2). Next, he crosses the poles in a specified running exercise (see 3). He steps farther forward and must parry the shot from goalkeeper B (see 4).

Variations

* Vary or change the running style: low side step (see running path to 1 and 2).
* Add a transition action after possession: throw-out into a mini goal (see A').
* Add a transition action: high throw from C or the coach and throw-out into a mini goal.
* Organize as a competition:

    Which goalkeeper scores the most goals on the mini goal in three minutes?

    Change the practicing goalkeepers after scoring five times on the mini goals.

5.1.7   Legwork—low balls (3)

Execution

Goalkeeper A jumps with legs together over the hurdle (see 1) and receives a low pass in the corner of the goal (see 2). After the save (see A'), the goalkeeper quickly moves back to the hurdle and crawls, or dives, under it (see 3). Next he receives another shot into the corner of the goal (see 4).

Coaching

* Clear the ball to the outside/parry to the front/avoid falling backward.
* Keep your eyes forward while jumping or diving.

Variations

* Add more jumps: triple two-leg jump (forward/backward/forward).
* Vary or change the passes (e.g., waist-high and high shots).

5.1.8   Reacting (1)

Execution

Various and different marking cones or agility poles are set up in front of the goal. Depending on the desired degree of difficulty, they are positioned closer (short reaction time) or farther (longer reaction time) away from the goal. The shooter (see B) takes low shots on the goal (see 1). He places the balls so they can alternately approach the goal without coming into contact with a cone or touching one of the pieces of pieces of training equipment. The trajectory changes accordingly, forcing the goalkeeper to react very quickly.

Coaching

★   Low body position on the balls of the feet/light on the feet/hold hands in front of the body.

Variation

★   Change the starting position: eyes on the goal (turn after signal from the coach).

5.1.9   Reacting (2)

Execution

Goalkeeper A positions in the center of the marked field. The field is marked with four different colored cones. The coach starts the action by calling two different colors. The goalkeeper runs around those cones (see 1 and 2) in the called order. As he does, he keeps his eyes on shooter B. Next he steps forward off the field (see 3) and parries the low shot by goalkeeper B (see 4 and A").

Coaching

★ Keep your eyes forward while running around the cones.

★ Maintain a low center of gravity while running around the cones.

★ Shorten the distance to the shooter: step up to the ball/shorten the angle.

Variations

★ Specify the cone by calling a number (1 = RED, 2 = BLUE).

★ Call non-existent colors or numbers to increases attentiveness.

★ Increase the number of cones the player must run around: call 3 or 4 colors.

★ Control the load by decreasing the distance between cones or touching the cones.

★ Add a follow-up action: throw-out into a mini goal after the save (see A").

5.1.10 Catching high balls (1)

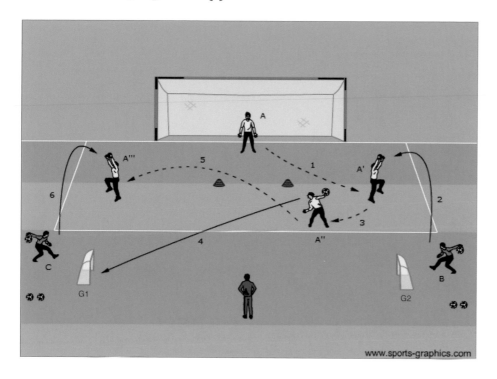

Execution

Goalkeeper A runs toward thrower B (see 1) and does a one-legged jump to meet B's throw (see 2) in order to catch the ball at the highest point possible (see A"). He turns (see 3) and throws the ball to the other side into mini goal G1 to quickly continue the play (see A" and 4). Next he runs through the cone goal with his eyes on the field (see 5) and, like the first action, catches the throw by C (see 6) and then continues the game with a throw-out on G2. The sequence continues. The practicing goalkeepers change regularly.

Coaching

- ★ Jump for the ball from the left (see A') with the left foot (right leg = body protection).
- ★ Jump for the ball from the right (see A") with the right foot (left leg = body protection).
- ★ Targeted low throw-out to be controlled by an imaginary teammate.
- ★ Keep eyes forward.
- ★ Timing/catching the balls at the highest point possible (see 2 and 6).
- ★ Vary or change the running style: low side step (see 5).

5.1.11   Catching high balls (2)

Execution

The goalkeeper positions in the goal and awaits crosses alternately from the right (see player C) and the left (see player B). Various obstacles are set up in front of the goal. During the run up (see 2) to the cross (see 1) the goalkeeper must run around these obstacles and cannot touch them. The markers represent opposing players and force the goalkeeper to look up from the ball and scan the periphery. The goalkeeper catches the cross (see 3), changes his running direction (see 4), and throws out the ball on mini goal G1 for a quick continuation of play. Next player C crosses, and after catching the ball, goalkeeper A throws out on mini goal G2. The crossing players vary the trajectory and placement of the balls.

Coaching

  - ★ Change the line of vision (alternate between ball and players).
  - ★ Jump for the ball from the left (see B) with the left foot (right leg = body protection).
  - ★ Jump for the ball from the right (see C) with the right foot (left leg = body protection).
  - ★ Time and catch the balls at the highest point possible (see 2 and 6).

5.1.12   Throw-out and punt

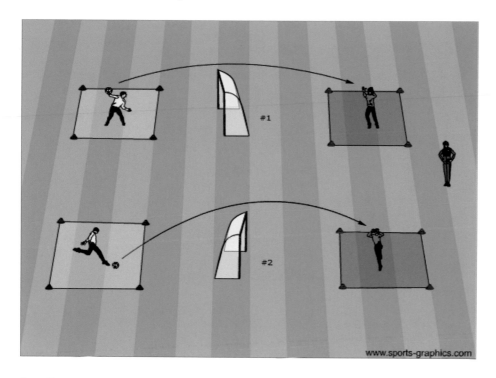

www.sports-graphics.com

Execution

Two goalkeepers are positioned across from a mini goal and practice punching and throwing techniques by passing, crossing, punching, and throwing the ball back and forth over the goal.

Variations

#1: The goalkeepers throw the ball to the partner over the large goal while alternating hands. The second goalkeeper catches the ball. As a variation, the ball is caught as a dropkick directly after impact. The throw that follows the catch should be fluid and quick for a fast continuation of play.

#2: The goalkeepers pass, cross, punch, and throw the ball to the partner over the large goal, alternating feet. The second goalkeeper catches the ball. As a variation, the ball is caught in the air at the highest point possible. To catch the ball, the goalkeeper jumps on one leg, alternating the left and right foot. Another variation would be to volley the ball out of the air or dropkick it to the opposite side.

6 TEAM BUILDING

A functioning team is characterized by good group cohesiveness. In this chapter we outline versatile and entertaining drills and games to address individual elements of typical teamwork. During the drills and games, players must communicate with each other, pay attention to each other, help, and support each other. In all scenarios, multiple players act together or compete against each other.

Empathy **Teamwork**
Together **Team building**
Teamspirit

6.1 TEAMWORK

Chain competition

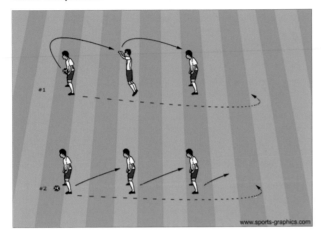

Multiple teams face off in small groups of at least three players and must complete a certain distance. The respective passing player continues the chain (see running path). #1: Throw the ball overhead. #2: Pass the ball between the legs like a football snap.

Ball transport

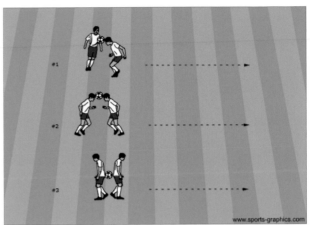

Multiple teams face off in groups of two and must complete a certain distance without letting the ball touch the ground. #1: Carry the ball head to chest. #2: Carry the ball head to head. #3: Carry the ball back-to-back.

Group run

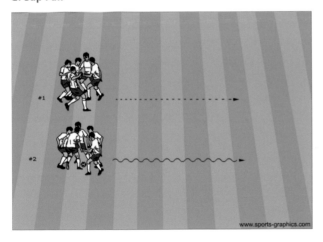

Multiple teams compete against each other in small groups and must complete a certain distance. Players hold hands. #1: Running ABCs. #2: Complete while passing or juggling.

One-leg hop

Multiple teams compete against each other in small groups and must complete a certain distance. They also must hold on to the foot of the person in front of them and together hop on one leg.

Throwing and catching 1

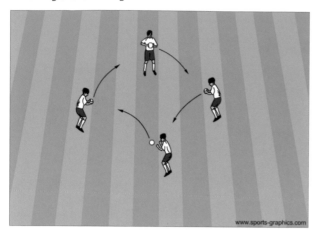

Players are in groups of four, and each player has a ball. The balls must be passed clockwise or counterclockwise as quickly as possible.

Throwing and catching 2

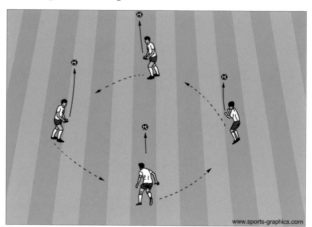

Players are in groups of four, and each player has a ball. Players throw the own ball up in the air and catch the ball of the partner to the right or left.

Sorting

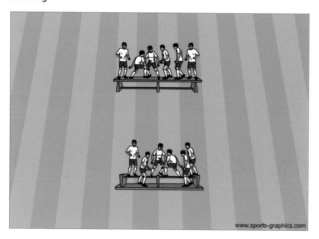

Players spread out on a bench in no particular order. Players must get organized without touching the ground and without speaking. **Variation:** Organize according to age, height, or date of birth.

Jumping rope

Players must jump rope together as a group. **Variations:** Come in together, or come in individually. Do a certain number of jumps, or jump as many times as possible.

Jumping rope

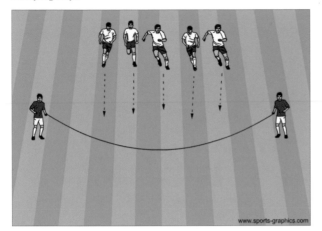

Players must run through the jump rope a a group without jumping or touching the rope. **Variation:** Players go all at the same time or one after the other without pausing, or they can go in pairs.

Flying

Players must complete a certain distance as a group while carrying a teammate. **Variation:** Guide and control a ball through the carrying players.

Field running

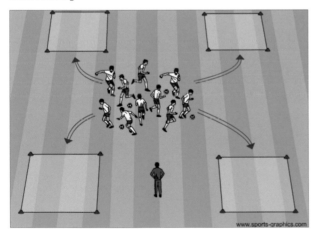

Multiple players spread out in the center with or without a ball. The coach calls a number. Players must spread out on the fields according to the number called. Each field must have a ball on it. The remaining players stay in the center.

Supporting legs

Multiple players spread out on a small field. The coach calls two numbers. The first number denotes the group size, and the second the exact number of permitted supporting legs. **Example: #1:** 2/2, **#2:** 3/4, and **#3:** 3/3.

Dribbling chain

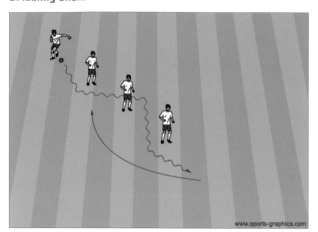

Together players must complete a certain distance as fast as possible as a group. The last player dribbles through all of his teammates, passes the ball to the last player, and positions at the front of the chain.

2-on-2 challenge

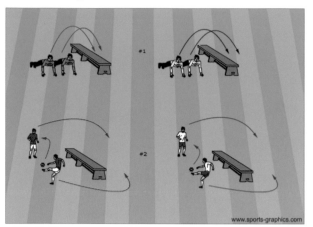

Players compete against each other in pairs. **#1:** Which team is the first to complete 20 push-ups? Cross the bench after two push-ups. **#2:** Which team is the first to juggle 20 times? Cross the bench after five touches.

Trust fall

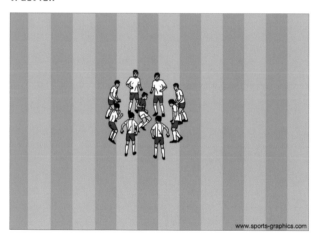

Players form a tight circle around one player in the middle. The player in the middle lets himself fall with eyes closed and body taut. The outside players catch him.

1-on-1 equilibrium

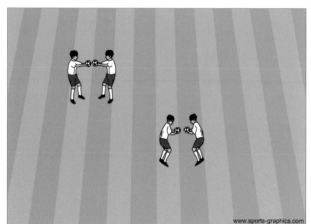

Two players each hold a ball in their hands and try to push each other off balance in a 1-on-1. Only the balls can touch. **Variation:** Complete the exercise on one leg.

Rock-paper-scissors

Pairs of players play rock–paper–scissors. The loser must perform a movement task: **#1**: three push-ups; **#2**: three straight jumps; **#3**: three knee-bends; **#4**: three one-leg straight jumps.

Caterpillar

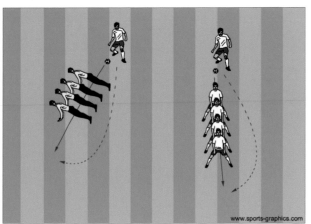

One player with a ball passes the ball to the head of the group, chases the ball, plays the ball back to the last man in the group, and positions at the head so the entire group moves forward.

Flying carpet

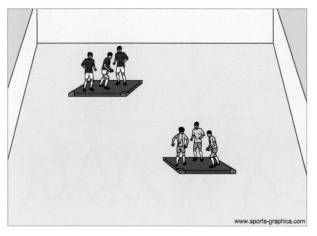

Multiple players stand on a mat. The mat must be turned all the way around without a player touching the floor. Which team finishes first?

Mass revolt

Multiple payers position in a group so only their posteriors and backs touch. Now players must move from a seated to a standing position as a group without using their arms.

5-on-1 with task

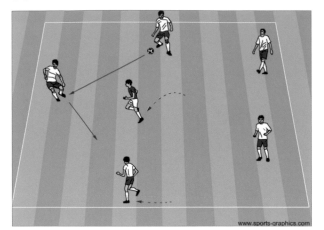

1-on-1 with task

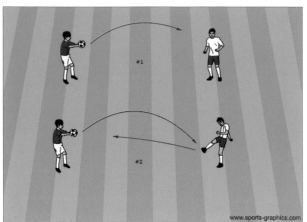

In a 5-on-1 game, each pass is accompanied by a command and a task. The respective receiver must perform the task, or he becomes the defender: #1: "Direct" (one touch); #2: "Two" (two touches); #3: "Right" (pass with the right foot); or #4: "Left" (pass with the left foot).

Players throw each other a ball in 1-on-1 play and accompany each throw with a command and associated task: #1: no command (return header) or "Catch" (catch the ball); #2: command "Right" (pass the ball back with the right foot) or "Left" (pass the ball back with the left foot).

Figures

The players talk and coordinate to build the following pyramids.

7 BACKGROUND KNOWLEDGE

The sport of soccer can be viewed against the backdrop of sports science and training theory. This chapter, Background Knowledge, offers a soccer-specific glance at general and superordinate principles of training planning and design, followed by a realistic view on how coaching can influence and control a competition.

Principles Guidelines
Coaching
Training management
Managing training loads

7.1 SOCCER-SPECIFIC TRAINING PRINCIPLES

Training generally focuses on improving the sport-specific performance and its systematic increase. Targeted training is subject to general and specific training principles that are based on the specific training design.

General and organizational training principles

* Promote fun and joy in the sport and in moving.
* Variety, versatility, and motivation in training.
* Positive reinforcement of the desired behavior.
* Training complexity is in line with the players' actual performance level.
* Realistic training (train content that is required in a game).
* Complex coaching in frozen situations (stop the game and directly discuss the situation).
* Sensible load and intensity management (injury prevention).
* Sensible exercise structure (no long rebuilding phases).
* Methodical training structure (from simple to complex and from familiar to unfamiliar).
* Determine key areas of emphasis and train those intensively.

Child-appropriate training principles

* Age-appropriate training (don't demand too little or too much).
* Optimal use of training time and preferably brief explanations (create little waiting time).
* Have a ball for each child (facilitates lots of repetitions).
* Facilitate a sense of achievement for every player (ensure lots of actions on the ball).
* Child-appropriate language (use language with imagery and vivid comparisons).
* Facilitate genetic learning (allow mistakes; let children test themselves).
* Include basic forms of movement in training (running, jumping, throwing, catching, falling).
* Complex training (use children in multiple playing positions).
* Offer support (demonstrations, learning with a model).
* Simple rules, small groups, and short playing times.

Non-sport principles

* Be a role model (positive language, sport-appropriate behavior, dress like a coach).
* Aspire to giving each player equal attention and equal treatment.
* Develop a community (team spirit, team presence, respect, tolerance).
* Take into account development outside the sport (puberty, private and professional situations).
* Personal development (independence, responsibility, maturity).

7.2   SOCCER-SPECIFIC TRAINING MANAGEMENT

A traditional training unit consists of warm-up, main unit, and cool-down. During the design of the individual training phases, the coach has certain parameters that he can variably use and change to accurately manage the training. By using and practicing with the available tools, he manages the load intensity and the training content:

* Field sizes
* Team sizes
* Rules of the game
* Playing time and break design
* Type and number of goals
* Audible and visual signals
* Coaching conduct

7.3   COACHING FOR TRAINING AND GAME MANAGEMENT

Training and competitions are generally managed through coaching. Coaching can be done not only by the coach, but also by the players themselves. Easy-to-understand coaching instructions and concise commands can form a basis for successful coaching. In the following sections, we introduce individual coach's instructions and their significance to training and competition. To avoid confusion, it is a good idea to explain the coach's instructions to the players before using them. Furthermore, it is consequential that the selected and explained instructions should be issued in a concise and sustained manner.

7.3.1   Defensive coaching with individual tactics

Offensive thinking	A player is asked to perform a courageous and offensive action.
Defensive thinking	A player is asked to perform a reliable defensive action.
Deeper	A player is asked to position himself closer to the own goal.
Narrower	A player is asked to position himself closer to his opponent's goal.
Hold the center	A player is asked to move to the center and stay there.
Left shoulder	A player is asked to look over his left shoulder to be aware of players behind his back.
Right shoulder	A player is asked to look over his right shoulder to be aware of players behind his back.
Shoulder check	A player is asked to look over his left or right shoulder to be aware of players behind his back.
Confront	While playing against the ball, one player is asked to confront the opposing player in possession in order to buy time for the team to get organized.
Approach	While playing against the ball, one player is asked to approach the opposing player in possession and pressure him.
To the ball	A player is asked to approach and actively confront the opposing player in possession or a loose ball.
Touch the ball	During play without the ball, a player is asked to engage in a duel and attack the opposing player in possession to win the ball.
No hands	A player is asked to engage in a duel without unnecessary use of his hands to avoid drawing a foul.
No foul	A player is asked to engage in a duel without unnecessary foul play to avoid a dangerous free kick by the opponent.
Clear ball	A player in possession or close to gaining possession is asked to clear the ball.
Fall	A player is asked to let himself fall in the direction of the own goal.

7.3.2   Offensive coaching with individual tactics

Offensive thinking	A player is asked to perform a risky and offensive action.
Open position	A player is asked to position in an open playing position to be able to see and observe a large part of the field.
Left shoulder	A player is asked to look over his left shoulder to be aware of open spaces or teammates behind him.
Right shoulder	A player is asked to look over his right shoulder to be aware of open spaces or teammates behind him.
Shoulder check	A player is asked to look over his left or right shoulder to be aware of open spaces or teammates behind him.
Head up	A player is asked to look up to observe his surroundings.
Higher	A player positioned in front of the player in possession is asked to position closer to the opposing goal.
Push forward	A player is asked to position closer to the opposing goal.
Calm	A player in possession is asked to keep calm.
Tempo	A player in possession is asked to perform his next action at top speed.
Risk	A player in possession is encouraged to show willingness to take risks.
Man on	During play with the ball, the player in possession is given the helpful information that an opponent is closing in from behind.
Rebound	A player waiting for the ball is asked to play a direct return pass to the passing player.
Square up	A player waiting for a ball is asked to control the pass and square up to the opposing goal.
Forward	A player is asked to perform an offensive action prior to dribbling or passing, for example.
Pass	During play with the ball, a player in possession is asked to separate from the ball using a pass to speed up the game or avoid opponent pressure.
Direct	During play with the ball, a player in possession is asked to play a direct pass to speed up the game or avoid opponent pressure.
1-on-1	During play with the ball, the attacker in possession is asked to engage in offensive 1-on-1 to get past an opponent.
To the goal	During play with the ball, the attacker in possession is asked to move toward the opposing goal and approach the goal from a wing position.
Finish	A player in possession is asked to take a shot on goal to take advantage of a good shooting opportunity.
Touch and go	A player in possession is asked to play a pass to a teammate and immediately run to get open.
Overlap	A player is asked to overlap a player in possession to create playing opportunities.

7.3.3   Defensive coaching with group tactics

Transition	A group of players is asked to switch to defense after losing the ball.
Positions	Players are asked to quickly occupy their individual positions.
Compress	During play without the ball, a group of players is asked to narrow the field and close off the spaces the opponent wants to play in.
Center	During play without the ball, a group of players is asked to man and safeguard the center of the field.
Drop	During play without the ball, a group of players is asked to drop behind the ball to allow the team to get organized.
Press	During play without the ball, a group of players is asked to run toward the opposing players in possession and pressure them.
Doubling up	Two defending players are asked to jointly put pressure on the opposing player in possession.

7.3.4   Offensive coaching with group tactics

Transition	A group of players is asked to switch to defense after winning the ball.
Positions	Players are asked to quickly man their individual positions.
Possession	During play with the ball, a group of players near the player in possession is asked to keep the ball in the own ranks with safety-minded play and to take little risk.
Vacate	During play with the ball, a group of players near the player in possession is asked to vacate a space that is compressed by the opponent and play on other open spaces.
Switching play	During play with the ball, a group of players near the player in possession is asked to leave a space that is compressed by the opponent and switch the ball to the other side of the field.
Fan out	During play with the ball, a group of players is asked to increase the distances between players to open up space and increase the distances between opposing players.
Push up	A group of players behind the ball is asked to push up toward the teammates in possession.
Depth	During play with the ball, players positioned in front of the player in possession are asked to continue moving toward the opposing goal.
Running lanes	During play with the ball, a group of players in front of the player in possession is asked to run in specific running lanes to offer passing options to the player in possession.

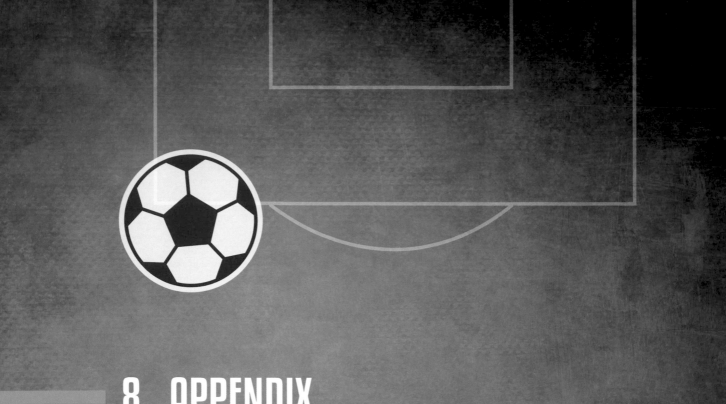

8 APPENDIX

8.1 LEGEND

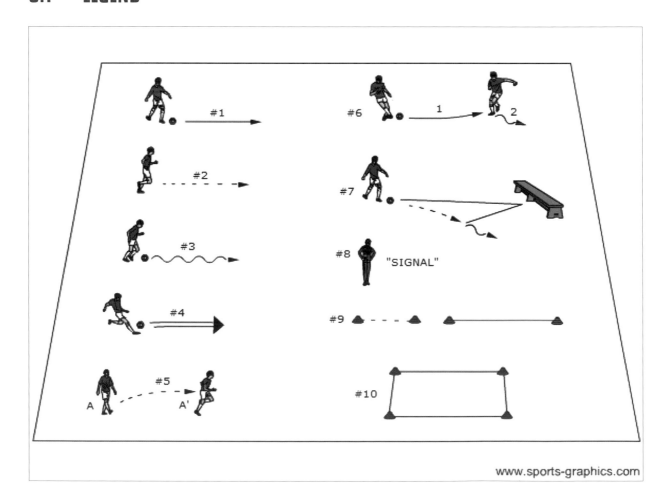

Meaning of individual elements in the depicted drills

#1   Passing lane (solid line)

#2   Running lane (broken line)

#3   Dribbling (wavy line)

#4   Shot (double solid line)

#5   The same player A runs to a new position A'.

#6   The order of passing, running, and dribbling lanes is numbered in ascending order. The pass (see 1) is followed by one-touch ball control (see 2).

#7   The player passes a ball against a turned-over bench and then handles his own ball.

#8   The coach gives a visual or audible signal.

#9   Marked goals and lines.

#10   Playing zone

8.2   DEFINITIONS AND READING SUPPORT

Drill	Training exercise with specified running/passing lanes and technical content.
Game	Training exercise with playing fields, teams, scoring opportunities, or playing objectives.
Individual tactics	Planned/targeted behaviors by an individual player.
Group tactics	Planned/targeted behaviors by a group.
Team tactics	Planned/targeted behaviors by the entire team.
Pressing	Defensive behavior aimed at winning the ball/pressuring the opponent.
Offensive pressing	Pressing in the opposing half.
Midfield pressing	Pressing in a zone at a level with the centerline.
Defensive pressing	Pressing in the own half.
Counterpressing	Pressing immediately after losing the ball.
Pressing zone	Zone on field where pressing takes place.
Pressing victim	Opposing player in possession to be pressed.
Pressing start	Command/signal to start pressing.
Defensive coaching	Commands/coach's instructions during opposing possession.
Offensive coaching	Commands/coach's instructions during own possession.
Coach's behavior	Coach's behavior while instructing/explaining during training and during competitions.
Coach's instructions	Catchwords/verbal signals to direct training and competition play.
Coach's commands	Catchwords/verbal signals to direct training and competition play.
Positions	GK (goalkeeper) RWB (right wing back) LWB (left wing back) RCB (right center back) LCB (left center back) 6er (central midfielder) LF (left forward) RF (right forward)
Start cone	Marking cones to designate a starting position.
Bib	Shirt to identify team affiliation.
Passing loop	Passing sequence with the same starting and ending position for constant repetitions.
Passing relay	Passing sequence with specified passing stations and passing order.
Passing triangle	A triangle marked with cones in which players complete passing sequences.
Passing square	A square marked with cones in which players complete passing sequences.
Out-of-bounds zone	A zone on the field that cannot be played in or entered.
Passing zone	A zone on the field that must be negotiated in passing play.
Dribble zone	A zone on the field where players must dribble.
Passing line	A line that must be crossed by passing.
Dribble line	A line that must be crossed by dribbling.
Passing lane	Route/distance of a targeted pass.
Dribble lane	Route/distance of dribbling with the ball at the foot.

Passing distance	The distance of a pass between two players.
Coach's ball	Pass played by the coach/pass played into the game by the coach.
Coach's signal	Audible (e.g., whistle/shout) or visual (e.g., raised hand) command.
Command	Communication among players (coach's instruction).
Starting signal	Audible or visual command to start an action.
Neutral player	Neutral player as passer or receiver for a player in possession.
Brief dribble	A player's brief dribble as a preliminary action to a follow-up action.
First touch	A player's first contact with the ball after receiving a pass.
Skipping	Running style on the balls of the feet (quick and brief ground contact).
Side step	Sideways running style.
High-knee skips	Skipping run with high knees.
Single-leg stance	Standing on one leg with the other knee raised and bent.
Two-leg jump	Jumping with both legs.
Single-leg jump	Jumping with one leg.
Roll-in	Continuing the game by hand (rolling).
Kick-in	Continuing the game by foot (pass/cross).
Dribble-in	Continuing the game with a dribble.
Free leg	Leg/foot with which a player plays the ball.
Passing leg	Leg/foot with which a player passes the ball.
Receiving leg	Leg/foot with which a player controls a pass.

8.3 REFERENCES

Heim, C., Frick, U. & Prohl, R. (2007): *Futsal in der Schule – eine Chance für den Fußball?* Frankfurt am Main: Institut für Sportwissenschaften, Johann Wolfgang Goethe-Universität.

8.4   PHOTO CREDITS

Cover design:	Claudia Sakyi
Cover photos:	©Thinkstockphotos/iStock/jessicahyde
Inside book layout:	Andreas Reuel
Jacket photos:	Catharina Peppel (www.catharinapeppel.de) author's photo
	Background illustration: ©Thinkstockphotos/iStock/jessicahyde
Inside photos:	Page 16: ©frommfotograf, Andreas Fromm
	All photos in chapter 3.2, Soccer-specific athletic training (strength, flexibility, stabilization, and coordination), were taken by Alexander Seeger. The copyrights are the property of the author.
Graphics:	All graphics accompanying the drills and games were created with Sports-Graphics (www.easy-sport-software.com).
Composition:	www.satzstudio-hilger.de
Editing:	Elizabeth Evans

ACKNOWLEDGMENTS

I would like to thank Stephan Kerber, Andree Fincke, Oliver Dittberner, Stefan Wolgast, Lewe Timm, Uwe Jahn, André Reinhold and Loïc Favé.

THE SECRET OF GERMAN SOCCER COACHING

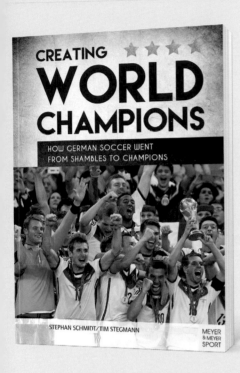

Stephan Schmidt, Tim Stegmann

CREATING WORLD CHAMPIONS

How German Soccer Went From Shambles
to Champions

184 p., 6 1/2" x 9 1/4", in color
90 Halftones, 27 Illustrations, 6 Charts
Paperback
ISBN 9781782550938

$ 19.95 US/$ 29.95 AUS
£ 13.95 UK/€ 18.95

Soccer players and coaches alike admire the German national team for their combination of individual qualities and teamwork, leading to some of the most creative soccer being played during the 2014 World Championship. The roots for the German team's success can be found in the youth training practiced in German soccer clubs. Most professional soccer clubs have their own youth academy where the next Bundesliga stars are formed. In this book, the system used for German soccer youth development is explained with particular emphasis on the different paths that young players can take on the road to success. World Champions and rising star players present their individual stories and some of the exercises that improve their strengths and remove their weaknesses. This book contains many interviews with former Bundesliga stars, soccer experts, and youth and professional coaches as well as an overview of the youth development program of an ambitious amateur club. Some of the star players interviewed include Marco Reus, Manuel Neuer, and Shkodran Mustafi as well as rising stars Sebastian Rode and Maximilian Arnold. This book is for everyone who's interested in the German Soccer Association's talent nurturing and different perspectives on the preparation of young players for a professional soccer career.

All information subject to change. © Thinkstockphotos/photodisc_Ryan McVay

MEYER & MEYER Sport
Von-Coels-Str. 390
52080 Aachen
Germany

Phone   +49 (0) 2 41 - 9 58 10 - 13
Fax   +49 (0) 2 41 - 9 58 10 - 10
Email   sales@m-m-sports.com
Website www.m-m-sports.com

All books available as e-books.

MEYER
& MEYER
SPORT

COACH LIKE
JOSÉ AND PEP

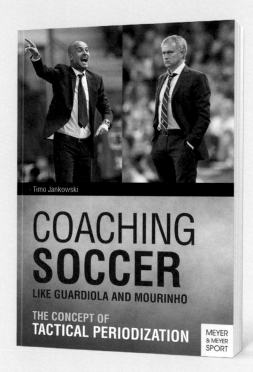

Timo Jankowski

COACHING SOCCER LIKE

GUARDIOLA AND MOURINHO

The Concept of Tactical Periodization

248 p., 6 1/2" x 9 1/4", in color

67 Halftones, 120 Illustrations

Paperback

ISBN 9781782550723

$ 19.95 US/$ 29.95 AUS

£ 12.95 UK/€ 18.95

A soccer player is more than the sum of his parts: endurance, speed, shooting technique, passing technique, and many more. All of these factors need to be turned into one system to create good players. Traditional training theory doesn't achieve that because each skill is trained individually. This is why the concept of Tactical Periodization has become the preferred training theory for many of the current most successful soccer coaches: Pep Guardiola, José Mourinho, Diego Simeone, André Villas-Boas, and many others train according to these principles. By creating match-like situations in practice, players learn to link their technical, tactical, and athletic abilities to match intelligence. They will learn to transfer their skills to soccer matches and they can improve endurance, technique, and tactics all at the same time while enjoying the practice sessions more. For this book, the author has evaluated and analyzed hundreds of training sessions and has tailored exercises to specific demands. All exercises are performed with a ball so that players learn to apply each skill to the game. Every coach will find numerous exercises in this book to help them create better and more efficient practice sessions so they can improve their players' and the team's performance. With Tactical Periodization, your team will become better and be successful on the next match day!

THE ULTIMATE SOCCER FITNESS

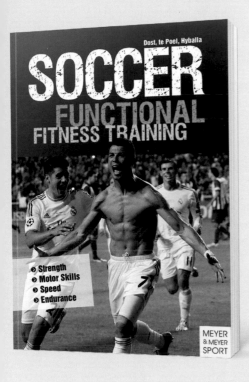

Dost, te Poel, Hyballa

SOCCER FUNCTIONAL FITNESS TRAINING

Strength I Motor Skills I Speed I Endurance

448 p., 6 1/2" x 9 1/4", in color

573 Halftones, 83 Illustrations, 57 Charts

Paperback

ISBN 9781782550907

$ 34.95 US/$ 51.95 AUS

£ 23.95 UK/€ 32.95

The world's best soccer players are incredibly fit, fast, lean, and strong. Achieving this level of athleticism requires a rigorous soccer fitness training program applying the most effective drills, exercises, and core training methods. In Soccer: Functional Fitness Training, the authors present numerous drills for this training. Based on the latest the findings in sports science and on the authors' long-term coaching experience, they present an extensive practical guide to help you improve your team's performance through core training, soccer specific exercises, and drills. The exercises can be used for amateurs and professional players, youth and adults alike. Your players can learn how to score the most exciting and acrobatic goals, how to tackle without fouling, and how to avoid injuries. The drills in the book create typical match situations to help your team prepare for the game and stay motivated. Many of the fitness exercises require no extra equipment and rely only on bodyweight, thus targeting many different muscles at once. The book is easy to use on the pitch and the ideal tool to turn youth players into the next Cristiano Ronaldo, Zlatan Ibrahimovic, or Bastian Schweinsteiger.

All information subject to change. © Thinkstockphotos/photodisc_Ryan McVay

MEYER & MEYER Sport
Von-Coels-Str. 390
52080 Aachen
Germany

Phone   +49 (0) 2 41 - 9 58 10 - 13
Fax   +49 (0) 2 41 - 9 58 10 - 10
Email   sales@m-m-sports.com
Website   www.m-m-sports.com

All books available as e-books.

MEYER
& MEYER
SPORT